Madame Alexander
COLLECTOR'S DOLLS

The current values in this book should be used only as a guide. They are not intended to set prices, which vary from one section of the country to another. Auction prices as well as dealer prices vary greatly and are affected by condition as well as demand. Neither the Author nor the Publisher assumes responsibility for any losses that might be incurred as a result of consulting this guide.

Additional copies of this book may be ordered from:

COLLECTOR BOOKS
P.O. Box 3009
Paducah, Kentucky 42001

@$19.95 Add $1.00 for postage and handling.

Copyright: Patricia R. Smith, Bill Schroeder, 1978
ISBN: 0-89145-054-8

Printed by IMAGE GRAPHICS, Paducah, Kentucky

Madame Alexander
COLLECTOR'S DOLLS
by
Patricia R. Smith

EDITORS: Madame Beatrice Alexander
Karen Penner

COLLECTOR BOOKS

Published by Collector Books
P.O. Box 3009
Paducah, Kentucky 42002

DEDICATION

This book must be dedicated to two people. First to Madame Alexander because without her there would not have been a book. Second, to my husband, Dwight F. Smith, because without him, also, there would not have been a book. My thanks to both Madame Alexander for her dolls and help and Dwight for the many hours spent, not only photographing, but for the many, many hours spent in his darkroom developing and printing a large amount of negatives sent to us by others.

FOREWORD

by

Madame Beatrice Alexander

"A thing of beauty, is a joy forever."
I believe that children should look like dolls and dolls to look like children. At a very early age, I became aware that the love of a doll by a child has the same depth as the love of a mother for her child. One who has the capacity to appreciate is as fortunate as I am to be appreciated.

Madame Alexander

Madame Alexander
March 9, 1977

CREDITS

All photographs are by Dwight F. Smith except the following:
Cover photo of Madame Alexander by Mort Saye, Palm Beach, Fla.
Partridge, Perkins, Lago, Cook & Vinton by Jim Habersetzer of Seattle, Wash.
Mandeville-Barkel Collection by Bob Gantz of Cornwells Heights, Pa.
Elizabeth Montesano (Yesterday's Children) by Isolde Jackson of Amherst, N.Y.
Jeannie Niswonger by Terry Crosier of Winter Haven, Fla.
Donna Maish by Ron Hensel of Dyer, Ind.
John Axe by himself.
Houston & Arnold by Phyllis Houston.
Joan Amundsen—Faye Iaquinto by Joan.
Sandy & Robin Rankow by herself.
B. Ermansons by herself.
Jeannie Gregg by O.D. Gregg.
Marge Meisinger by Michael and Diane Scheer.
E. Chisman by herself.
Ruth Price by herself.
Kathryn Fain—Lois Harbert by Kathryn.
Betty Motsinger by herself.
Charmaine Shields by herself.
Sally Betscheider by herself.
Ernestine Howard by herself.
Renie Culp by Leroy Seeley of Puyallup, Wash.

Others who helped and to them, also our gratitude: Jay Minter, Anita Pacey, Amy Zwickle, Virginia Jones, Connie Chase, Marie Ernst, Bessie Greeno, Peggy Boudreau, Bessie Carson, Pat Raiden, Helen Faford, Kathy Walter, Barbara Monzelluzzi, Barbara Baker, Kay Shipp, Alice Capps, Mae Teeters, Margaret Weeks, Kathleen Flowers Council, Jean Haydn, Ernestine Howard, Linda Krattlie, Angie Landers, Billie Nelson Tyrrell, Pearl Clasby, Alma Carmichael, Patricia Urban, Shirley Bertrand, Gloria and Eileen Harris, Lucy Buffington, Sharon Pressler.

Contents

A great many words have been written about Madame Alexander, herself and her dolls, over the past 52 years. She has appeared in national publications, in collector's books and one can find a large amount of newspaper coverage. All the accounts are glowing ones, but even with hundreds of words flowing cleanly across dozens of pages, they fail to tell about the real Madame Alexander.

We all accept the fact that Madame Alexander is a "Lady of distinction," a "legend in her own time," and all concede to the fact that she has made a greater than normal success of her life. But wanting to know more, we must look at the psychological makeup of this very remarkable lady, Beatrice Behrman-nee Alexander.

Parents and environment play a major part in the patterns of everyone's personality but major is the substance we are born with, the ability to adapt these patterns to our God-given ambitions. If it could be said that success might be inherent, then Beatrice Alexander had a head start.

Maurice Alexander left Odessa, Russia for Germany as a young boy. As he grew, so did his interest in the toy field. He met and married an Austrian girl, Hannah Pepper in 1891 after coming to the United States. He was befriended by the firm of Foulds & Freure, toy importers, and eventually opened the first Doll Hospital in the United States (1895) where not only dolls were repaired but new dolls were sold and bric-a-brac and antiques were repaired and sold also.

Beatrice Alexander, along with three sisters, Rose (Mrs. Harry Schreckinger), Florence (Mrs. Robert Rapport) and Jean (Mrs. Maurice Disick) were born above this shop, surrounded by a constant flow of beauty and taste. Not only in items finding their way through the shop, but Hannah Alexander surrounded herself and family with beautiful things, no matter how simple the home was. For example, the area behind the shop was turned into a beautiful garden, a place of restful beauty just a step away from the everyday chores.

As a child Beatrice was able to judge "beauty" and appreciation of beauty based on her own mother's ability to transmit the "experience" to her children, but also, Beatrice seemed to be born with a deep, true love of beautiful things. Even as a young child a Dresden figurine could capture her imagination as vividly as the children's classics she loved to read.

Beatrice Alexander was a dynamic, extremely energetic and very ambitious child that was often referred to as the "fiery" one of the Alexander children. It was these very attributes which allowed her to survive a world where others faltered and fell by the wayside.

After graudating from Washington Irving High School (N.Y.C.) in 1912, Beatrice married Mr. Phillip Behrman, on June 30, 1912. Their daughter, Mildred, was born in 1915. At this point in time, Beatrice grew more and more restless, needing and wanting her freedom to express herself through an artistic enterprise. She needed a home of her own, decorated to her own tastes and more than that, an outlet for the pent up longing to "do something." At times she felt as an artist denied a canvas on which to paint. Ambition dictated not only a longing for a home but also for a business that she and her husband could call their own. This same ambition called for action and where a great many want but never do, Beatrice found ways to follow through, which is the fact that decides true ambition.

Ambition is tempered with environment and Beatrice had always been compassionate and deeply understanding, and rather intrigued with the emotions of little girls, who gently placed their dolls into the hands of her father, "the Doctor," to repair. She saw beauty and excitement of a re-found friend, when the child came to the "hospital" to reclaim her doll. These emotions have never left Beatrice Alexander and helped to fulfill her own dreams. She saw that these dolls represented not only a friend but a part of the child's mind that was developing, along with the dreams of childhood that make every little girl a princess and every little boy a king. This beauty of childhood was reflected in the eyes of the child for her doll. The doll represented security in an insecure world, it represented dreams in a stark world and it foresaw the fulfillment of the future. Beatrice Alexander had felt the importance of a doll in helping to bring beauty and comfort, and yes, even understanding to a child. Dolls helped in the development of personality.

It was during World War I when doll imports and parts were strictly unavailable when Beatrice's parents had very few dolls to sell or repair as the United States had not yet been able to compete with the huge European concerns. During this period, to help through these years, Beatrice created a little Red Cross Nurse doll and a baby doll of cloth.

Always feeling that a child should have reality, yet webs of dreams sewn into her dolls, during 1923, Beatrice Alexander made a doll that was a portrait of her daughter Mildred. With this charming doll, the strong encouragement of friends, a new commercial doll company was born and became the Alexander Doll Company. During the first months of the company's existence, the four sisters worked together, painting faces and making bodies, always under the watchful, yet playful eye of the oldest, Beatrice. Each took turns painting the faces and all helped to sew the delightfully designed clothes that seemed to spring from the depths of Beatrice's mind like an unending circle.

Beatrice's husband, Phillip Behrman, was working in the personnel department of a large New York hat concern and she really felt that he needed something of his own. Since her own small business had grown to the point that she couldn't handle it alone, she thought it would be great for him to come into the business with her. At first he disagreed but finally gave in and together they built a company beyond their dreams. By the late 1950's the Alexander Doll Company had three factories, with one being in White Plains (plastic and vinyl division) and two in the New York area. By the 1960's they employed over 600 persons.

The Alexander Doll Company was actually built out of the talents of its founder. It is recognized that talents are born along with our first taste of life but it is not often that we see talents extended to their fullest capabilities. For success is not arrived at without the intense desire and the will to fight for the achievement of a self set goal. Beatrice had the talent and also the ambition, the zeal to run after, to hold onto the goal and dream she carried with her from the time she was a little girl. The goal was the artistic self-expression of beauty, as she saw it.

It must be remembered that during the early years when the Alexander Doll Company was breathing new breaths, but had not yet breathed a sigh of success, that the "business" world was made of men. Women found themselves as "assistants" and very, very rarely "boss" in anything. Even though Beatrice Alexander Behrman was basically a creator, a painter of ideals on cloth and in the form of dolls, she had to also be a business woman. Beatrice had it rough those first years but she survived and this fact is to her greatest credit. Her ambition, pushed by a seemingly bottomless lake of energy, allowed her to create, to extend herself beyond the home, her office, and to become her own person.

These first Alexander dolls were of cloth. The very first had flat faces but it was not long before she began to make the dolls with dimensional facial features. Inherent to her childhood, she created dolls from the classics, the poems of Eugene Fields, Longfellow, Tennyson, the stories of Lewis Carroll, Dickens and a favorite, Louisa May Alcott.

The book "The Little Women" by Louisa May Alcott inspired Madame Alexander to give her conception in dolls of the four sisters. She brought these to the office of the newspaper woman, Mary Margaret McBride, 52 years ago and Miss McBride was so enchanted that in a long article in her paper (World Telegram) and she concluded this article with, "Not only does Madame Alexander put soles on her dolls but also puts souls into them." This article gave Madame Alexander great encouragement to continue in the business world and it was the very first publicity that Madame Alexander received.

Neither the newspaper article by Mary Margaret McBride, nor the book had pictures so Madame Alexander used her own interpretation of the cloth dolls. The later movies seemed to echo her own designs. If her love for the "Little Women" stems from her own home, then of the four sisters, she would have to be "Jo." Each of the Little Women dolls ever produced by the Alexander Doll Company were outfitted to the best of this creative artist's ability, but the first in cloth, she loved so much and took such pains to make perfect that she felt their warmth, as if they, too did have souls.

Some place success on awards and if success is rightfully measured that way then few, in the doll world, would be as successful as Madame Alexander. For example, the year 1951 brought the Fashion Academy Gold Medal and she again captured this high award in 1952, 1953 and 1954. Also during the 1950's she was asked by the British Government to make three dolls to represent Queen Elizabeth, Princess Elizabeth and Princess Margaret Rose. The occasion was the visit of Their Majesties to South Africa and the dolls were to be presented to the Government of South Africa. The dolls were attired in Royal gowns made of the finest silks, satins and laces trimmed with seed pearls and rhinestones.

Two dolls were requested, in 1955, by the United States Government to be presented to a little Latvian girl, Dace Epermanis, who was the 150,000th displaced person to enter the United States after World War II. The dolls were a Statue of Liberty doll and a Statue of Freedom doll.

Some feel the most outstanding dolls created by Madame Alexander was the 1953 "Coronation" set or referred to also as the "Recessional" set. This set consists of 36 dolls depicting Queen Elizabeth II leaving the Palace, leaving Westminster Abbey after the Coronation with six maids of honor, carrying the train of the new Queen. Also included in this set is the Duke of Edinburgh, the Queen Mother, Princess Margaret Rose, Anthony Eden, Winston Churchill, The Archbishop, The Admiral and Princess Ann and Prince Charles who were not at the Coronation but whom Madame Alexander felt should have been there. All 36 dolls are dressed in exact detail. Valued at $25,000.00 then, the dolls were donated to the Brooklyn Children's Museum where it is frequently on display. The dolls were on display at Abraham and Strauss (in Brooklyn) during the Coronation Week in May of 1953. The entire grouping of dolls was shown on CBS-TV, 3 hours before films of the Coronation reached the United States.

Among Madame Alexander's honors for achievement is her life-time Honorary Membership in the Brooklyn Institute of Arts and Sciences. Her dolls are shown in many parts of the world in various countries' museums. In May of 1954, exhibition of her dolls by the Public Relations Bureau of the Savings Bank Association of New York, with dolls depicting the fashions of the past 100 years. Late in 1954, copies of these dolls were sold in stores throughout the United States.

Madame Alexander's International dolls of all the United Nations have received highest recognition and honored by U.S. Ambassador Goldberg at the 1965 United Nations Day celebration at New York's City Hall, where the full line of the dolls were on display.

In 1968, the Smithsonian Institute placed two Madame Alexander dolls in their fine doll collection. Madame Alexander made for them, the Madame Doll, inspired by the Madame Doll Book, complete with hidden pocket and pearls to represent the Revolutionary Period and her famous Scarlett O'Hara portraying the Civil War Period.

A few museums featuring Alexander Dolls are the St. Valentine Museum, Richmond, Va.; the Sandwich Museum in Mass.; the Museum of City of New York, and Museum of Yesteryear in Florida. Upon request Madame Alexander made dolls that represented the various cultures of the United States and these were presented to the Congressional Club of Washington D.C. for permanent exhibit. A like set went to the Children's Trust Museum in New Delhi, India and are part of the American Collection there.

Playthings Magazine of February 1931 has an announcement that Madame Alexander personally designed a group of costumes for little girls to go along with their dolls. (Dolls were cloth). Then again in 1946-1947 with matching dresses of the Margaret O'Brien dolls. In 1964, Madame Alexander once again designed and distributed a child's line of clothing by opening "Madame Alexander's Tots, Inc." These clothes matched the dolls costumes. This venture was discontinued in 1966 because demand was so great that it would have interferred with the doll production.

The Alexander Doll Company has always made a practice to supply certain stores with "exclusive" dolls and, or wardrobes. One can find these exclusive yearly models in the older FAO Schwartz, Wanamakers and Marshall-Fields catalogs. (In the 1962 section of this book, there are a few shown). These dolls had different names in the store catalogs, such as Miss Judy, Simone and Milly. Their wardrobes were extensive and expensive. These "exclusive" designs have been discontinued.

All Madame Alexander dolls are beautiful, be they ladies, girls or babies, but this beauty is nothing but the reflection of the beautiful woman herself. Madame Beatrice Alexander is outstanding, true, because of her dolls, but the dolls are because of her!. Her success came from the fact that she believes in the things that she does...., and that in essence is two things, herself and people.

Some of the Alexander employees have been with her for 30 or 40 years and as long as they can continue to work, she plans to keep them on. She respects her people and with young common sense and the wisdom of age, she is more tolerant and understanding of their needs. She makes life a pleasure by the simple fact of a very ancient guide, "Expect not, respect much and love will come." This does not mean that Madame Alexander is, or ever was, "soft," for despite friendship, she is a demanding employer and expects the very best from each person, who are not only paid by her inspiration but well compensated besides.

One fine example of just how far Madame Alexander's friendship can go is reflected in the case of Diane Allen. Madame Alexander first got involved in the Allen case through one of her employees who was Diane's aunt. After the case was explained to her that Diane Allen was accused of murdering her husband, whom she did stab during a domestic quarrel, and convicted of manslaughter by an all male jury, despite the medical examiner's testimony that Leonard Allen did not die of his knife wounds, she started looking into the case.

Since Diane Allen had spent 18 months in jail on a six month to 10 year sentence, her four children were being cared for by her aunt, sister and mother. Madame Alexander began fighting to bring the mother back to her children. She made calls and trips to offices of the public defender, the superintendent of Diane's correctional facility, to state Rep. Don Hazelton (D. West Palm Beach). Through the confident approach of Madame Alexander into the case and the success of Rep. Hazelton, the case was put before the State Probation and Parole Department, who finally agreed to the release of Diane Allen. She is now home with her children and will start all over again, thanks to someone who saw fit to "become involved."

Even though "retired," this great lady of the doll world, manages to stay busy, not only helping others personally, but in her activities and philanthropies. She is active in the support of American Friends of the Hebrew University in Israel and the Albert Einstein College of Medicine in New York. Her activities also cover the Women's League for Israel which helped to found Beth Haluzot, which is five homes for young women in Israel, where 1200 annually receive vocational training and job placement. As stated before, she keeps a hand in the doll business also.

Since her husband died 10 years ago, the company has actually been supervised by her son-in-law, Richard Birnbaum, and grandson, William Alexander Birnbaum. Her daughter, Mildred (Mrs. Richard Birnbaum) is an artist and consultant of the company. Madame Alexander is still president of the company and although not there every day, has at least six years ahead designed and ready for production

This book contains listings of a great many known dolls by the Alexander Doll Company and the contents has over 1000 dolls created by this amazing woman but that only touches the corners, as she has actually created over 5000 dolls, so there are a great many that are not shown, only because of lack of availability to include them. When looking over the lists and photographs, the reader may sense that Madame Alexander is "mid-Victorian" and of the "old school" but in doing so, can't they say to themselves, "How beautiful!" For Madame Alexander has always been inspired by the beauty beheld in a child's eyes and has always designed a doll with the child in mind, never cutting corners and always with the thoughts of a development of the understanding of history accompany each doll.

The latest "new" dolls from the Alexander Doll Company are the First Edition of the First Ladies (Presidents wives). Considered by a great many to be Madame Alexander's finest creations, these dolls have created such an impact on the doll world that production must continue into 1977 (and maybe into 1978) to fill the orders already received for them. Madame Alexander will add new Presidents' First Ladies to the series as time goes on and they will be presented in rotation with the next six to be: Emily Donelson, seventh presiding lady who was Mrs. Andrew Jackson Donelson. 1820 to 1836. She served in lieu of Rachel Donelson Jackson, wife of President Andrew Jackson. Sarah York Jackson (Mrs. Andrew Jackson, Jr.) Presiding lady the last year of the Jackson administration. 1837. Angelica Van Buren, eighth presiding lady. 1839-1841 and wife of Abraham Van Buren. Jane Irwin Findlay (Mrs. James Findlay) was ninth presiding lady in lieu of Anna Symmes Harrison, wife of President William Henry Harrison. 1841. Letitia C. Tyler (Mrs. John Tyler was tenth presiding lady, 1841 and 1842 although Julia G. Tyler was presiding lady of this tenth administration from 1844 to 1845). (Madame Alexander will produce one of these). Sarah Childress Polk, wife of James Kox Polk was eleventh presiding lady. 1845 to 1849. Betty Taylor Bliss-Dandridge, serving in place of her mother, Margaret Smith Taylor (wife of President Zachary Taylor) was the twelfth presiding lady. 1849 to 1950.

To sum up the lady who is Madame Alexander, we quote a letter from her to this author; "As far as your analyses of me

as a "Tough, demanding and at times arrogant (this question was in regard to her having survived a very tough and rough business world), I take pleasure in correcting you. It was never necessary for me to be these things. I have always been able to walk away from all ugliness and surround myself with people of my own caliber, no matter who they were. I choose my employees, my customers and trades people as I choose my friends and have found if you are honest and kind you can bring out the best in a human being. I am patient and tolerant and I don't have to win all the time. After all these fifty-two years in business, I have not been damaged or disillusioned, I have been greatly rewarded."

The following lists only cover dolls used many times over for various personalities.

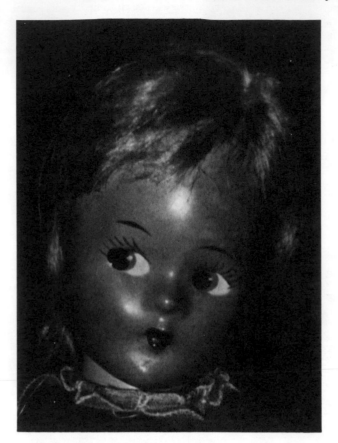

7½" (8") Tiny Betty. Has one piece body and head. Is all composition with painted on shoes/socks. The eyes are painted to the side. The right arm came slightly curled. Some of the later dolls were marked Wendy Ann/Mme. Alexander/New York U.S.A. The early ones were just marked Mme. Alexander (generally) 1935 to 1939.

Hawaiian	Cinderella
American Girl	Fairy Princess
American Child	Czech.
Persia	France
Belgian	Norwegian
Colonial	Swedish
Danish	School Girl
Egyptian	Red Cross Nurse
Russian	Bride
Scotch	Bridesmaid
Spanish	Mexican
Pan American (Pollera)	Heidi
S. American Child-Carmen	Carmen
Dicken's Characters	Dolls of Month
Kate Greenaway	Bo Peep
Dilly Dally Sally	Lazy Mary
Little Boy Blue	McGuffey Ana
Little Jack Horner	Dutch
Goldilocks	Jugo-Slav
Mistress Mary	Peasant
Topsy-Turvy	Brazil
(also with Quint heads)	Jack & Jill
Hansel & Gretel	Eva Lovelace
Polly Put Kettle On	Chinese
Red Riding Hood	Finnish
Alice In Wonderland	Normandy
Ding Dong Dell	Polish
Little Women	Burma

9" & 11" "Little Betty." Used for storybook. Fairytale and Nursery Rhyme dolls. Fully jointed all composition with painted eyes. Some have swivel waists. Had both modeled hair and mohair/human wigs. Barefooted. 1937 to 1941. Some bodies will be marked Wendy Ann.

McGuffey Ana	Virginia Dare
Egyptian	Brazil
Peasant	Sleeping Beauty
Swiss	Sunbonnet Sue
Fairy Tales—Dumas	Colonial
Day of the Week Dolls	Princess Elizabeth
Mexico	Jack & Jill
Hansel & Gretel	Spain
Danish	Little Women
Carmen	Doris Keane
Norewegian	Flora McFlimsy
Scotch	Alice In Wonderland
Red Cross Nurse	Fairy Princess
Dilly Dally Sally	American Girl
Red Riding Hood	Bo Peep
Eskimo	French

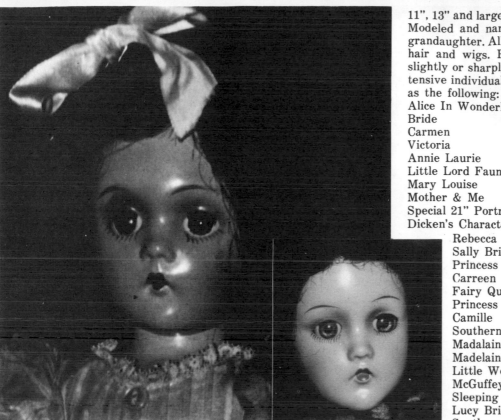

11", 13" and larger "Wendy Ann." 1937 to 1948. Modeled and named for Madame Alexander's granddaughter. All composition. Has both molded hair and wigs. Painted and sleep eyes. Both slightly or sharply bent right arms. Had an extensive individual wardrobe as well as released as the following:

Alice In Wonderland	Wendy Bride
Bride	Orchard Princess
Carmen	Posey Pat
Victoria	Queen
Annie Laurie	Cinderella
Little Lord Faunteroy	Princess Flavia
Mary Louise	Flora McFlimsy
Mother & Me	Southern Belle
Special 21" Portraits	Bridesmaid
Dicken's Characters	Maid of Honor
Rebecca	Cathy
Sally Bride	Fairy Princess
Princess Rosetta	Juliet
Carreen	Marm Lisa
Fairy Queen	Scarlett O'Hara
Princess	Zorina Ballerina
Camille	Ginger Rogers
Southern Girl	W.A.V.E.
Madalaine DeBain	Military Dolls
Madelaine	Sonja Henie
Little Women	(closed mouth)
McGuffey Ana	Ballerina
Sleeping Beauty	Suellen
Lucy Bride	Queen Alexanderine
Southern Belle	Judy
W.A.A.C.	

"Princess Elizabeth" 13", 14", 15", 16", 17", 21", 24", and 27". The 13" and 16" also came with closed mouths. All composition with sleep eyes, open mouth and many had human hair wigs. The Princess Elizabeth was first released at the Coronation of her father, King George VI just a short time after the abdication of her uncle. This mold was used for the following dolls also and they are marked Princess Elizabeth. 1937 to 1946.

Kate Greenaway
Princess Margaret Rose
Carreen
McGuffey Ana
Cinderella
Suellen
Miss Victory
Flora McFlimsy
Princess Doll
Snow White
Babsie Skater

5

"Margaret O'Brien." 1946-1947. All composition. Far as known there was a Margaret O'Brien doll made in hard plastic but the Margaret mold was used for various dolls. The composition dolls will be noted, the remainder will be hard plastic dolls. Hard plastic: 1948 to 1956.

Margaret O'Brien (Compo)
Alice In Wonderland (Compo)
Alice In Wonderland (hard plastic)
Hilda (Black compo.)

Wendy (Peter Pan)	Poor Cinderella
Piper Laurie	Cinderella, Ballgown
Bride	Queen Elizabeth
Peggy Bride	Blue Danube
Princess Margaret Rose	McGuffey Ana
Prince Charming	Lucy Bride
Mary Rose Bride	Dressed For Opera
Little Women	Civil War
Fairy Queen	Karen
Babs Skater	Hedy Lamar
Mary Martin	Louisa
Cynthia	Beau Art Dolls
Edwardian	Glamour Girls
Bridesmaid	Me & My Shadow Series
Stuffy (boy)	Century of Fashion
Wendy Bride	Little Men
Godey	Ballerina
Prince Phillip	Groom
Victoria	Karen Ballerina
Renoir	Majorette
Royal Wedding	
Lady Churchill	
Sir Winston Churchill	
Cherry	
Wendy Ann (hard plastic)	
Margot Ballerina	
Snow White	
Nina Ballerina	
Story Princess	

"Maggie." All hard plastic. 1948 to 1956. (1956 used for Little Women only).

Maggie Walker	Little Men
Kathy	Evening Gown
Annabelle	Victorian
Garden Party	Century of Fashion
Picnic Day	Ballerina
Cherie	Tommy Bangs (boy)
Alice In Wonderland	Little Women
Beau Art Dolls	Peter Pan
Little Men	Ball Gown
Glamour Girls	Victoria
Me & My Shadow Series	Polly Pigtails
Betty (Sears)	Bridesmaid
Maggie Teenager	Alice

7½" & 8" "Wendy Ann/Wendy/Wendy-kins/ Alexander-kins. Wendy Ann was named for and modeled from Madame Alexander's grandaughter (both composition and hard plastic) and Billy for her grandson (William). 1953 to date. First were straight leg non walkers (left) followed by walkers (right). Wendy Ann passed away at the age of 20 and the "Ann" was dropped by company during 1955.

Quiz-kin	Bo-Peep	Cousin Mary
Bill	Romeo	Charity
Bride	Bridesmaid	French Flower Girl
Ballerina	Alice In Wonderland	Blue Boy
Queen	Rodeo	Aunt Pitty-Pat
Agatha	Davy Crockett Boy	Bobby
Bible Characters	Davy Crockett Girl	Faith
Hansel	Cousin Karen	Miss Muffet
Cinderella	Apple Annie	Parlour Maid
Baby Angel	Billy	Pinky
Minister	Little Melaine	Nana
Baby Clown	Goya	Prince Charles
Southern Belle	Cheri	Amanda
Red Boy	Little Women	
Alexander-kins	Little Ice Queen	
Wendy-kins	Gretel	
Peter Pan	Red Riding Hood	
Groom	Lady In Waiting	
Blue Danube	Best Man	
Mary Louise	Dude Ranch	
Guardian Angel	Nurse	
Curly-Locks	Rose Fairy	
Juliet	Cherry Twins	
Scarlett O'Hara	Mary, Mary	
Wendy Bride	Flower Girl	
Mombo	Pierrot Clown	
Drum Majorette	First Communion	
Cousin Grace	Aunt Agatha	
Colonial	Princess Anne	
Little Southern Girl	Lucy	
Little Godey	American Girl	
Victoria	McGuffey Ana	
Ice Skater	Graduation	
Melaine	Cousin Marie	

If two dates appear after the following International dolls, it is the year they were discontinued.

African (1966-1971)	Greek Boy (1965-1968)
Argentine Boy (1965-1966)	Gretel (1966 to date)
Betsy Ross (1966 to date)	Indian Boy (1966)
Spanish Boy (1964-1968)	became Hiawatha (1967-1969)
Cowboy (1967-1969)	Israeli (1965 to date)
Denmark (1970 to date)	Korea (1968-1970)
Ecuador (1963-1966)	Morocco (1968-1970)
Hawaiian (1966-1969)	Polish (1964 to date)
German (1966 to date)	Russian)1965 to date)
Hansel (1966 to date)	Swedish (1961 to date)
India (1965 to date)	Turkey (1968 to date)
Indian Girl (1966)	Vietnam (1968-1969)
became Pocahantas (1967-1970)	Amish Girl (1966-1969)
Irish (1964 to date)	Belgium (1972 to date)
Japanese (1968 to date)	Brazil (1965 to date)
Miss U.S.A. (1966-1968)	China (1972 to date)
Peruvian Boy (1965-1966)	Czechoslavakia (1972 to date)
Priscilla (1966-1970-	Dutch Girl (1961 to date)
Colonial 1962-1965)	Eskimo (1966-1969)
Rumania (1968 to date)	French (1961 to date)
Spanish Girl (1961 to date)	Greek Girl (1968 to date)
Thailand (1966 to date)	Hungarian (1962 to date)
Tyrolean Girl (1962 to date)	Indonesia (1970 to date)
United States (1974 to date)	Italy (1961 to date)
Amish Boy (1966-1969)	Mexico (1964 to date)
Argentine Girl (1965 to date)	Norway (1968 to date)
Boliva (1963-1966)	Portugal (1968 to date)
Canada (1969 to date)	Scottish (1961 to date)
Gowgirl (1969-1970)	Swiss (1961 to date)
Dutch Boy (1964 to date)	Tyrolean Boy (1962 to date)
English Guard (1966-1968)	Yugoslavia (1968 to date)
Finland (1968 to date)	Great Britian (1977)

Although this doll started out in 1953 as Winnie Walker, we shall use the name "Cissy." All hard plastic with vinyl over plastic arms (Few have one piece arms). Jointed knees and most are walkers. Adult figure. 1953 to 1962. The 1962 doll was used for Queen only.

Miss Flora McFlimsey	
Agatha	Gainsbourgh
Sweet Violet	Classics
Debutante Series	Maggie Walker
Bride	Me & My Shadow Series
Fashion Parade	Binnie
McGuffey Ana	Mary Louise
Models Formal Gowns	Binne Walker
Melanie	Century of Fashions
Story Princess	Princess
Portraits of 1958	Skater's Waltz
Winnie Walker	Margot Ballerina
Elaine	Lady Hamilton
Flower Girl	Scarlett O'Hara
Queen	Active Miss
Bridesmaid	Godey
Wendy Bride	Ballerina

"Elise" 16½" tall. All hard plastic with jointed elbow, vinyl arms. Has jointed knees and ankles. 1957 to 1964. The 1966 to date plastic and vinyl Elise will be shown by herself.
Bride
Lucy Bride
Scarlett
Ballerina
Ball Gown
Bridesmaid
Queen
Model
Renoir

"Cissette" is 10-11" tall, all hard plastic with high heel feet, jointed knees and was introduced in 1957 to 1963. A great many outfits were made for this doll and we will list, here, only the major ones:

Gainsbourgh	Lady Hamilton
Ballerina	Klondike Kate
Barbary Coast	Margot
Gibson Girl	Tinker Bell
Liesl & Brigitta	Portette: (1968-1973)
Agatha	Southern Belle
Melinda	Queen
Denmark	Scotch
Germany	Latin America
Queen Elizabeth	Bride
Internationals	Gold Rush
Bridesmaid	Fairy Princess
With Wigs	Godey
Scarlett	Renoir
Jenny Lind	Sleeping Beauty
Ireland	Swiss
India	

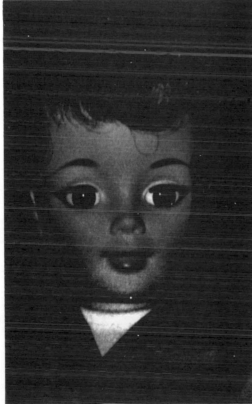

21" "Jacqueline-Portraits." Uses the Cissy body. 1961-1962 only. The Portraits, using this doll, started in 1965 to date. THEY ALL HAVE THE SAME MOLD MARKS/DATE OF 1961, NO MATTER IF MADE IN 1965 or 1975. Left: Jacqueline with dark eyes. Right: Lady Hamilton with blue eyes. 1966, the Coco doll was used for Portraits, all others this one.

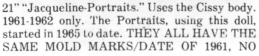

Bride	Scarlet	Southern Belle	Cornelia
Godey	Queen	Melanie	Renoir
Lady Hamilton	Gainsbourgh	Magnolia	Agatha
Renoir Mother	Mimi	Goya	Jenny Lind
			Madame Pompadour

Those made with the Coco mold (1966 only): Madame Doll, Melanie, Lissy, Godey, Scarlett and Renoir. This doll also sold as Judy (FAO Schwarz) and Simone (Marshall-Field) and Margot (Marshall-Field)

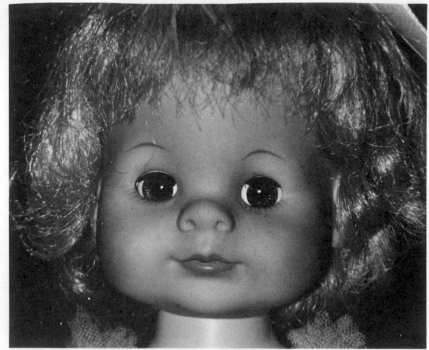

"Janie." 12" Uses same body as Smarty. 1964 to 1971.

Suzy	Marta
Lucinda	Brigitta
Fredrich	Michael
Rosie	

"Polly." 17" all vinyl with long slender limbs.
1965. Leslie: to date. Marie: to 1971.

Ballerina	Leslie (Colored)
Bride	Milly (Marshall Field-1968)
Maria	

"Mary Ann." 14" This doll has been used extensively from 1965 to date.

Ballerina	Jenny Lind
Little Granny	Bride
Lucinda	Grandma Jane
Renoir Girl	Liesl
Scarlett	Blue Boy
Wendy	Renoir Child
Orphan Annie	Snow White
Rebecca	McGuffey Ana
Heidi	Sleeping Beauty
Jenny Lind/cat	Gidget
Madame Doll	Alice In Wonderland
Peter Pan	Poor Cinderella
Louisa	Riley's Little Annie
Degas Girl	Cinderella, Ball Gown
Pinky	

"Elise" 17" Uses the Polly body. All vinyl. From 1966 to date.
Portrait Elise
Nancy Drew (12" version)
Maggie
Bride
Ballerina
Formal
Marlo Thomas
Little Women (12" version)
Maria (Sound of Music)

Little Women. 16." From book by Louisa Mae Alcott. (1832-1888). Trademark 344-080 in 1933. The movie this same year included Jean Parker as Beth, Joan Bennett as Amy, Kathryn Hepburn as Jo, Frances Dee as Meg and Spring Byington as the Mother of the March girls, Marme. The Little Women dolls have played a major part in the history of the Alexander Doll Company and there were only a very few years when a set of these dolls were not available to their customers.

Blue Boy. 16." Inspired by Gainsboro's painting.

Pinky. 16." Inspired by Reynold's painting.

Dicken's (Charles) Characters. 16" Little Emily, Little Dorrit, Little Nell, Oliver Twist, Amy and David Copperfield. These first appeared late 1933 and into 1934.

"Agnes" 18." From the Oliver Twist novel. 1934 cloth with original wrist tag. Red print dress with white pinafore with red trim. (Courtesy Sandy Rankow). Shown with David Copperfield dressed in tones of brown. (Courtesy Mandeville-Barkel Collection)

Freddie Bartholomew shown with W. C. Field in M.G.M's version of David Copperfield. 1935. Madame Alexander generally was inspired by literature long before a movie on a given subject, was made but usually released her dolls along with the movie.

Although Alexander Doll Company cloth dolls go past the 1935 date to today's date, we use 1935 for convenience.

Construction of the early cloth dolls were basic with bodies and limbs of pink cotton. The limbs are sewn on and the heads are "jointed" to turn. The mask type faces are of felt style suede material and were hand painted in oils. The very early ones by Madame Alexander, herself, or one of her three sisters. The painting is artistically done with most eyes looking to the side, several highlights, with painted iris and pupil. There is a red dot on the inside corners of the eyes and the eyebrows are one stroke. The mouths are generally "bow" shaped. The mohair wigs were attached to a cotton base and either glued or pinned on. The clothing is mostly cotton, with undies of organdy or cotton and made in one piece. The clothes are tagged but the dolls are not.

The most early dolls of cloth were make believe ones taken from Beatrice Alexander's own imagination. Soon she began applying her gift of design to the make believe characters from ficition. The instant success was Alice in Wonderland from Teniel's book.

Alice In Wonderland. 16." Trademark 304,488, August. 14, 1930. Book by Charles Lutwidge Dodgon—pseudonym — Lewis Carrol (1832-1898).

Alice In Wonderland. 16." Re-issue 1933. Trademark 334,921. The Paramount movie, Alice In Wonderland was released in 1933. Alice was played by Charlotte Henry, W.C.Fields was Humpty Dumpty, Edna Mae Oliver as the Red Queen. Others were Gary Cooper, Cary Grant, Charles Ruggles, Jack Oakie, Richard Arlen and Alison Skipworth.

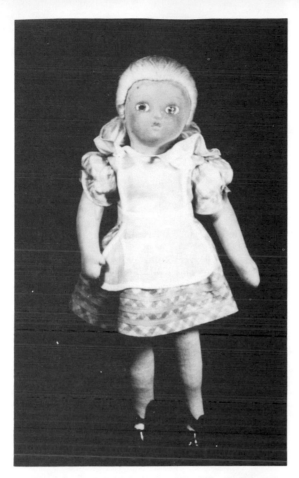

16" "Alice In Wonderland." All cloth with pressed, raised features, all hand painted in oils. Original. (Courtesy Mandeville-Barkel Collection)

Alice is shown here with the Mock Turtle who was played by Cary Grant and the Gryphon, played by William Austin.

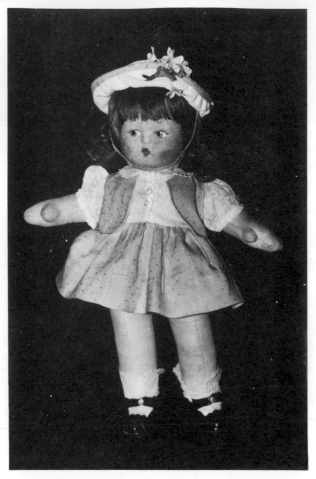

18" "American Tots." All cloth little girl. 1935-1937. Human hair wig (Also came with yellow yarn hair). Face mask with oil painted features. Original. Tag: Madame Alexander/New York, USA.

These are actually Beau Brummel and Belle Brummel of 1935. By 1939 the Belle Brummel had evolved to being dressed as a little school girl.

Tippie Toe and Pitty Pat, inspired by Eugene Field's poem.

American Tots. 16" Dressed in little child fashion. 1935-1937.

American Babies. 16." Exceptionally dressed as infants.

Kate Greenaway.

Grave Alice. 18" Laughing Allegra, Edith With Golden Hair, Hiawatha, Evangeline and Priscilla, inspired by Longfellow's poems. All 18."

McGuffey Ana. 16." Inspired by the McGuffey Readers. Trademark: 350,781.

Re-issue Alice in Wonderland. 14" Along with Tweedle-Dum and Tweedle-Dee.

Goldilocks. Poet Robert Southey, in England, wrote the first "Three Bears" but the poem had an old woman instead of little girl and as the story was repeated there it was called "Silver Hair and the Three Bears" and it was in U.S. that she became a child named "Goldilocks."

Doris Keane, (1881-1945). Star of Edward Sheldon's "Romance" in 1913.

Babbie. 16" Inspired from Little Minister. The R.K.O. movie starred Katherine Hepburn. Brown mohair wig in bangs. Brown eyes. Red skirt/yellow print blouse. Laced wide belt.

Eva Lovelace. Inspired by Morning Glory (1933). Katherine Hepburn played the lead and won the Academy Award for her performance. 24." Long set in eyelashes, long thin legs.

Cherub Babies. New born Babies.

Beatrice Behrman (nee Alexander) made many cloth dolls through the years, as she always felt that the softness and beauty of these dolls will always have an appeal to children. The company also produced a continuing line of stuffed animals, both "oil cloth" washable ones and long pile rayon ones. During the 1930's, the company produced a great variety of stuffed toy dolls, that is dolls with "animal characters." It was through an error in research that we listed the rabbit dolls (Vol. II) as being Suzie Q and Bobby Q, when they are actually Beau Brummel and Bell Brummel of 1935.

The following is a list of stuffed dolls/animals produced from 1934 through 1936. Most are based on known characters.

Oliver Twistail, David Twistail, Emily, Agnes, Cornelia, March Hatter, Mrs. March Hatter, Aunt Betsy, David Quack-a-field, Mrs. Quac-a-field, Smoky Tail, Beau and Belle Brummel, Sir Lapin O'Hare and "fiancee," Dottie Dumbunnie (the Rabbit Haress), Molly Cottontail, Dicksie and Ducksie, Riding Hood, Lady Lovelace, Buck Rabbit, Mrs. Buck Rabbit, Mrs. Snoopie Goes A Marketing, Gibson Girl, Sandy and Nan MacHare, White Rabbit.

During the 1936 and into the 1937 season, Alexander made cloth Dionne Quints, along with the composition ones. These came in sizes 16" and 24." Bodies were pink cotton and they have hand painted features with brown eyes and dark brown mohair wigs.

Little Lord Fauntleroy. Trademark 374,270. 1936. From book of same name by Frances Hodgson Burnett (1849-1924). The movie this same year starred Freddie Bartholomew.

Baby Genius. All cloth of "So-Lite" design. 1937.

Alexander Rag Time Dolls: Movie "Alexander's Rag Time Band" (1938), starred Alice Faye and Tyrone Power.

So-Lite line of dolls. 10," 12," 18," 20" and 24" sizes. 1939.

Bobby Q and Susie Q. Based on comic strip. 1940.

Playmate Line. With over-sized dolls. 1940-1942.

Little Shaver. Inspired by Elsie Saver's paintings of Victorian children. 1941. The Trademark 125,515 (Dec. 2, 1919) was sold to the Alexander Company. Little Shaver dolls were made in five sizes.

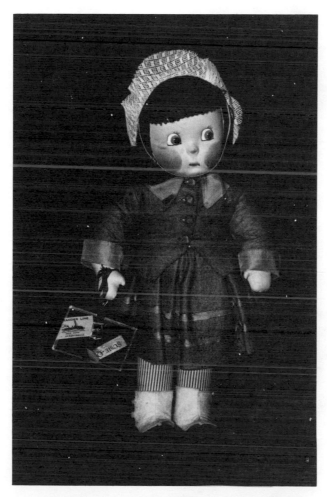

16" Character from Susie Q comic strip. Cloth with felt clothes and yarn hair. Painted features. 1940. (Courtesy Jay Minter)

Playmate line with over-sized dolls. 1940-1942.

29" "Playmate" 1940. 25½" waist and 21" head. All cloth with stitched fingers, due to size also has cardboard inserts for soles. One piece yellow panties and blouse. Apron type skirt is blue. Yellow yarn hair. Marks: Madame/Alexander/ New York U.S.A. (Courtesy Jayn Allen)

Shows body of the extremely large cloth doll. Country Cousin of 1942 also came in the 29-20" size.

Little Shaver, inspired by Elsie Saver's paintings of Victorian children. 1941. The Trademark #125,515 (Dec. 2, 1919) was sold to the Alexander Company. Little Shaver dolls were made in five sizes.

10" "Little Shaver" Mask face with stockinette, wired and posable body and limbs. Auburn floss hair. 1937-41. Tag: Little Shaver/Madame Alexander. Came in five sizes. (Courtesy Peggy Boudreau)

17" "Funny" All checked cloth with yarn hair. Tag: Madame Alexander. Dress tag: Funny/ Madame Alexander. #50-1963. This doll, along with the cloth Muffin became a regular part of the Alexander line and is still available.

Country Cousins. 10," 26" and 30" sizes. Boy and girls. 1942.

Cuddly. Mask face with plus body and limbs. 10½" and 17" sizes. 1942.

Funny. 18." 1961. This all cloth doll has been made continuously since then.

Muffin. 14." 1961. Has been made continuously since the. In 1965-1966, this doll was made in the 19" size also.

Pachity Pam and Pachity Pepper. 15." From book of same name. 1965-1966.

Good Little Girl (16" in pink) and Bad Little Girl (16" in blue) from book of same name. Book illustrations by Eloise Wilkin for Golden Books. 1965-1966.

Carrot Top. 18" 1967.

14" "Muffin" All cloth with yarn hair and felt features. Dress is flowered. This one is 1972 although this doll has been made continuously since 1963. Catalog reprint.

Madame Alexander has always been a sharp business woman and few areas try the endurance as the Toy Industry and dolls, in particular. Madame Alexander always tried to temper the coldness of business with the soft warmness of ideals that came to life for her, in a special way, for her dolls were meant to be cultural, to help educatie children, to help their interest in the Arts, dancing, theater and good books.

When Alexander's dolls are looked at squarely, one sees Beatrice Alexander's own reactions take form. For example, when campus riots were going strong, she introduced silver haired and bespeckled "Grandma Jane" and truly hoped "She" (Grandma Jane) would help bring little girls closer to their grandmothers and respect for family life"....or after reading Gone With The Wind (1936) was so impressed, not by Scarlett's personality or fight to survive but her sympathies were aroused by the starving Scarlett's generosity in "sharing/a carrot, the only thing she could find, with her Negro maid." There has been an almost continuous "Scarlett" doll since then.

As the book, Gone With The Wind (1936) began to sell well and due to Madame Alexander's own impressions, she secured the rights to make the doll characters and infused her own ideas into the design of the clothes for these "Southern

Belles" (Girls) and Scarlett, along with Melanie and two younger sisters, Carreen and Suellen.

Madame Alexander has always seemed to have the talent to recognize a "winner" and kept her high ideals of what a doll should be and represent. She has always seemed to manage to introduce a doll based on a book, poem, etc. prior to it being released as a movie or a break of National Publicity, in some way. Another example, besides Gone With the Wind, would be Alice In Wonderland, for she tied in with the book, registered the doll and had the doll on the market (1933), the same year the movie was released.

During 1935, Madame Alexander received the rights to make dolls based on the stories of the "Little Colonel" by Annie Fellows Johnston, from her heirs. By doing so, she was able to introduce her Little Colonel dolls the same time the Shirley Temple movie "Little Colonel" was being released, thereby gaining a lot of free publicity.

Early in 1935, the guardians of the Dionne Quints accepted Madame Alexander's offer and she has sole United States rights to make these dolls. The first ads appeared in 1935 and the dolls were offered in the 7½" size with painted sleep eyes, 17½" with cloth body, 23" with cloth body, 10½" and also the all cloth ones. A set of five was offered in a white enameled bed, kiddie cars and a ferris wheel. By March of 1936 the Quints were offered in their "home" with nursery furniture along with a nurse (Yvonne Leroux). Dr. Defoe was placed on the market early in 1936 (1937 was issued as a Priest, Minister and Doctor). Late in 1936 came the Quint-O-Bile, holding a set of 5-7½" dolls, swing-facing each other, and by the fall of 1937 came the promotional tour with nurse Yvonne Leroux, nurse of the Dionne Quints. At each stop, she appeared on the radio and made visits to stores where the Alexander Quint dolls were sold, to meet the children and their mothers and to talk of the Quints.

It was during 1935 and into 1936 that Madame Alexander designed the Baby Jane doll, a chubby faced little girl with smiling mouth and eyes. Baby Jane was Universal star, Juanita Quigley and played Baby Jane in Imitation of Life, along with Claudette Colbert. When older, she left films to enter a Convent and still later, left the Convent to marry.

Madame Alexander introduced the Jane Withers' dolls in 1937, after negotiating with the family. Jane, herself, is a doll collector and in recent years has said that she never did care for herself as a doll. The closed mouth, painted eye version was first and done by Bernard Lipfert in the 13" size, then came the 16", 18" and 20" sizes. The ads for these dolls all show that the 13" size only came with a closed mouth but recently it has been reported that collectors own Jane Withers dolls with closed mouths in the other sizes also.

May 12, 1937 was the Coronation to the Throne of England, of King George VI, father of Princess Elizabeth and Margaret Rose. By October, 1937, Madame Alexander had a Princess Eliabeth doll on the market. As a little girl attending her father's coronation, she wears a tiara with a miniature British crown. The dolls came in sizes of 11", 13", 14", 16", 21", 22", 23", 24" and 28." The 13" (marked Alexander and with the circle-X) has a closed mouth and others have open mouths. In 1938 and 1939, the dolls had evolved into a "little girl/Princess" image with riding habit, party dresses and little girl dresses and it must be remembered that the Princess Elizabeth marked doll was used in a great variety of other dolls. It must also be noted that composition, often times, shrunk or swelled after leaving molds, so doll sizes can vary as much as 1½."

The following is list of small composition dolls.

Tiny Betty. 7" to 8" with one piece body and head. Eyes painted to side. Painted on black shoes with white socks. Bent right arm. 1935 through 1939. All clothes removable.

Little Women (1936-39)
Jack & Jill (1938-39)

Bo Peep (1938-39)	Brazilian (1935-37)
Cinderella (1935)	Hawaiian (1936)
Lazy Mary, Will You Get Up (1936)	Colonial (1937-38)
Dilly Dally Sally (1937)	Goldilocks (1938)
Little Boy Blue (1937)	Mistress Mary (1937)
Eva Lovelace (1935)	Topsy (1935-36)
Little Jack Horner (1937)	Gretel & Hansel (1937)
Lola, Lila Bridesmaids (1937)	Polly Put Kettle On (1937)
Penny, Lila Bridesmaids (1937)	Red Riding Hood (1936)
Pan American (Pollera) (1936)	Alice In Wonderland (1935)
Peasant (1936)	Red Cross Nurse (1937)
School Girl (1937)	Mexican (1936)
American Girl (1938)	Belgium (1935-38)
Chinese (1936)	France (1936)
Czech (1935-37)	Danish (1937)
Dutch (1935-39)	McGuffey Ana (1935-39)
Bride (1935-39)	Egyptian (1936)
Finnish (1935-37)	Polish (1935-36)
Normandy (1935-38)	Persia (1936)
Norweigan (1936)	Russian (1935-36)
Swedish (1936)	Scotch (1936-39)
American Child (1938)	Heidi (1938)
Ding Dong Dell (1937)	Spanish (1935-39)
Fairy Princess (1939-40)	Burma (1939)

Carmen, inspired by Geraldine Farrar in opera, "Carmen" (1936-39)

Doll of Month Club: Jan. Mittens, hood and full skirt. Feb. Lacy dress with ribbons, hearts and flowers. Mar. Apron and carries rake. Apr. Rain coat. May. Full length gown, flowers in hair. June. Organdy dress with roses. July. Bathing suit/bag with towel, pail and shovel. Aug. Sheer organdy short sleeve party dress. Sept. School dress/bag. Oct. Unknown. Nov. Pilgrim costume. Dec. Unknown.

Little Betty. 9" and 11." Fully jointed with painted eyes. Had both molded hair and wigs. Barefooted. 1936 to 1941.

McGuffey Ana (1935-39)	French (1936-39)
Danish (1938)	American Indian (1937-39)
Bride (1936-41)	Jack & Jill (1939)
Little Women (1937-41)	Scotch (1938)
Egyptian (1936)	Mexico (1938)
Hawaiian (1937-39)	Hansel & Gretel (1938)
Carmen (1937-41)	Dilly Dally Sally (1938)
Bridesmaid (1937-39)	Virginia Dare (first child
Eskimo (1937-39)	from England born in U.S. (1940)
Peasant (1938-39)	Alice In Wonderland (1939)
Norwegian (1938)	Red Cross Nurse 1939
Brazil (1938)	Doris Keane (Romance) (1936)
Spain (1937-38)	Fairy Princess (1939-40)
Jugo-Slav (1937-39)	Princess Elizabeth (1937)
Red Riding Hood (1939)	Sunbonnet Sue (1937)
Swiss (1935-38)	Sleeping Beauty (1941)
Colonial (1936-39)	Fairy Tale Characters
Bo Peep (1938)	from Dumas (1940)
Days of Week Dolls (1936-38)	American Girl (1937)

Wendy Ann. 11", 12", 13", 14" and larger. 1937 to 1940 with "face" used to 1947. Modeled and named for Madame Alexander's Grandaughter, designed by Madame Alexander. Swivel waists and came with both molded and painted hair. Both painted and sleep eyes and came with either sharply bent right arms and slightly curved ones. Had individual wardrobes and was issued as:

Alice In Wonderland	Carmen
Flora McFlimsy (without "e")	Ballerina
Bridesmaid	Cinderella
McGuffey Ana	Bride
Little Women	

The 1936-1937-1938 Wendy Ann day of the Week dolls were: Washing on Monday; Gardening on Tuesday; Ironing on Wednesday; Cleaning on Thursday; Marketing on Friday;

Baking on Saturday; Party on Sunday.

The later composition dolls had far greater quality than the early ones and when the Alexander dolls were made of the later composition, they generally are far superior to many manufacturers of the day. It must be noted that the same "face" was used with different hairstyles/clothes to make different personalities. For example, the Princess Elizabeth doll was used for not only Princess Elizabeth but also for Snow White, McGuffey Ana, Flora McFlimsy, Kate Greenaway, Cinderella, Miss Victory and others. The following listing shows introduction dates with many being issued for several years. This listing will be done by years and the dolls of those years will be shown following the list. The name appearing right after each listing is the "face" used that year.

It must be remembered that not all dolls made were shown in the company catalogs and also that a same catalog photograph was shown year after year when actually the doll did remain the same but the costume was changed.

1935

Betty. Patsy style doll with bent right arm and "bow" mouth.

Betsy. 12" only. Painted eyes. (Also in 1934), Marked "it" on back. Doll was purchased from another company.

Betty Character Dolls. McGuffey Ana, Cinderella, etc.

Tiny and Little Betty. 7" to 9."

Baby Betty. 10." Also in 1936 and 1937. Very bent baby legs.

Baby McGuffey. 12" only.

David Copperfield. (Tiny Betty)

Little Colonel. 8½" to 23." Trademark 362,009. Came in nine different outfits. 13" size has closed mouth. Slight dimples and Shirley Temple style curls. All had the photo from book (head of little girl) on clothes tag. (Betty).

Baby Jane. Laughing eyes, open mouth child representing Juanita Quigley, child star.

1936

Marcella Doll line.

Dionne Quints. Trademarks: 374,274; Quins, 374,269, Five Babies, 374,273; Quinties, 374,271.

Five Little Peppers. Trademark 374,268. Book written in 1880 by Margaret Sidney (Harriet Mulford Lothrop: 1844-1924)

Babsie. Baby with moving tongue.

Little Cherub. 11." Rosebud mouth. Pink or blue organdy dress/bonnet.

Slumbermate. (to 1937). Cloth and composition. Closed, sleeping painted eyes.

Alice In Wonderland. (Little Betty)

Round the World Dolls. (Tiny and Little Betty)

Doris Keane. Star of Edward Sheldon's play "Romance."

1913 production. (Betty)

Wendy Ann. 11," 13," 15," 17" and 21." Molded and named for Madame Alexander's Grand daughter.

Romeo and Juliet. (to 1937). Inspired by movie of same name. Leads played by Norman Shearer and Leslie Howard. (Betty and Wendy Ann, 1937)

Little Lord Fauntleroy. Trademark 374,270. The 1937 movie starred Freddie Bartholomew. (Wendy).

Old Fashioned Girl. Based on book by Louisa Mae Alcott. (Betty)

Princess Doll. 13" and 15." Has dimples.

1937

Carmen. Inspired by Geraldine Farrar in the opera "Carmen." Green velvet skirt with pink satin top. (Tiny, Little Betty and Wendy Ann)

Camille. From Dumas classic. Metro film (1936) starred Greta Garbo and Robert Taylor. (Wendy Ann)

Round the World Dolls. (Tiny and Little Betty)

Princess Elizabeth. At the time of her father's coronation.

Princess Margaret Rose. Sister of Elizabeth. Pale blue chiffon gown (Prin. Eliz.)

Snow White. Trademark 363,240. This very first doll was 13" and had painted eyes. Came with both open and closed mouths. (Prin. Eliz.)

Seven Dwarfs. Fully jointed.

Zorina Ballerina. 17." Gold lame bodice, pleated short net (white) skirt. Gold lame head scarf with white feathers. (Wendy Ann)

Scarlett O'Hara. From Margaret Mitchell's book. Trademark 392-003. Came in 10," 11," 13," 14," 16," 17," 18" and 21" sizes. (Wendy Ann)

Carreen and Suellen. 14" size only. Sisters of Scarlett (Wendy Ann)

McGuffey Ana. Inspired by the McGuffey Readers. Trademark 393,886. Re-issued early 1950's and again in 1965. (Prin. Eliz.) Also in 9" size (little Betty) 11" and 13" sizes have closed mouths.

Jane Withers. 15," 17" and 20" with open mouths. 13" and 13½" with closed mouths. Some of the larger sizes have been reported with closed mouths but none seem to appear in the old ads on the dolls.

Annie Laurie. Trademark 401,099. (Wendy Ann)

Princess Alexandria. Trademark 401,004. Cloth body baby.

Little Genius. Cloth body baby.

Precious. Cloth body baby.

Baby McGuffey. Cloth body baby.

Norma Shearer and Leslie Howard shown from a scene in Romeo and Juliet. 1936. (Thalberg Production). The doll inspired by this movie may be seen in the color section. The doll was not released until 1937.

This studio picture shows Freddie Bartholomew showing Baby Jane — Juanita Quigley a safe way to celebrate the 4th of July. Note cuff protectors on Freddie.

Tweeny-Twinkle. Trademark 392,002. (Doll unknown)

Neva-Wet Baby line. Trademark 392,942.

Madelaine DuBain. For FAO Schwarz. In French costume of 1880. Sold 1937, 1938, 1939. (Wendy Ann)

Dionne Quints. Repeats of 1936.

Dr. DeFoe. Same doll used for Priest, Minister and Doctor.

Pinky Baby.

1938

Scarlett O'Hara. Various costumes. (Wendy Ann)

Alexander Rag Time Dolls. Cloth dolls in turn of century costumes. The 1938 movie "Alexander's Rag Time Band" starred Alice Faye and Tyrone Power.

Sleeping Beauty. (Prin. Eliz.)

Snow White. (Prin. Eliz.)

Princess Elizabeth. Repeat with costume changes.

Princess Margaret Rose. 15" and 18." Sister to Elizabeth. (Prin. Eliz.)

McGuffey Ana. (Little Betty and Prin. Eliz.) Repeat with costume changes.

Kate Greenaway. (Prin. Eliz.)

Three Pigs and Wolf. Fully jointed.

Dionne Quints. Repeat.

Ballerina. (Wendy Ann) 14" and 17."

Round the World Dolls. (Tiny and Little Betty)

Princess Alexandria. Repeat of 1937.

Dicken's Characters. 14." Tiny Tim, Little Nell and David Copperfield. (Wendy Ann)

Cookie. Raising arm made her head turn from side to side.

Sally Bride. 14," 18" and 21." (Wendy Ann)

Portraits. 21." Mary Louise, Godey Lady. Camille dressed in pale green with dotted swiss overskirt, lace trimmed. Full sleeves narrowing down arms. Green or blue sash. Black shoes. Very large picture straw hat. White pantalettes. Has brown eyes. Carmen. Victoria of 1850. Marm Lisa, from book by Kate Douglas Wiggins. Princess Flavia, from Prisoner of Zenda. Heroine in this 1938 movie was Madaline Carroll. (all Wendy Ann). These same portraits were made again in 1946 along with others.

1939

Flora McFlimsy (without "e"). From McGuffey Readers. (Prin. Eliz.)

McGuffey Ana. With costume changes. (Prin. Eliz.)

Lucy Bride. (Wendy Ann)

Dionne Quints. Repeat.

Cinderella. Metal tiara, organdy gown with matching ruffle at hem. Puff sleeves and lace trim. 14," exclusively at Sears, Roebuck (1940). (Prin. Eliz.)

Snow White. (Prin. Eliz.)

Kate Greenaway. (Prin. Eliz.) Different outfits.

Scarlett O'Hara. (Wendy Ann) Costume changes.

21" Portrait doll Princess Flavia from the movie Prisoner of Zenda. This doll was repeated in 1946 and had a clover tag attached to the arm. Another view may be seen in color section. (Courtesy Renie Culp)

Shows scene from The Prisoner of Zenda which starred Ronald Colman and Madaline Carroll. The part played by Madaline Carroll is Princess Flavia. The Princess Flavia doll may be seen in the color section.

Carreen and Suellen. Sisters of Scarlett. (One Wendy Ann, one Prin. Eliz.)

Juliet. (Wendy Ann)

Sleeping Beauty. (Wendy Ann)

Queen Alexandrine. (Denmark). 21" only. (Wendy Ann)

Jeannie Walker. Patent 2,328,704. First made in 1939 but not registered until Sept. 7, 1943.

Round the World Dolls. (Tiny and Little Betty)

Little Women (Wendy Ann)

Mother and Me. Trademark 431,899 (in 1940). (Wendy Ann and Little Betty)

Sonja Henie. Open and closed mouth versions. (Closed mouth-Wendy Ann)

Cathy. 21" and 17." Inspired by Bronte's (Emily) novel Wuthering Heights. In the 1939 movie, Cathy was played by Merle Oberon and Heathcliffe by Laurence Oliver. (Wendy Ann)

Posey Pat. Red hair in braids and brown eyes. 14" and 21." (Wendy Ann)

This photo from the 1939 movie Withering Heights shows Cathy and Heathcliff on the Moors. (Merle Oberon and Laurence Oliver)

1940

Butch McGuffey. Trademark 432,898. One of Alexander's first boy dolls.

Baby McGuffey. Cloth and composition.

Madelaine. Different than one sold through FAO Schwarz. Trademark 433,208. (Wendy Ann)

Little Angel. (Unknown)

Ginger Rogers. Three different outfits. (Wendy Ann)

Sonja Henie. Repeat with new costumes.

Honeyette Baby.

Clover Kid. (Unknown)

Sleeping Beauty. (Wendy Ann). Repeat. 14½."

Anna Ballerina. Inspired by famous Russian Ballerina, Anna Pavlova (Wendy Ann)

Fairy Princess. (Tiny and Little Betty)

Southern Girl. (Wendy Ann). Style of the Scarletts.

Scarlett O'Hara. (Wendy Ann). Repeat with costume changes.

Little Women. (Wendy Ann)

Kate Greenaway. Repeat. (Prin. Eliz.)

Fairy Queen. (Wendy Ann). 14½" and 18."

Bride and Bridesmaids. (Wendy Ann and Prin. Eliz.)

Rebecca. In three sizes. Inspired by book of same name by Daphne DuMaurier. This year's film starred Joan Fontaine and Laurence Oliver. (Wendy Ann)

Ginger Rogers starred in a number of movies but will not be remembered for any great skill in acting but will be remembered for her fantastic ability to dance, especially her routines with Fred Astair.

1941

Bride. (Wendy Ann)

Lollie. Made with Lov-Le-Tex latex. Trademark 444,850.

Kate Greenaway. (Prin. Eliz.)

Baby McGuffey. Arms and legs of latex.

Kitty Baby. Composition head, cloth body and latex limbs.

Kitty Baby. Composition head, cloth body and latex limbs.

Scarlett O'Hara. Repeat. (Wendy Ann)

Southern Girl. Scarlett style clothes. Both brown and blue eyes. (Wendy Ann)

McGuffey Ana. Repeat with costume changes. (Prin. Eliz.)

Flora McFlimsy. Repeat. (Prin. Eliz.)

Sonja Henie. In different outfits.

Babsie. Skater (roller). (Prin. Eliz.)

1942

June Bride. In 7," 9," 15," 18," and 22" sizes. (Wendy Ann, Tiny and Little Betty).

Carmen. In red dotted organdy dress. 7" to 22." (Wendy Ann, Tiny Betty)

Scarlett in various outfits. (Wendy Ann)

Southern Girl in various outfits. (Wendy Ann) in four sizes.

McGuffey Ana in six sizes. (Prin. Eliz.)

Jeannie Walker. Repeat.

W.A.A.C. (Wendy Ann)

W.A.V.E. (Wendy Ann)

David O. Selznick made the film of DuMaurier's story Rebecca in 1940. Directed by Alfred Hitchcock and starred Joan Fontaine and Laurence Oliver.

W.A.A.F. (Wendy Ann)

Soldier. (Wendy Ann)

Skating Doll. (Sonja Henie)

Fairy Princess. In four sizes. (Wendy Ann)

Kate Greenaway. In five sizes. (Prin. Eliz.)

Mother and Me. Repeat with clothes changes. (Wendy Ann and Little Betty)

Baby Genius. With molded hair and wigs.

So Lite Dolls.

Special Girl. 22" and 24."

Slumbermate. Sleeping baby.

Portraits. 12 dolls, all using Wendy Ann, dressed in "exhibition" gowns. This group was very expensive selling for $175.00. Included were June Bride, Carmen, Mary Louise, Renoir, Rebecca, Groom, Judy, Camille, Orchard Princess, King, Queen, Princess Rosetta. Discontinued after 1942, due to war, and continued again in 1946.

Butch. In three sizes.

Baby McGuffey. In five sizes.

1943

Due to very limited production during War time (World War II) there were very few dolls on the market. Only three were offered, but some dealers used up stock from the 1942 and into 1944 years: Military dolls, Jeannie Walker, Sonja Henie and the So Lite clothes dolls.

1944

Miss Victory. (Prin. Eliz.)

Bride in two sizes. (Wendy Ann)

Bridesmaid in three sizes. (Prin. Eliz.)

Flowergirl in three sizes. (Prin. Eliz.)

Southern Girl in two sizes. (Wendy Ann)

Princess Doll in two sizes. (Prin. Eliz.)

McGuffey Ana in four sizes. (Prin. Eliz.)

Little Women. (Wendy Ann)

Flora McFlimsey. (Prin. Eliz.)

1945

Judy. 17." (Wendy Ann)

Ginger Rogers. In three outfits. (Wendy Ann)

Gene Tierney. 15" Inspired from movie "Dragonwyck." Sequined, off shoulder, white gown. (Wendy Ann)

Bride. 17" and 22." (Wendy Ann)

Bridesmaid. 15," 18" and 21½." (Wendy Ann)

Maid of Honor. 18." (Wendy Ann)

Flowergirl. 16," 20" and 24." (Prin. Eliz.)

Southern Girl. (Wendy Ann)

Little Women. (Wendy Ann)

Princess Rosetta. 21" only. (Wendy Ann)

1946

Wendy Bride, in satin. Two sizes. (Wendy Ann)

Bridesmaid. In three sizes. (Wendy Ann)

Little Women. (Wendy Ann)

Flowergirl. In three sizes. (Prin. Eliz.)

Margaret O'Brien. Dressed in original movie/real life costumes. 14½" 18" and 21." All eye colors were used and wigs from ash blonde to dark brown.

Margaret O'Brien Ballerina. From "The Unfinished Dance" based on story "LaMort du Cygne," also starring Cyd Charisse, Danny Thomas and Karin Booth (Prima Ballerina)

Alice in Wonderland. (Margaret)

Fairy Queen. 14½" and 18." (Wendy Ann)

Margaret Rose (Princess). 15," 18" and 21." (Margaret)

Hulda. 18." (Margaret)

Karen Ballerina. 15," 18" and 21." (Margaret)

Sleeping Beauty. 15," 18" and 21." (Wendy Ann)

Baby Genius. In five sizes.

Baby McGuffey. 11" only.

Portraits Series of 12. All 21" and using the Wendy Ann and Margaret molds. June Bride, Carmen, Mary Louise, Renoir, Groom, Judy, King, Queen, Camille, Orchard Princess, Princess Rosetta, Rebecca.

1947

Alice in Wonderland. 14½," 18" and 21." (Margaret)

Bitsey and Butch. 11" and 12."

Hilda. Colored little girl. (Margaret)

Margaret O'Brien. Costume changes.

Little Women. First in hard plastic. (All Margaret, in this first set)

Royal Wedding. 21" (Margaret). Queen Elizabeth, elder daughter of King George VI and Consort Queen Elizabeth and Prince Phillip, Duke of Edinburgh. Married in Nov. 1947.

16" "Baby Jane." (Child actress Juanita Quigley) All composition. 1935-36. Head marked: Baby Jane/Reg. Mme. Alexander. Dress tag. Universal starlet/Baby Jane Madame Alexander. (Courtesy Billie Nelson Tyrrell)

14" "Little Colonel" All composition with blue tin sleep eyes. 1935. (Betty). Has re-placed wig as all the Little Colonels had blonde, curly styled wigs. (Courtesy Virginia Vinton)

Full view of 8½" "Little Colonel." Original. 1935-1936. (Courtesy Marge Meisinger)

8½" "Little Colonel." 1935-1936. All composition. Painted brown eyes. Wig over molded hair (Hair pushed back to see bangs). Original. Tag: Picture as on "Little Colonel" book/Trademark/Little Colonel/Alexander Doll Co./New York. (Courtesy Marge Meisinger)

Unless this emblem is on the tag, it is very unlikely that a "questionable" Little Colonel is actually one.

14" "Little Colonel" 1935. Pink satin dress with matching bonnet. Black vest and patent shoes. Blue tin eyes and slight dimples. Replaced wig. (Betty). (Courtesy Roberta Lago)

12" "Nurse." 1935. All composition with painted blue eyes and molded blue bow in hair. Nurse costume came on doll when she was purchased with a very fine unmarked set of quintuplets in original costumes, with Dionne bed and booklets. Marks: none. (Courtesy Ruby K. Arnold)

19" "Betty" 1935. All composition. Blue sleep eyes but also came with brown eyes. Dark eye shadow. Bent right arm. Had paper tag: Betty/Madame Alexander. (Courtesy Karen Penner)

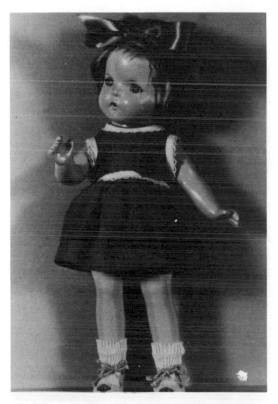

13" "Betty" 1935. All composition with blonde mohair wig over molded hair. Blue tin sleep eyes. Rosebud style mouth. Not original. Bent right arm. Body identical to the Princess Elizabeth. (Courtesy John Axe)

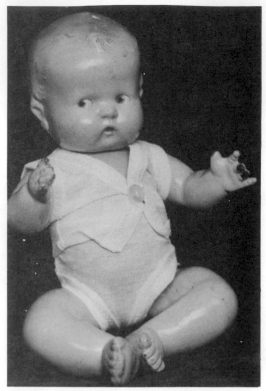

10" "Baby Betty" 1935. All composition with extreme bent baby legs with toes curled down. Molded hair with short curls in back. Painted blue eyes to side. Marks: Madame/Alexander, on back. Not original. (Courtesy Elizabeth Montesano of Yesterday's Children)

13" Unidentified. All composition with blue painted eyes to the side. Blonde mohair wig. Closed mouth. Separate jacket and skirt of brushed (fuzzy) pink material. White cotton blouse. Racoon fur trimmed jacket and muff. Pink furry tiny hat stapled to hair. Ca. 1935-1937 Marks: are only partly readable:————BE/ Ale————er. (Courtesy Elizabeth Montesano of Yesterday's Children)

9" "McGuffey Ana" 1935. All composition. Painted eyes to side. Tag: Madame Alexander/ U.S.A. Reg. No. 350,781. Deep rose with white pinafore. Also came in pink and with lace trimmed pink organdy. All three have straw hat with flowers. (Courtesy Jay Minter)

7". "David Copperfield" All composition with one piece body and head. Painted on black shoes. Charles Dicken's character. Freddie Bartholomew played David in the 1934 movie. Marks: none on doll. Tag: Charles Dicken's David Copperfield / Madame Alexander / New York U.S.A. 1935. (Tiny Betty) (Courtesy Jane Thomas).

12" "Betsy" All composition with painted blue eyes and yellow blonde molded hair. Doll is marked "I T," on back with dress tag: "Betsy/ Madame Alexander/New York. One piece bloomer style underclothes. Pink, dress with white collar and cuffs. Matching bonnet. Both arms are bent. 1934-1935. (Courtesy Jay Minter)

12" "Baby McGuffey" Cloth with composition head and hands. Pink dress with flowered pinafore. Wig over molded hair. Marks: "Baby McGuffey" / Madame Alexander, etc. (Courtesy Marie Ernst)

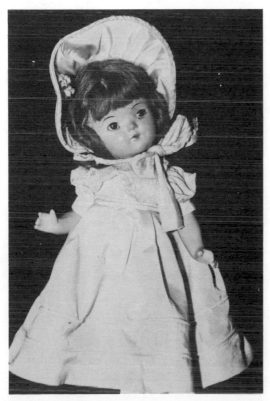

13" "Princess" All composition. Tin blue sleep eyes and slight dimples. (Betty-Little Colonel). Bent right arm. 1936. This doll made year before Princess Elizabeth's father was crowned. Tag: Princess/Madame Alexander, etc. (Courtesy Helen Faford)

Close up face of Princess (Betty). (Courtesy Helen Faford)

13" "Princess" All composition. Bent right arm. Brown tin sleep eyes. Dimples. Human hair wig. (Betty-Little Colonel) Pink taffeta gown with black bows. Tag: Princess/Madame Alexander/ New York. (Courtesy Alma Carmichael)

20" One of the "Marcella Dolls" of 1936. All composition with pale blonde mohair wig, brown sleep eyes, open mouth. Peach organdy dress with straw and peach organdy bonnet. Tag with red lettering: Madame/Alexander/New York. This doll is similar to the Little Colonel doll but is a better quality composition. (Courtesy Elizabeth Montesano of Yesterday's Children)

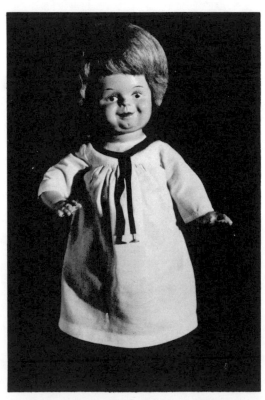

14" "Dr. DeFoe" All composition with painted eyes and gray mohair wig. 1936. Clothes not original. Marks: none. (Courtesy Mandeville-Barkel Collection)

14" "Dr. Defoe" and set of 7½" "Dionne Quints." 1936. Painted eyes and mohair wigs. Original except pins. Marks: Dionne/Alexander, on head and Alexander, on bodies. (Courtesy Mandeville-Barkel Collection)

7½" "Dionne Quints" 1936. All composition with painted eyes and molded hair toddlers. This set also came with bent baby legs and also with wigs. Original pastel shade dresses and bonnets. (Courtesy Jay Minter)

7½" Set of "Dionne Quints" in their own Ferris Wheel. The seats bear the individual names of the children. 1936. (Courtesy Sandy Rankow)

7½" "Dionne Quint" toddler with wig. Original romper suit with matching beret. 1936.

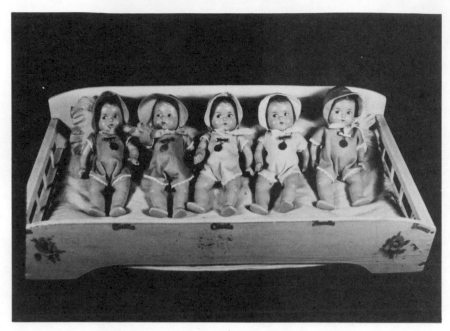

7½" "Dionne Quints." All original in wooden
bed. 1936. (Courtesy Carrie Perkins)

10½" "Dionne Quints" All composition with
brown sleep eyes, curved baby legs. Dresses are
pale shades of organdy with names embroidered
on bibs. Very lightly molded hair that is spray
painted brown. Marks: Dionne, on head. Madame Alexander, on backs. 1936. (Courtesy
Jeannie Gregg)

14" Set of "Dionne Quints" with wigs and sleep eyes. Clothes are copies of the originals. 1936. (Courtesy Sandy Rankow)

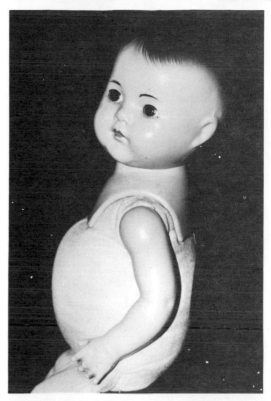

17" Cloth bodied "Dionne Quint" 1936. Swivel composition shoulder head and plate. Molded hair and brown sleep eyes. (Courtesy Connie Chase)

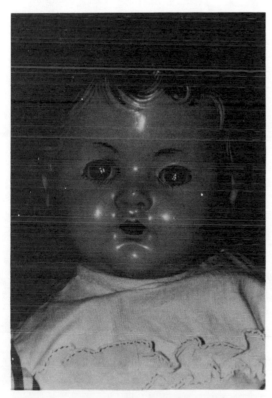

17" Cloth bodied "Dionne Quint" with swivel shoulder plate to show the difference in hair molding. This one has "heavy" molding and others have light/or brush stroked hair at the sides. 1936. (Courtesy Alice Capps)

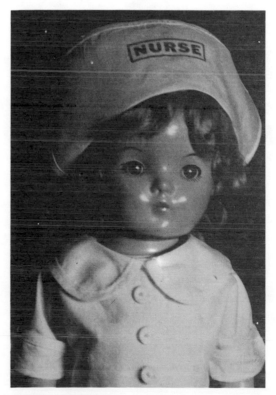

13" "Nurse" 1936. All composition with blue tin sleep eyes. Glued on mohair wig. Came to original owner with set of marked Dionne Quints and a Dr. DeFoe. Marks: none. (Betty) (Courtesy Ruby K. Arnold)

31

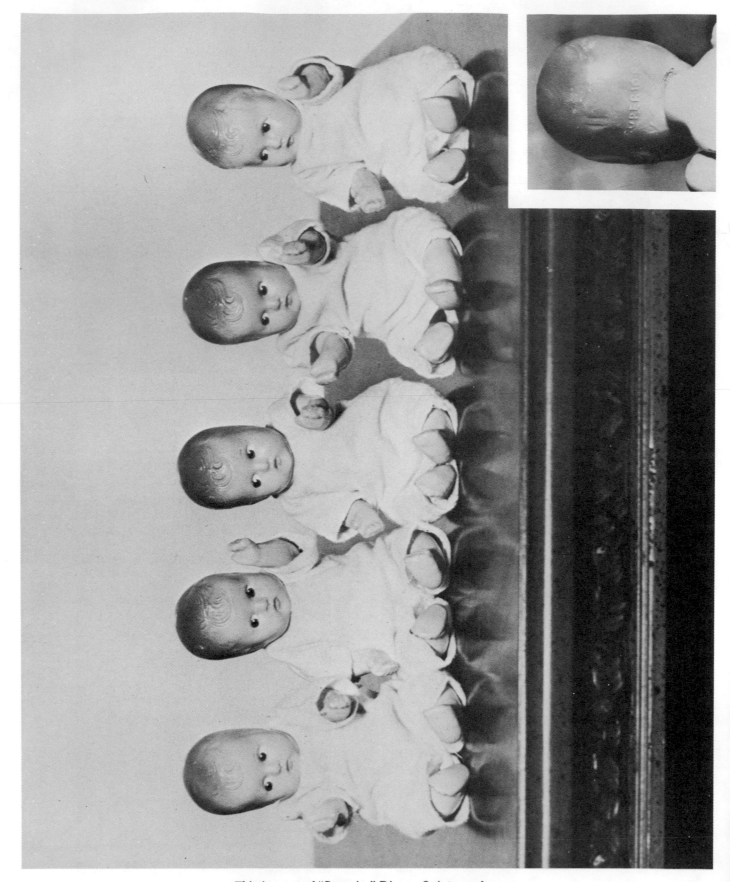

This is a set of "Superior" Dionne Quints made in Canada and only, other than Alexander, authorized dolls. All composition. Ca. 1935. (Courtesy Ernestine Howard)

7" "China" 1936. All composition with one piece body and head. Black wig with painted blue eyes to side. Painted on shoes and socks. Original. Marks: Mme/Alexander, on back. (Tiny Betty)

7" "Red Riding Hood" 1936. All composition with painted on shoes and socks. Red polka dotted dress with with white lace trim organdy apron. Red cape. (Tiny Betty). (Courtesy Glorya Woods).

7½" "Carmen." Bahaan costume is basic green with pink satin bodics. White yarn shawl over shoulder. Beads at wrist with tiny ivory cassenette. 1936 to 1942. (Tiny Betty) Marks: Mme/Alexander, on back. Tag: "Carmen"/Madame Alexander, etc. All Rights Reserved.

8" "Pollera," the Pan American child. 1936. All composition with painted eyes to side. Painted on shoes and socks. (Tiny Betty). Dress is red dots on white with lace trim. (Courtesy Sandy Rankow)

8½" "Little Betty Gardening on Tuesday" 1936. (One of the Day of the Week dolls). All composition with painted eyes to side. One piece body and head. (Courtesy Jay Minter)

7" "Amy" from Little Women. All composition. (Tiny Betty). 1936. (Courtesy Jeannie Niswonger)

7" Tiny Betty as "Beth" of Little Women. 1936. All composition with painted blue eyes. One piece body and head. Painted on shoes and socks. Dress is yellow with red roses and white pinafore. Marks: Mme/Alexander, on back. Tag: Madame Alexander, etc. (Courtesy Pat Raiden)

7" "Swedish" All composition with glued on mohair wig. Painted eyes to side. Marks: Madame/Alexander/New York. 1936.

9" "France" All composition. (Little Betty). 1936. (Courtesy Jeannie Niswonger)

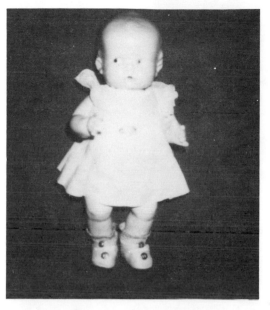

11" "Little Cherub" All composition with painted eyes. Original pale blue organdy dress, blue stockings and had matching pale blue bonnet. (Courtesy Patricia Urban)

9¼" "Egyptian" 1936. All composition with light brown tones. Fully jointed. Black mohair wig. Painted brown eyes to side. Original white cotton dress. Marks: Mme Alexander/New York, on back. Tag: Egyptian/N.Y. U.S.A. (Little Betty) (Courtesy John Axe)

Shows body view of 9¼" Egyptian/N.Y. U.S.A. tagged Alexander. Legs connected by hooks. (Courtesy John Axe)

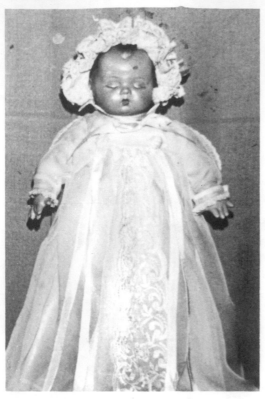

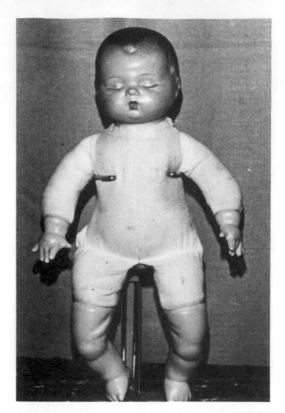

21" "Slumbermate" 1936-37. Cloth body with composition legs, gauntlet hands and head. Painted closed eyes. Original christening gown and matching bonnet. Marks: Alexander, on head. (Courtesy Jeannie Gregg)

Shows the body and construction of the 1936 Slumbermate.

21" "Madelaine DuBain" All composition and original. Made exclusively for FAO Schwarz, 1937-1938-1939. In French costume of 1880. (Wendy Ann) (Courtesy Connie Chase)

7" "Hansel" All composition. Red satin pants with net top and felt vest. 1937. Tag: Fiction Doll "Hansel" Mme. Alexander on body. (Courtesy Ann Keepers).

7½" (8") "Dutch" 1937. Painted on shoes and socks. Tag: Dutch/Madame Alexander/New York/All Rights Reserved. Arm tag: Created by / Madame / Alexander. (Courtesy Jeannie Gregg)

7" "Little Bo Peep" All composition. (Tiny Betty) 1937. (Courtesy Jeannie Niswonger)

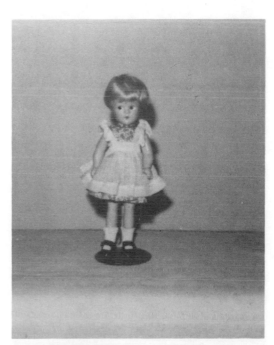

8" "Tiny Betty" All composition with eyes painted to side. In "School Girl" flowered dress and pinafore. 1937. (Courtesy Sandy Rankow)

9" "McGuffey Ana" All composition. (Little Betty) 1935 39. This is one from 1937. (Courtesy Jeannie Niswonger)

9" "Eskimo" All composition. (Little Betty) 1937. (Courtesy Jeannie Niswonger)

9" "McGuffey Ana" 1937. All composition with painted eyes. (Little Betty) Marks: Mme. Alexander/New York, on body. Tag: McGuffey Ana/Madame Alexander, etc. (Courtesy Mandeville-Barkel Collection)

9" "Hawaiian" All composition (Little Betty) 1937. (Courtesy Jeannie Niswonger)

9½" "American Girl" 1937. All compostion with side glance painted eyes. Blue and white checked dress. Straw hat. Marks: Mme/Alexander on back. Tag: American Girl/Madame Alexander. (Little Betty) (Courtesy Jay Minter)

9" "American Indian" All composition (Little Betty) 1937. (Courtesy Jeannie Niswonger)

9" "Spain" All composition. (Little Betty) 1937-1938. (Courtesy Jeannie Niswonger)

9" "Jugo-Slav" All composition. (Little Betty) 1937. (Courtesy Jeannie Niswonger)

12" "Carmen" All composition. Sleep eyes. 1937. (Wendy Ann). (Courtesy Jeannie Niswonger)

11" "Wendy Ann" All composition. Blue tin sleep eyes. Both arms are straight. Marks: Wendy Ann/By Madame Alexander, on tag. 1937.

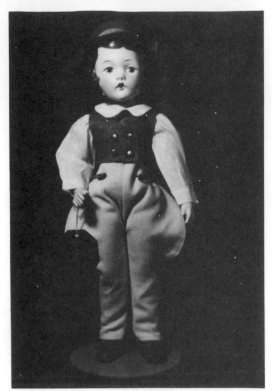

14" "Wendy Ann" 1937. All composition with molded, painted hair. Painted eyes and swivel waist. All original. Marks: Wendy Ann/Mme. Alexander, on head. Tag: Wendy Ann/Mme. Alexander, etc. (Courtesy Mandeville-Barkel Collection)

14" "Wendy Ann" All composition. Right arm is bent. Marks: Wendy Ann, on back and tag. 1937.

15" "Princess Elizabeth" At time of the Coronation of her father. 1937. Open mouth. Dress is pink with silver shoes and tiara (Center piece of tiara gone). Side part human hair wig. Marks: Princess Elizabeth/Alexander Doll Co., on head. These marked Princess Elizabeth "faces" were used for many different dolls and the original clothes are the only way to tell who they were meant to be. (Courtesy Jay Minter)

13" "Princess Elizabeth" All composition with side part blonde mohair wig, blue tin sleep eyes. Dimples and bent right arm. (Betty) 1937. Closed mouth. Tag: Princess Elizabeth/Mme. Alexander. (Courtesy John Axe)

18" "Princess Elizabeth" at the time of her father's Coronation. 1937. All composition with sleep eyes/lashes. Open mouth/four teeth. Blue-greyish (faded?) gown of taffeta, with matching bag. Silver tiara and shoes. (Courtesy Jay Minter)

24" "Princess Elizabeth" 1937. All composition with human hair wig. Sleep eyes and open mouth. Original. Marks: Princess Elizabeth/Alexander Doll Co., on head. Tag: Princess Elizabeth/Madame Alexander, etc. (Courtesy Mandeville-Barkel Collection)

13" "McGuffey Ana" All composition. 1937. All original minus poke bonnet. Marks: +, on head. 13, on body. Tag: McGuffey Ana/Madame Alexander, etc. (Courtesy Mandeville-Barkel Collection)

41

Jane Withers. Born April 12, 1926 in Atlanta, Ga. to Walter and Lavine Withers. Two year old Jane was entered in Atlanta's Boston Academy to study tap, ballet and character dancing, from there to a radio show, "Aunt Sally Kiddie Review." Later she had her own show, "Dixie's Dainty Dewdrop," doing imitations. Her mother took her to Hollywood in 1932. By 1937 she was sixth in the box office ratings. After being out of the movies four years (1947) she married William Moss, Jr. and had three children, Wendy, William and Randy. Divorced in 1953, she married Ken Errair in 1955 and they have two sons, Kenneth and Kendall. Her husband died in a plane crash in 1968.

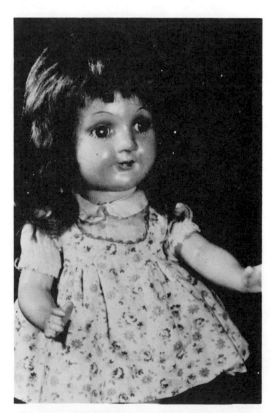

13" "Jane Withers" Closed mouth version. Original dress tagged. Mohair wig. 1937. (Courtesy Mary Partridge)

13" "Jane Withers" Closed mouth version. All composition with blue sleep eyes/lashes. Bent right arm. Marks: Jane Withers/All rights reserved/Madame Alexander, etc., on dress tags. 1937. (Courtesy Connie Chase)

17" "Jane Withers" All composition. Open mouth. 1937. (Courtesy Mandeville-Barkel Collection)

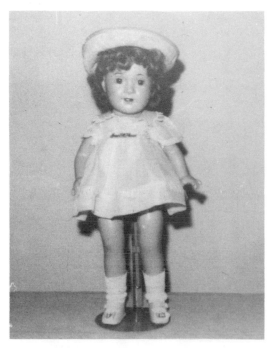

18" "Jane Withers" All composition. Wears original gold script pin with her name. 1937. (Courtesy Sandy Rankow)

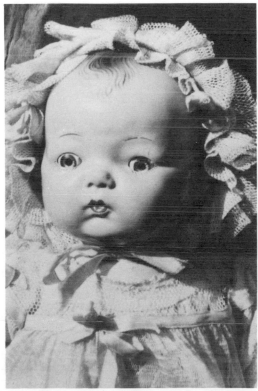

23" "Pinkie" Cloth with composition head and gauntlet hands. Blue sleep eyes. All original pink cotton-net and pink satin ribboned baby dress and matching bonnet. 1937. (Courtesy Phyllis Houston)

23" "Pinkie Baby" of 1937. Cloth with composition head and gauntlet hands. Original christening outfit with really fine lace on bonnet and trim. Clover tag: Madame Alexander. (Courtesy Elizabeth Montesano of Yesterday's Children)

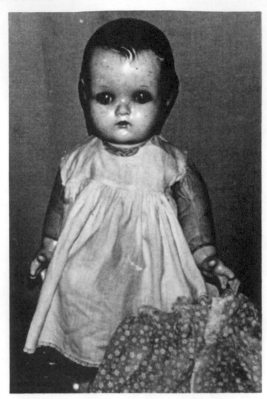

18" "Little Genius" 1937. Brown sleep eyes. Cloth body with composition arms, legs and head. Dress is white self color print with scalloped hem, lace trim at neck and hem. Original and tagged. (Courtesy Jeannie Gregg)

12" "Precious" Composition head with composition lower arms and legs. Cloth body. Blue sleep eyes. Original clothes are tagged: "Precious"/Madame Alexander, etc. Booties not original. 1937. (Courtesy Robin Rankow)

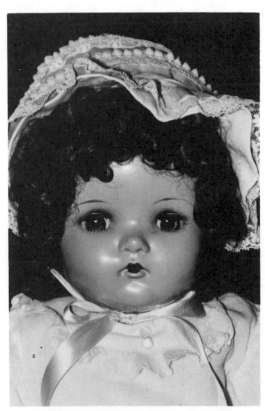

24" "Genius Baby" Composition with cloth body. Came with wigs and also molded hair. 1937. (Courtesy Alma Carmichael)

11" "McGuffey Ana" Closed mouth. Dressed in pink satin with white organdy apron. 7" Dionne toddler in pink and 7" Cinderella also in pink (Tiny Betty). The McGuffey is 1937, Dionne Quint is 1936 and the Cinderella 1935. (Courtesy Shirley Bertrand)

9" "Norwegian" All composition, waist not jointed. Glued on blonde mohair wig, painted blue eyes. Marks. Wendy Ann/Mme. Alexander/New York, on back. Norwegian/Madame Alexander, on tag. 1938. (Courtesy Virginia Jones)

9" "Scottish Girl" 1938. All composition with glued on blonde wig and painted blue eyes to side. Marks: Wendy Ann/Mme. Alexander/new York, on back. Tag: Scotch/Madame Alexander. Waist is not jointed. (Courtesy Virginia Jones)

9" "Swiss" All composition (Little Betty) 1938. (Courtesy Jeannie Niswonger)

11" "Mexico" (Little Betty) All composition. Painted blue eyes to side. 1938.

9" "Dilly Dally Sally" (Little Betty) All composition with eyes painted to side. Dress is deep yellow polished cotton with black cotton pinafore decorated with flowers. Flower trimmed black straw hat. 1938. (Photo and doll courtesy Ann Keepers)

9" "McGuffey Ana" All composition. Painted features. All original. Tag: McGuffey Ana / Madame Alexander/All Rights, etc. Alex, on head and Alexander on back. 1938. (Courtesy Jay Minter)

9" "Little Bo Peep" All composition. (Little Betty) 1938. (Courtesy Jeannie Niswonger)

9" "Danish" All composition. (Little Betty) 1938. (Courtesy Jeannie Niswonger)

9" "Peasant" All composition. (Little Betty). 1938. (Courtesy Jeannie Niswonger)

13" "Wendy Anns" 1938. All composition with swivel waists. Sleep eyes. Human hair wigs. All original. Left has original price tag of $2.98. Marked body and clothes: Wendy Ann/Madame Alexander, etc. (Courtesy Mandeville-Barkel Collection)

24" McGuffey Ana" 1938. Shown with Flora McFlimsy of 1939. Flora has freckles across her nose and is dressed in yellow with brown trim. Both are marked Princess Elizabeth. (Courtesy Shirley Bertrand)

16" "McGuffey Ana" Shown in Alexander ads of Sept. 10, 1938, but name spelled without the "e." All composition. Blonde human hair wig in braids. Brown sleep eyes, open mouth with four teeth and metal tongue. Brown eye shadow. Marks: Princess Elizabeth/Alexander Doll Co., on head. Tag: McGuffey Ana/Madame Alexander, etc. (Courtesy John Axe)

47

14" "Sally Bride" 1938. All composition with dark red mohair wig. Blue sleep eyes. (Wendy Ann). Marks: Mme. Alexander. All original except veil. This same gown with flower trim at neck and slightly lower neck line, and doll with black mohair wig is the Scarlett O'Hara Bride. (Courtesy John Axe)

16," 9," 24," and 13" "McGuffey Anas" All are marked Princess Elizabeth except 9" one. 16" — 1939; 9" & 13" — 1937; 24" — 1938. (Courtesy Mandeville-Barkel Collection)

16" "Snow White" 1938. All composition. Black human hair wig, green sleep eyes. Closed mouth. Four long painted lashes at corners of eyes only. Marks: Princess Elizabeth/Alexander Doll Co., on head. Original. Tag: Madame Alexander, etc.

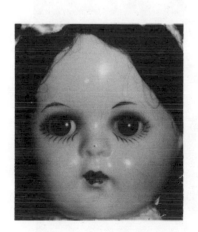

13" "Snow White" All composition. Original. Marks: Mme. Alexander, on head. 1938.

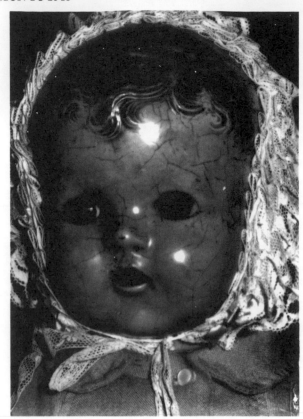

24" "Princess Alexandria" Cloth body with composition head, arms and legs. Open mouth with four teeth. Brown sleep eyes/lashes. Straight legs. Marks: none. 1938. This doll has been played with much love and is not in the best of condition, but the hair outline shows well for identification. Prices will be based on a mint and original doll.

The **great event** of **1939** was the movie Gone With the Wind starring Clark Gable and Vivien Leigh. Based on the Margaret Mitchell book of 1936. Based first on the novel, Madame Alexander's Scarlett dolls began before the movie's release. She also made Southern Belle and Southern Girl dolls before the book or the movie had been released.

SCARLET O'HARA

One of the most continuous dolls from Madame Alexander, has been her Scarletts (Southern Girl), with their beautifully designed clothes from Pre-Movie late 1936, 1937 and early 1938 on through the release of the movie in 1939. With just the novel, Madame Alexander designed "Southern Lady" clothes that would later reflect in the movie.

Since some of the most desirable compositions are the Scarletts, we thought perhaps collectors would like to know a little how the movie Scarlett came about.

An agent gave galley proofs to M.G.M. of the massive Civil War novel by unknown Atlanta novelist named Margaret Mitchell, in May of 1936, before the novel was released to the public. M.G.M. (L.B. Mayer) could see no reason to put $65,000 in it and said "no."

Agent Annie Lauric Williams gave a set of the enormous pile of galley proofs to Mervyn LeRoy and wife, who was a producer for Warner Brothers, as he was boarding a train in New York. After reaching California, Mrs. LeRoy, the daughter of Jack Warner, took it to her father and told him she thought the contract star of Warner's was perfect for the part. This star was Bette Davis.

Bette Davis was leaving to do a picture in England and was doing it in an act of defiance for not getting better parts and greater artistic freedom. Warner told her he had bought a great book for her to play the lead, called "Gone With The Wind." Her reply was "I'll bet that's a pip" and went off to England, soon to her regret. After Davis was gone, Warner saw no need to buy the book rights, so did not. He did get Davis back by suing her in an English Court for breach of contract, forcing her to return.

Lilly Messenger, story editor at R.K.O., was reading "Gone With The Wind" proofs on her way to Bermuda and became very excited at the prospects of a movie. She obtained a second set of proofs and gave them to R.K.O.'s star, Katherine Hepburn. Then gave her set to Pandro Berman, R.K.O.'s leading producer. As he read, he was impressed but more so with cost and production problems he could foresee. He doubted if the New England actress, Katherine Hepburn could be a believable Scarlett.

By the time that Katherine Hepburn finished the novel proofs, she was convinced that she would be great as Scarlett so she kept up daily pressure of begging and wheedling everyone at R.K.O. to buy the movie rights of the book.

Meanwhile, the idea of "Gone With The Wind" was being pushed in other quarters and it had been offered to David O. Selznick. Selznick, at first, had turned the idea down saying for one thing, that the asking price was too much for a small independent production company like his. Then he began having second thoughts and told the story of "Gone With The Wind" to Ronald Colman. Colman wanted the part of Rhett Butler and volunteered to spend time in the South changing a British accent for a Southern one.

The book was released and sold an amazing 176,000 copies in the first three months. Selznick finally offered $50,000 and was accepted. This was a straight purchase of the movie rights, without a percentage of the box office profits and this amount was divided equally by the author, Margaret Mitchell and the publisher Macmillan. Margaret Mitchell paid a standard 10% agent's commission to Annie Laurie Williams.

In a short few weeks the novel had sold 300,000 copies and Louella Parsons gave out the news of the Selznick purchase (at $65,000). The conjector of who would play Scarlett and Rhett became as pronounced as Roosevelt's re-election, the Dionne Quints, King Edward VIII and Wallis Simpson or Adolf Hitler's next move. This speculation went on for a great length of time, for when finally into production, the film took two and a half years reaching the screen.

Note: Lewis J. Selznick, David's father, had instilled a deep respect for the "classics" in him and when at Metro Studios, young Selznick hired author Hugh Wapole to adapt David Copperfield for the screen. After its success he did more of his childhood classics—Anna Karenina, Tale of Two Cities and the Little Women. Later came Little Lord Fauntleroy, The Garden of Allah and Prisoner of Zenda.

Walter Plunkett noted for historical costume design was signed to a 15 week contract to create costume designs for "Gone With the Wind" and stayed the full two and a half years.

In the novel, Scarlett seems to wear a lot of green so Walter Plunkett (costume designer) went to Atlanta to research and ask author Margaret Mitchell why. She replied that green happened to be her favorite color and its repeated use was quite unconscious and also that Selznick was entitled to dress Scarlett in any color he pleased.

While in Atlanta, Walter Plunkett was besieged with offers of Southerners to sell him their Grandmother's old wardrobes. He did not buy any but brought back swatches of fabric actually clipped from dresses of the period in Southern Museums. These swatches went to a textile firm in Pennsylvania and this firm was to supply the cotton for costumes in return to the rights to market the "Gone With The Wind" prints.

Walter Plunkett began making costumes and uniforms by the hundreds. His seamstresses kept busy, along with weavers, who made homespuns of the period. Two looms were kept busy as well as milliners, shoemakers, metal men to solder the skirt hoops and he even had a woman brought out of retirement because she knew how to construct antebellum corsets.

Selznick was still undecided about the cast and sent out hundreds of cards to P.T.A. groups all over the country, asking who they thought would be best in the leading roles. The results were an overwhelming popular choice for Scarlett was Bette Davis, followed by Katherine Hepburn, Tallulah Bankhead and others. Rhett Butler was seen in their eyes as Clark Gable and Ronald Colman. Selznick then approached Jack Warner to see if he was willing to discuss a loan out agreement for Bette Davis.

For 25 percent of the box office gross, Jack Warner volunteered to provide part of the financing, plus Bette Davis and Errol Flynn as the stars. Selznick was tempted, except for the Errol Flynn part of the deal. The young Tasmanian had made an impact as the swashbuckling star of Captain Blood but Selznick didn't, as yet, think Flynn had skill as an actor. Bette Davis, who wanted to play Scarlett very badly, felt the same way and she refused to co-star with him. Warner refused to break up the package deal.

Bette Davis looked around for a Southern story and came up with Jezebel. Rushed into production at Warners, Jezebel took eight weeks to film and it bore a great similarity to "Gone With The Wind." Selznick was furious when he saw it and complained to Warner's because of the obvious "lifts" from his picture. At least one scene was cut before a general release, the scene of the conversation after dinner, on the South's chances in a war with the North. Bette Davis gave one of her best performances in Jezebel and the movie was a success.

Next on Selznick's list was Tallulah Bankhead, who was from Alabama, the granddaughter of a Civil War hero, Senator John Hollis Bankhead and daughter of Congressman William B. Bankhead (D). Tallulah Bankhead was established on the stage, both in London and on Broadway. She was known for her colorful, extravagant personality. Her reputation was not the best and her exhibitionisms were quite well known, but she was offered a scene test and she read the novel, convinced that only she could play Scarlett.

On December 20, 1938, Tallulah came to Hollywood. On the 21st she made a Technicolor test wearing a costume that Garbo had worn in Camille. As the first test for the part, Tallulah did three scenes from the book as the negotiations with Broadway playwright, Sidney Howard to do the screen script were not completed.

Selznick was uncertain on many counts, but mainly that Tallulah wouldn't be convincing in the early scenes when Scarlett is sixteen and so she was unsigned for the part, despite a huge campaign in the South, headed by her aunt, Marie Bankhead Owen, who spearheaded letters, telegrams and copies of editorials of the Southern Press that poured into the Selznick offices.

Now the novel had sold over a million copies and M.G.M was wondering if they had made a big mistake in rejecting the film rights. The world already considered their star, Clark Gable, as Rhett Butler. So in March, when Selznick sounded out M.G.M. on conditions for loaning Gable, the answer was full distribution rights of the film. Selznick had signed an exclusive contract with United Artists that ran through 1938 and he could not do as M.G.M. wanted. So he started to negotiate with Goldwyn for Gary Cooper. At this same time he was seriously considering another Southern actress, Miriam Hopkins for Scarlett, but shortly this idea was dropped and then replaced with thoughts of Norma Shearer.

Norma Shearer was married to Irving Thalberg (one strong M.G.M. boss) and had first claim on everything at M.G.M., including dressing rooms to movie parts and no expense was spared on a Shearer picture. For example, in making Romeo and Juliet, the capulet garden scene took up the entire Stage 15, largest sound stage in the world. The balcony scene took five weeks to shoot and the total cost of the film was over two million dollars.

During this "pre-filming" period of "Gone With The Wind," Norma Shearer's husband (Irving Thalberg) died and she ended up fighting a bitter battle with Mayer over her inherited share of the company profits. She did make a secret screen test for the part of Scarlett but again Selznick felt her too mature (37) to play the younger Scarlett and decided to let the public decide for him. He let columnist Walter Winchell pass the news that she was being considered for the part, onto his (Winchell's) eight million radio listeners. The rsponse was the role was too undignified, as well as she did not have enough "fire" for the role.

It was then that Selznick announced he would look for an unknown girl to play Scarlett. He really wasn't convinced an unknown could handle the long and complex part but it did keep the picture in the public eye. Selznick assigned executives to cover different areas of the United States to interview candidates.

Hundreds of actresses from little theatre groups, debutants and students of college drama auditioned for the role. Atlanta socialite, Catherine Campbell, read for the role. She later married newspaper heir, Randolph Hearst and became the mother of Patty Hearst. Another Southern girl to read for the part was Alicia Rhett.

Selznick invited all the Hollywood Studios to send their stock players to audition. Among the R.K.O. starlets was a newcomer, Lucille Ball. She never felt she would be right for the part, but read it anyway. Another to test was a beautiful hat model from New York named Edyth Marrener, who was spotted by Selznick's wife, Irene. Her test was amateurish and she did not get the role. Edyth Marrener went on to become a great actress by the name we all knew her: Susan Hayward.

By the end of 1938 Selznick needed more money and indeed there were a great many jokes about him and "Gone With The Wind! He told his backers about the latest offer of his Father-in-law, Louis B. Mayer. This offer was outright purchase, repayment of complete investment and hiring him as producer. The backers came up with an additional $1,250,000 which was half the cost up to that time but Selznick had to provide the other half. He went to M.G.M. and started to work out a deal for Gable. By June the deal was worked out with M.G.M. loaning Gable and contributing the $1,250,000 toward production costs in exchange for distribution rights and a sliding scale percentage of the gross.

With Gable settled as Rhett Butler and a deadline of February 1939 for him to begin work on the picture, finding a Scarlett became foremost in priority.

Paulette Goddard was given a screen test and the results were good, for in appearance she came close to Selznick's idea of Scarlett with her bold looks and spirited personality. But she lacked acting experience and Selznick put her under contract and hired English stage actress, Constance Collier to coach her. Paulette was not yet a movie star but she received a form of celebrity with much publicity in regard to her affair and/or marriage to Charlie Chaplin (never known for sure, which was true.)

Louella Parsons had started calling Paulette, Scarlett O'Goddard and mail came pouring in from Women's Clubs protesting her role due to her being suspected of being the mistress of Chaplin. The protests increased and were picked up by the press. A threat of boycott of the movie now hung in the air and the idea of Goddard playing Scarlett was dropped.

Over the next few months Katherine Hepburn was once again considered and Lana Turner tested for Scarlett under her real name, Jean Turner, but in her case, lack of experience was evident.

Thus to the end of 1938 the following had been considered for the part of Scarlett:

Alicia Rhett	Joan Bennett
Jean Arthur	Lana Turner
Norma Shearer	Bette Davis
Joan Fontaine	Catherine Campbell
Loretta Young	Susan Hayward
Miriam Hopkins	Tallulah Bankhead
Paulette Goddard	Marcella Martin
Joan Crawford	Lucille Ball

The men who were considered for Rhett Butler were, along with Clark Gable: Basil Rathbone, Errol Flynn, Gary Cooper and Ronald Colman.

Still without a Scarlett, Selznick's backers gave him to January 19, 1939 to begin shooting the picture. The night of December 10, 1938 the City Desks of the Los Angeles newspapers began receiving calls that the Selznick back lots were on fire. The sky over Culver City were red and glowing to light up the sky.

The reporters rushed to the scene and found a fire. Atlanta was burning. The first scene for "Gone With The Wind" was being filmed. All the Technicolor's seven existing cameras were set up around the blaze to shoot from different angles. Three pairs of doubles for Scarlett and Rhett were filmed escaping from the burning, collapsing city on three identical buckboards. One of the cameras filmed a high brick wall (originally used in King Kong) at just about point blank range, as it disintegrates in an avalanche of flame. This same footage was one used in the final "Gone With the Wind" film and also again in the movie "Rebecca" at the burning of Manderly sequence.

This first filming of "Gone With The Wind" was a point of anxiety for many, especially Lee Zavity, the movies number one demolition expert. The burning of Atlanta was the most complex assignment he had ever undertaken. Ernest Grey, the Culver City Fire Chief dreaded the moment and envisioned the studio, as well as all of Culver City being destroyed. He had marshalled every available fire company in the area and the studio had increased its own fire department by addition of some 200 voluntary helpers. Everything went smoothly, to everyone's surprise and needless to say, delight.

During this first filming, Selznick's brother, Myron Selznick appeared on the observation platform, together with his dinner guests. He stated to his brother, "Here, genius, I want you to meet Scarlett O'Hara." In the fading glow, David Selznick was conscious of a pair of large, arresting gray-green eyes, a cascade of auburn hair and a slight trim figure beneath her mink coat. Her voice let every consonant pound firmly into place with exact emphasis. She laughed and her voice became full throated, a trick she shared with many trained actresses.

It was thus that Vivien Mary Hartley, born in Darjeeling, India in 1912 to British parents, to become Vivien Leigh and this night of December 10, 1938, she became, for all times, in many memories—Scarlett O'Hara.

After editing this manuscript, Madame Alexander sent along an interesting item about her Scarlett dolls so I am sharing this as a direct quote from her letter.

"This is how I was inspired to creat a Scarlett doll. When the book was launched, I responded quickly and bought the book. It is the only book that I ever started from the beginning and did not put it down until finished. I was so enchanted that I remember starting it Saturday morning after breakfast and never left my room until Sunday. I stayed up all night reading and it is remarkable that I did not feel any need for sleep. Fortunately, my dear husband brought a tray of food to me. On Monday I was in my studio and started to work and I am happy to report that everything went smoothly and I had to make no corrections. She (Scarlett) has been very rewarding and has made many people happy. The next event was M.G.M. (Metro-Goldwyn-Mayer) sending out publicity that they were looking for an actress who would play Scarlett. For almost two years, wherever I went I heard people speculating on who would play Scarlett and Rhett Butler.

Long before the decision was made I presented my conception of Scarlett to M.G.M. and three days later, I received my contract from M.G.M. to do Scarlett O'Hara dolls. After all these many years, I am still amazed with my conceptions of Scarlett O'Hara.

When Vivien Leigh was picked I presented her with a doll when she left to make an appearance in Richmond, Va. to publicize the movie. I was told by many people, that when they saw the doll, they said to Vivien Leigh, "What a perfect likeness." I had no pictures of any kind from the book and this was my conception of how Scarlett looked with her heart shaped face, high forehead, black hair and green eyes."

14" "Scarlett" All composition. Green velvet coat over flowered print gown. Satin green hat and ties. 1939. Black wig with green eyes. From movie scene where Scarlett makes a dress from drapes of Tara. (Courtesy Jay Minter)

16" "Scarlett" All composition. 1939. Green sleep eyes. Gown is green with green and blue flowers. Bodice is Forest green as is matching bonnet. (Courtesy Sandy Rankow)

18" "Scarlett O'Hara" 1939. All composition and original. Black human hair and green sleep eyes. Has original price tag of $6.85. (Wendy Ann). Head and clothes marked. From movie, dressed patterned after one worn in dance scene at Twelve Oaks. (Courtesy Mandeville-Barkel Collection)

18" "Scarlett" All composition. Blue sleep eyes. Black mohair wig. Gown is blue flowers on white background. Styled from Ball scene of movie. 1939. Tag: Scarlett/Madame Alexander, etc. Sometimes supplies ran out on eyes and whatever color was handy was used. Variation of costume. (Courtesy Jeannie Gregg)

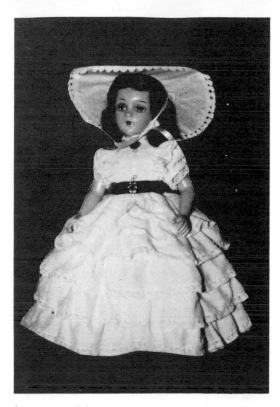

21" "Scarlett O'Hara" All composition. (Wendy Ann). Madame Alexander designed this white gown and hat with green velvet sash from the first scenes of the movie when Scarlett leaves the twins and runs across the lawn to greet her father. (Courtesy Ruth Price) England.

21" "Scarlett" All composition with human black hair wig, green sleep eyes and eyeshadow. 1939. Dress is green with orange flowers. The bodice is organdy with ribbon trim. (Courtesy Jay Minter)

Sonja Henie was born April 8, 1910 and grew up to be a woman of taste for luxury and business that made her one of the world's richest women. Sonja was the daughter of an Olso, Norway fur merchant. He father gave her skates when she was six years old and enrolled her in ballet classes. She was eight when she won her first figure skating championship and in 1927, she won the first of ten consecutive skating titles at Oslo and won three Olympic titles for 1928, 1932 and 1936. It was in 1936 that Darryl F. Zanuck signed her to a 20th Century-Fox contract and her movies over the next 12 years grossed $25 million. In 1948, she made her last film: "The Countess of Monte Cristo." She became an American citizen in 1941 and married Daniel Topping, divorcing him in 1946. Later married to Winthrop Gardiner, Jr., she divorced him in 1956. In 1956 she married her childhood sweetheart, Neils Onstad, who grew up to become a Norwegian ship owner. In August, 1968, the Onstads gave Norway an art museum and 250 of their paintings. She became ill with leukemia and after nine months, died on an ambulance plane flying her from Paris to Oslo on October 12, 1969.

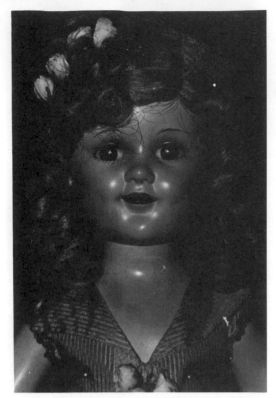

17" "Sonja Henie" All composition. All original. This outfit came in pastel colors. Hair in an original set. Wrist tag. Marks: Madame Alexander/Sonja Henie, on head. Pin says: Skate For Pleasure/Sonja Henie, but is not original to doll. These pins were given away at Ice Revues where Sonja was appearing but look nice with a larger doll. 1941. (Courtesy Jay Minter)

17" "Sonja Henie" to show close up of head. Some of these dolls appear to have "fatter" faces than others. (Courtesy Jay Minter)

14" "Sonja Henie" Original 1942 outfit. (Courtesy Sandy Rankow)

16" "McGuffey Ana" 1939. All composition and human hair wig. All original with original price tag of $3.95. Marks: Princess Elizabeth/Alexander Doll Co., on head. Tag: McGuffey Ana/Madame Alexander, etc. (Courtesy Mandeville-Barkel Collection)

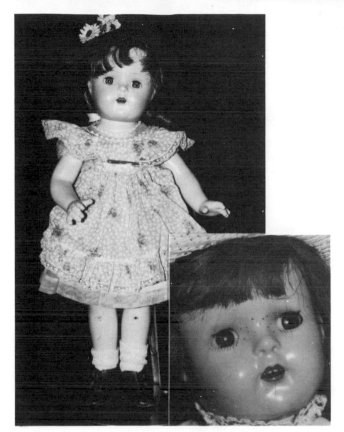

24" "McGuffey Ana" 1939. All composition with plaid cotton dress and organdy pinafore apron. Brown sleep eyes. Marked Princess Elizabeth. (Courtesy Sandy Rankow)

15" "Flora McFlimsy" All composition with glued on blonde wig of human hair. Freckles across nose. Open mouth/four teeth. Marks: Princess Elizabeth/Alexander Doll Co., on head. 1939.

14½" "Sleeping Beauty" 1939. (Wendy Ann) Long blonde human hair wig, red fingernails. Red velvet gown, gold slippers. All composition. Marks: Mme. Alexander, on head. Tag: Madame/Alexander/New York USA. The red velvet coat, hat and muff are part of trousseau / trunk. (Courtesy John Axe)

16" "Snow White" All composition. 1939. Yellow taffeta dress with net overdress trimmed with yellow ribbon and cluster of pink roses at neckline. Lavender cape and lavender silk hair ribbon. White imitation leather pointed toe shoes with rose satin bows on toes. Black hair and brown eyes with very pale complexion. Open mouth. Marked Princess Elizabeth. (Courtesy Virginia Vinton)

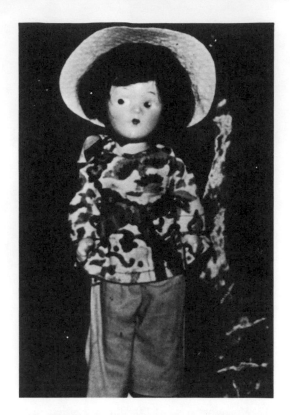

7½" (8") "Burma-Chinese" Black wig with blue eyes. All composition. 1939. Sold as both Burma and Chinese. This one has the tag: Chinese/Madame Alexander, etc. Wendy Ann/Mme. Alexander/New York, on back. (Courtesy Jeannie Gregg)

9" "Carmen" All composition. (Little Betty) 1939. (Courtesy Jeannie Niswonger)

9" "Swiss" All composition. Waist not jointed. Glued on mohair wig, painted blue eyes. Marks: Mme Alexander/New York, on back. Tag: Swiss/Madame Alexander/N.Y. U.S.A. 1939. (Courtesy Jeannie Niswonger)

14" "Wendy Ann" All composition with swivel waist, painted eyes and molded, painted hair. Original with both head and clothes marked. 1939. (Courtesy Mandeville-Barkel Collection)

7" "Fairy Princess" All composition with one piece body and head. Painted on black shoes. Pink satin dress with sequins. 1940. This same year the larger 14½" doll has the same design dress in deep red velveteen and two rows of sequin down the front and is "Sleeping Beauty." Tag: Fairy Princess/Madame Alexander, etc. (Courtesy of Helen M. Bohler).

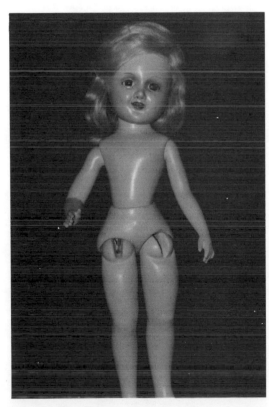

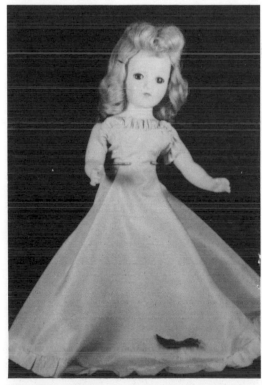

13" "Sonja Henie" All composition. Jointed waist. Dimples. Black eyeshadow. Marks: Alexander/New York, on back. 1940.

14" "Ginger Rogers" All composition. Same doll as the Scarlett O'Hara, WAVE, WAAC, etc. Blonde mohair page boy wig with green sleep eyes. Original pale green taffeta gown, blue velvet bows. Green slippers. 1939-40. (Courtesy Maish Collection)

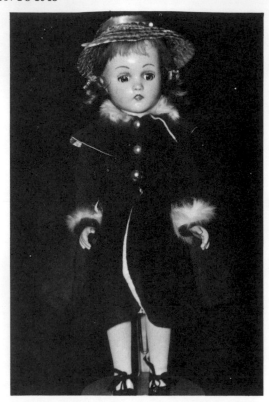

21" "Posey Pet" 1939 (Wendy Ann) All composition with brown eyes and red hair. Red/white striped dress with red velvet coat with fur trim. Tag: Posey Pet/Madame Alexander. There was a line of stuffed animals also called "Posey Pet." (Courtesy Jay Minter)

12" "McGuffey Ana" All composition. (Sleep eyed Wendy Ann). 1939. (Courtesy Jeannie Niswonger)

10" "Scarlett" 1940. One of smallest made. All compostion with black human hair wig, green sleep eyes and eyeshadow. Dress is green with blue stripes and red flowers. Marks: Alexander on head. Tag: Madame Alexander, etc. (Courtesy Jay Minter)

17" "Scarlett" All composition with black human hair wig, green sleep eyes/lashes and eyeshadow. Gown is rose and blue flowered. Very large straw hat. Marks: Alexander, on head. Tag: Madame Alexander, etc. 1940. (Courtesy Jay Minter)

18" "Scarlett" All composition. Original. Black hair and green eyes. 1940.

14" "Madelaine" 1940. All composition with brown sleep eyes/lashes. Painted lashes below the eyes only. Eyeshadow. Blue skirt with roses. Pink top. Marks: Mme Alexander, on head. Tag: Madelaine/Madame Alexander 1939. (Courtesy Marie Ernst)

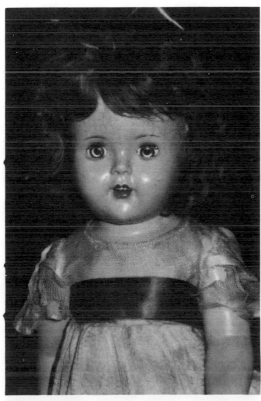

24" "Kate Greenaway" All composition with golden red glued on mohair wig. Blue sleep eyes/lashes. Open mouth/four teeth. Original yellow cotton net long gown. Ribbon is replacement. Marks: Princess Elizabeth/Alexander Doll Co. on head. Tag: Madame Alexander. 1940.

22" "Baby McGuffey" Cloth body with composition head and limbs. White organdy dress with lace trimmed scalloped hem. Matching bonnet with pink ribbons. Pink ribbons at wrists. 1940. (Courtesy Elizabeth Montesano of Yesterday's Children)

61

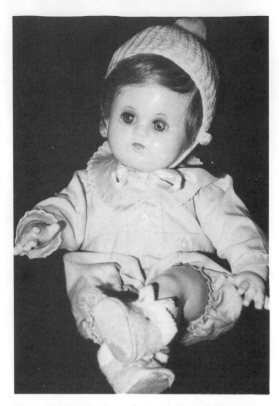

24" "Baby McGuffey" 1940 (Baby Genius) Cloth with composition head and limbs. Dress is blue checked as is bonnet with white pinafore. (Courtesy Roberta Lago)

11" "Butch" Cloth and composition. Blue sleep eyes. One of first boy dolls made. Marks: Mme. Alexander, on head. Butch/Madame Alexander, on tag. 1940. (Courtesy Kathy Walter)

11" "Scarlett O'Hara" 1941. All composition with black mohair wig. Green sleep eyes. All original. (Wendy Ann) Marks: none on doll. Tag: Scarlett O'Hara / Madame Alexander, etc. (Courtesy Mandeville-Barkel Collection)

14" "Southern Girl" 1941-42. Blue eyes. All composition. Black wig. Original gown of combination organdy and cotton with satin picture hat. Marks: Mme. Alexander, on head. Tag: Madame Alexander/New York U.S.A.

14" "Scarlett" All composition and original. 1941.

15" "Kate Greenaway" All composition. Blue sleep eyes. **Marks: Princess Elizabeth/Madame Alexander, on head.** Original. 1941.

21" "Bride" 1941. All composition with glued on light blonde wig. Satin bridal gown with floor length veil. Tag: Created by/Madame Alexander. (Courtesy Marie Ernst)

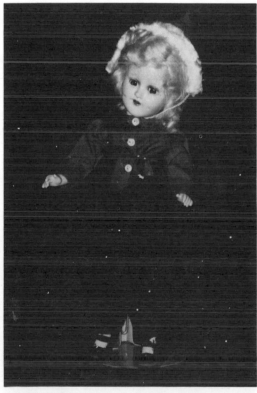

14" "Sonja Henie" Shown in an original ski outfit of 1941. (Courtesy Jay Minter)

14" "Sonja Henie" Original outfit for 1941-1942. (Courtesy Sandy Rankow)

15" "Sonja Henie" All composition. #3600-1941. Marks: Genuine Sonja Henie, on tag. Alexander Sonja Henie on head. (Courtesy Jeannie Gregg)

18" "Sonja Henie" In original outfit of organdy and velvet. All composition. 1941.

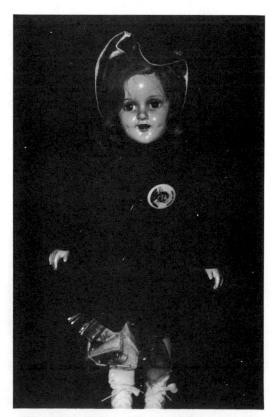

20" "Sonja Henie" All composition. Matching coat and hat are green satin lined dark green velvet. Pin says: Sonja Henie Ice Revue and not original to doll. 1941. (Courtesy Jay Minter)

14" "Sonja Henie" All original in biege and brown ski clothes. 1941. (Courtesy Shirley Bertrand)

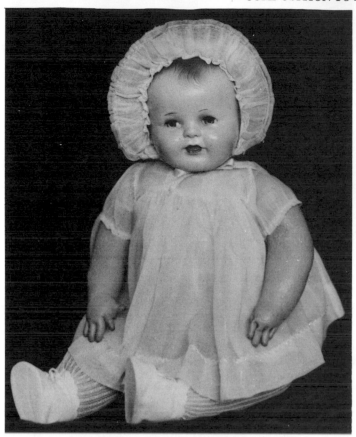

21" "Kitty Baby" 1941. Composition head with lightly molded hair, laughing blue sleep eyes, open/closed mouth. Stuffed latex body. Original clothes are pale pink organdy. Paper with her says: Pat. Applied For. Marks: Madame Alexander, on head. (Courtesy Jean Hadyn)

14" "Bride" All composition with brown sleep eyes, blonde mohair wig. Gown is organdy trimmed with lace with cotton net, lace trimmed long train style veil. 1942. #2150. Bridesmaid, also 15" from 1943. (Courtesy Renie Culp)

22" "Sonja Henie" In #3300-1942. Pink satin with fur trim and short jacket. (Courtesy Mary Partridge)

14" "Southern Girl" All composition with black wig and blue sleep eyes. All original yellow organdy dress and pantaloons. Green shoes. This outfit had green satin full length coat. Marks: Mme. Alexander, on head. (Courtesy Donna Maish)

14" "Sonja Henie" Closed mouth version. All composition and all original. Marks: Madame Alexander/Sonja Henie, on head. Tag: Madame Alexander, etc. 1942. (Courtesy Jay Minter)

14" and 9" "Mother & Me" 1942-43. Mother: Blue sleep eyes. Me: Brown painted eyes to side. These gowns are blue cotton net with matching ruffles, but came in different colors. Marks: Madame Alexander. (Courtesy Jay Minter)

23" "Special Girl" Cloth body with composition head on a composition shoulder plate, arms and legs. Blue sleep eyes. Marks: none. 1942. (Courtesy Marie Ernst)

23" "Special Girl" to show original clothes. Organdy dress with matching ruffles. (Courtesy Marie Ernst)

14" "Soldier" 1942. All composition and original. (Wendy Ann) Sleep eyes and mohair wig. Marks: Mme.Alexander, on head. Tag: Madame/ Alexander/New York/U.S.A. (Courtesy Mandeville-Barkel Collection)

14" "W.A.V.E." All composition with glued on dark blonde mohair wig, blue sleep eyes with eyeshadow. Original. Marks: Mme Alexander, o head. Tag: W.A.V.E./Madame Alexander. 1942.

67

14" "W.A.A.C." All composition with mohair wig, brown sleep eyes and black eyeshadow. Marks: Mme. Alexander, on head. Tag: WAAC/Madame Alexander/New York. Original with hat missing. 1942.

11" "Baby Genius" Compostion with cloth body and sleep eyes. All original. 1942. (Courtesy Phyllis Houston)

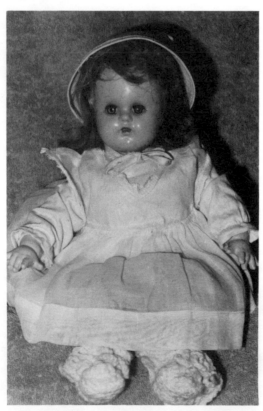

11" "Baby McGuffey" Cloth with composition head, legs and gauntlet hands. Same head used for "Butch." Wig over molded hair. Blue sleep eyes with eyeshadow. Booties and bonnet are not original. #240-1942.

14½" "An Armed Force Doll" With service un-identified. All composition (Wendy). Red mohair wig, blue sleep eyes. Clothes and cap are brown with eagle emblem on cap and eagle buttons on jacket. Brown leatherette purse with "V" on it. Tag: Blue script: Madame/Alexander/New York U.S.A. Ca. 1943-44.

18" "Jeannie Walker" 1943. All composition with wooden walker piece in crotch. Human hair wig and sleep eyes. Original. Marks: Alexander / Doll/Co./Pat. No. 2171281, on body. Tag: Jeannie Walker / Madame Alexander, etc. (Courtesy Mandeville-Barkel Collection)

16" "Flora McFlimsy" 1943. Head marked Princess Elizabeth. Red human hair wig and freckles. Coat (not shown) tagged Flora McFlimsy of Madison Square, etc. Hat not original. (Courtesy Mary Partridge)

16" "Flora McFlimsy" 1944. All composition. Human hair wig, sleep eyes and freckles. Open mouth. Marks: Princess Elizabeth/Alexander Doll Co., on head. Tag: Flora McFlimsy of Madison Square/Madame Alexander, etc. (Courtesy Mandeville-Barkel Collection)

21½" "Bridesmaid" 1944. High quality composition. Pink satin gown with gold trim. Carries matching muff. (Wendy). (Courtesy Sandy Rankow)

69

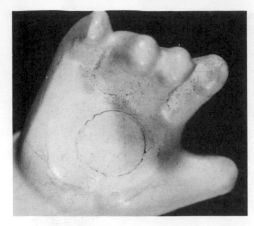

20" "Miss Victory" All composition with blue sleep eyes, open mouth but replaced wig. Magnets in hands, placed there by FAO Schwarz Co. (to hold items like a flag) Red skirt, white top with blue trim. Marks: Princess Elizabeth/Alexander Doll Co., on head. Tag: Madame Alexander/New York, etc. 1944. (Courtesy Marie Ernst)

This is a Sears catalog page for 1945. Left to right: "Bridesmaid" came in 15", 18" and 21½" sizes and her organdy gown came in various colors (pink-yellow and blue) The "Bride" came in 17" and 22" sizes and the "Flowergirl" came in 16", 20" and 24" sizes. Also came in yellow, pink or blue.

22" "Bride" (Wendy). All composition. 1945. Brown sleep eyes. (Courtesy Sandy Rankow)

18" "Bridesmaids" Part of the 1945 Wedding Party for Wendy Bride. All composition. (Wendy Ann). Left is pink, center is Maid Of Honor, in blue and the right hand one is in yellow. See color section for these dolls in color. (Courtesy Elizabeth Montesano of Yesterday's Children)

Dragonwyck costume doll shown in gown that is duplicate worn by Gene Tierney in a ball room scene from the movie. The doll came in 14" and 17" size. (Wendy Ann) 1945. Photo from the June 1945 Screenland magazine.

21" "Bridesmaid" 1946. All composition. Brown sleep eyes. White dress with pink and green decoration. Reddish brown mohair wig. Marks: Alexander, on head and body. (Courtesy Phyllis Houston)

This 1946 Ward's catalog shows top, left to right: "Princess Margaret Rose" in 15", 18" and 21" size. The sheer rayon dress is pink with natural straw hat trimmed with flowers. This gown also came in yellow and blue. "Hulda" came in 18" size only. Heavy rayon satin skirt with purple jacket of velvet and lace jabot. Flower hat with net veiling. Lower, left to right: "Karen Ballerina" in rayon net with satin bodice and gold rick-rack trim. Outfit came in blue, green, white and yellow.

Her hair is braided rayon yarn. Right: "Sleeping Beauty" came in 15", 18" and 21" sizes. Red rayon satin princess gown tied to wrist with braid. Gold braid coronet. Flowers in hair and one sleeve. Wig is mohair.

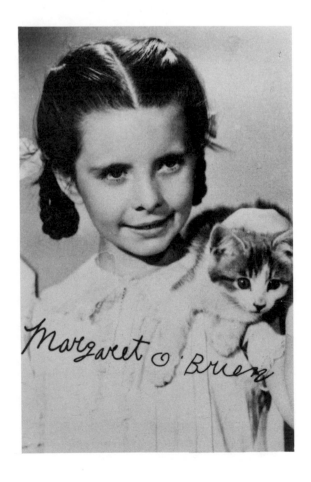

Angela Maxine O'Brien was born January 15, 1937 and her outstanding moment came in 1944 when she was presented with a miniature Oscar for "Meet Me In St. Louis" which also starred Judy Garland. Her favorite role was the "Unfinished Dance" in 1947 when she got to work with the Prima Ballerina, Karen Booth. Two other pictures were also her favorites: "Jane Eyre" in 1944 and "Madame Curie" in 1943. Margaret O'Brien dolls came in three eye colors: hazel, brown and blue. The wigs came in dark brown, and a reddish brown and in 1947 a dark ash blonde.

14" "Margaret O'Brien" 1946. All composition with glued on reddish-brown mohair wig in braids. Blue sleep eyes. Original dress. Shoes are replaced. (Courtesy Jay Minter)

14" and 17" "Margaret O'Brien" All composition with mohair reddish-brown wigs. Origial clothes and shoes. Tags: Margaret O'Brien/Madame Alexander, etc. 1946. Skirt and blouse on right are from the 1945 movie "Our Vines Have Tender Grapes." (Courtesy Mandeville-Barkel Collection)

24" "Margaret O'Brien" All composition. 1946. Dress is red with white collar, cuffs, hem and apron. (Courtesy Rankow)

19" "Margaret O'Brien" All composition. 1946. Soft red and white checked dress with organdy half apron. Straw hat trimmed with flowers. Marks: Alexander, on head and back. Tag, blue letters: Madame Alexander, etc. Green clover tag on arm: Madame Alexander. (Courtesy Elizabeth Montesano of Yesterday's Children)

18" "Margaret O'Brien" All composition and original. 1946-1947. This dress is one of the "Peplum Pals" from "Calling All Girls." (Courtesy Roberta Lago)

17" "Alice In Wonderland" 1946. Composition and using the Margaret mold. Original. (Courtesy Mary Partridge)

14½" "Fairy Queen" All composition. Brown sleep eyes. All original, minus wand. 1947.

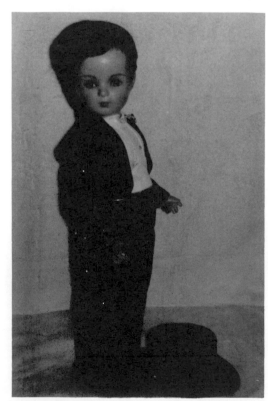

21" "Groom of the Royal Wedding Portrait Series. 1947. All composition with red mohair man's wig, amber eyes and pale pink lips. (Margaret). (Courtesy Shirley Bertrand)

14½" "Alice In Wonderland" All hard plastic with glued on blonde wig. Blue sleep eyes. Original blue dress and white pinafore. Marks: Alex., on head. Tag: Alice In Wonderland/by Madame Alexander, etc. 1948.

14½" "McGuffey Ana" All hard plastic with hairdo in long braids. Red-blonde hair (mohair), blue sleep eyes. Original. (Marks: Alex., on head. 1948. (Courtesy Jeannie Gregg)

1948

Madame Alexander was one of the first companies to change over to the use of hard plastics and begain using it extensively during 1948.

Fairy Queen. 14½" and 17." Pink rayon gown with gold braid trim. Green wings. Mohair wig with full bangs. (Margaret)

Baby Lovey Dove. First all hard plastic baby. 12" tall with molded hair.

Babs Ice Skater. 15," 18" and 21." Has marabou muff and hat plume. (Margaret and Maggie)

Old Fashioned Girl. From Louisa Mae Alcott book of same name.

Lucy Bride. 14" (Margaret)

Wendy Ann. 14½," 17½" and 20½." Has various little girl outfits. (Margaret)

Maggie. 15" only. Little girl fashions.

Alice In Wonderland. (Margaret)

Margaret O'Brien. Hard plastic.

Sweet Baby. Cloth body. Latex arms and legs. 18" and 20½."

Little Genius. 11." Cloth and hard plastic head, arms and legs.

MCGuffey Ana. 14½" All hard plastic. Red/blonde mohair wig. (Margaret)

Little Women. (Margaret and Maggie)

Karen. 15" and 18." (Margaret)

14" "Margaret O'Brien" All hard plastic. Original. White blouse, yellow-gold pinafore with red hair ribbons and trim. 1948. (Courtesy Mandeville-Barkel Collection)

15" "Amy" of Little Women, (played by Elizabeth Taylor as a dark blonde) All hard plastic with looped curls hairdo. Original. 1948. Uses the Margaret O'Brien face. (Courtesy Sally Bethscheider)

14" "Margaret O'Brien" as "Beth" in the movie Little Women. Apron not original. 1948. (Courtesy Mary Partridge)

15" "Meg" of Little Women. 1948. All hard plastic. (Maggie). Red plaid cotton gown with black bib front. Red plaid ruffle on cotton petticoat. (Courtesy Elizabeth Montesano of Yesterday's Children)

14" "Patty Pigtails" (Polly's little sister) All hard plastic with blue sleep eyes, platinum pigtails wig. Taffeta dress and hat with red snap shoes. (Courtesy John Axe)

1" "Little Genius" Cloth with hard plastic head, half arms and legs. Molded brown hair, sleep blue eyes. All original christening gown. Marks: Alexander, on head. Tag: Little Genius/Madame Alexander, etc. 1948. (Courtesy John Axe)

1949

Little Lady Doll. 21." Lady type with human hair in thick braids. Colonial silk dress with organdy bodice. Wide brim straw hat.

Wendy Ann. Repeat from 1948. (Margaret)

Mary Martin. As Nellie Forbush of South Pacific. (Margaret)

Hedy Lamar. Samson and Delilah. Black hair. 17." (Margaret)

Lucy Bride. (Margaret)

Babs Ice Skater. Repeat with costume change. (Margaret)

Nina Ballerina. 14½" and 17½" and 19" (Margaret)

Maggie Walker. 15" and 18."

Polly Pigtails. 14½," 17½" and 21" (Maggie). Named for the Pre-Teen publication "Polly Pigtails" of Parent's Magazine.

Patty Pigtails. 14" only. Polly's little sister.

Little Women. 15." Note: These costumes varied a great deal from the catalogs, ads and newspaper ads and some outfits were changed within the same year and from store to store (example: FAO Schwarz and Marshall Field) Even the later Alexander catalogs used same picture over and over when they differed from the actual releases.

Baby Genius. 16," 18" and 23." Cloth with hard plastic head and latex limbs.

Karen. 15" only. (Margaret)

Lovey Dovey. 19" cloth body, hard plastic head and latex limbs.

Bitsey and Butch. 12." Cloth body with COMPOSITION head and limbs.

Fairy Queen. 14½." (Margaret)

14" "Lucy Bride" 1948. All hard plastic. Satin gown with off waist gathers, puff shoulder sleeves and rhinestones on bodice. Veil may nto be original. (Margaret). (Courtesy John Axe)

14" and 17" "Polly Pigtails" All hard plastic with blue sleep eyes. Dark blonde pigtails. Plaid taffeta dresses and straw hats. Black shoes. Tag: Polly Pigtails/Madame Alexander. 1949. (Maggie face). She also came dressed in a broadcloth dress with floral design, puff sleeves and round collar. (Courtesy John Axe)

17½" "Nina Ballerina" Hard plastic with strawberry blonde glued on floss type wig. White ballet dress with silver trim. (Margaret) 1949. (Courtesy Robin Rankow)

17" "Babs, the Iceskater" All hard plastic with glued on blonde floss-like wig. Blue sleep eyes. Original satin outfit with fur trim. Marks: Alexander, on head. Tag: Madame Alexander, etc. 1949.

14" "Godey Lady" All hard plastic. (Margaret) Blue sleep eyes that appear to have a little green in them. Auburn hair in bun. Apricot colored gown of taffeta. Dress is styled longer in back. Tag: Godey Lady/Madame Alexander, etc. 1949. (Courtesy Sandy Rankow)

17" "Lucy Bride" 1949. All hard plastic with dark skin tones. Dark red glued on wig. Blue sleep eyes. Original satin gown with rhinestone trim. Missing is floor length viel.

14" "Babs" All hard plastic. Gold satin with white fur trim. Skates missing. This is the Maggie and the Margaret was also used for this doll. Tag: Babs Skating/Madame Alexander, etc. 1949.

17" "Hedy Lamar" All hard plastic. Not original. Doll was released with "Samson and Delilah" movie of 1949. Confirmed by Alexander Doll Co. (Margaret). (Courtesy Bessie Greeno)

This is a studio still of Hedy Lamar.

The 1949 version of Louisa May Alcott's "Little Women" starred Mary Astor (Marme), Margaret O'Brien (Beth), Janet Leigh (Meg), June Allyson (Jo) and Elizabeth Taylor (Amy). Peter Lawford played Laurie. Since Madame Alexander had the use of the "Little Women" rights since 1933 and had produced the Margaret O'Brien doll, this 1949 and 1950 set of "Little Women" dolls (hard plastic) did represent the actresses. The Elizabeth Taylor as Amy is a blonde.

14" "Jo" of "Little Women." All hard plastic with amber eyes and brown hair. Gown is red faille with inset blue velvet. White organdy inset sleeves and neck trim. 1949. (Maggie). Tag: Louisa M. Alcott's Little Women/by Madame Alexander. (Courtesy Jeannie Gregg)

14" Right: "Amy" in dress of blue background and rose figures. Loop curls. (Margaret face). 1949. 14" Left: "Beth" in dress of blue background and rose colored figures. (Maggie face). 1951. (Courtesy Jay Minter)

15" Standing: "Jo" with red gaberdine dress with blue velvet bib. Inset organdy sleeves. 1949. Sitting is "Beth" of 1950 with large hands and individual fingers. (Courtesy Elizabeth Montesano of Yesterday's Children)

14" "Cinderella" All hard plastic with blue sleep eyes. Original. Tag: Cinderella/Madame Alexander, etc. 1950. (Margaret face). (Courtesy Jay Minter)

14" "Prince Charming" All hard plastic with brown sleep eyes and caracul wig. Original clothes. Tag: Madame Alexander/New York USA. (Margaret face) 1950. (Courtesy Carrie Perkins)

1950

Mary Martin. In various outfits. 14." (Margaret)

Little Women. 14." (3 Margaret and 2 Maggie)

Peggy Bride. 14" and 18." (Margaret)

Poor Cinderella. 14." (Margaret)

Piper Laurie. 14." (Margaret)

Prince Charming. 14." (Margaret)

Bride. 14," 17" and 21." (Margaret)

Bridesmaid. 14" and 17." (Maggie)

Nina Ballerina. Variation of costume. (Margaret)

Wendy Ann. 14½" and 17½." Repeat with costume changes.

Maggie Walker. 15," 18," 21" and 23."

Alice In Wonderland. (Maggie)

Babs Ice Skater. Costume change.

Divine-a-lite Dolls. Trademark 573,313.

Lovey-Dovey. One piece latex with hard plastic head.

Godey, Renoir and Victoria. Beautifully dressed costume dolls. (Margaret and Maggie)

Cinderella. (Ball gown). 14" (Margaret)

Contessa. 14½" and 17." (Margaret)

14" "Mary Martin" All hard plastic with red caracul wig. Original white organdy over satin dress trimmed with bows. Also came in Sailor Suit. Earrings are glued on. Taken from movie "Show Boat." 1950. (Margaret face). (Courtesy Carrie Perkins)

14" "Piper Laurie" All hard plastic with red floss-like hair pulled to back of head in ponytail style. Blue sleep eyes. Clothes are rust colored polished cotton with dark brown trim and pearl buttons. (Margaret face). 1950.

14" "Godey Lady" (Margaret) 1950. All hard plastic. Peach taffeta dress and bonnet, trimmed with white feathers and tied with black velvet. Black patent shoes with pink bows on toes. Red hair caught in a "snood." Blue sleep eyes. (Courtesy Virginia Vinton)

14" and 17" "Alice In Wonderland" (Maggie face). All hard plastic. Light blue taffeta dresses and white organdy pinafores. 1950-51. (Courtesy Jay Minter)

14" "Nina Ballerina" All hard plastic wig glued on blonde wig. Blue sleep eyes. Unjointed ankles. Original. Marks: Alex., on head. Tag: Nina Ballerina/By Madame Alexander, etc. 1950.

18" "Peggy Bride" All hard plastic with blue sleep eyes. Blonde mohair wig. 1950. (Margaret face). (Courtesy Jay Minter)

18" "Babs" All hard plastic. 1950. (Margaret). Mohair wig. Tag: Babs/Madame Alexander, etc. (Courtesy Mandeville-Barkel Collection)

17½" "Wendy Ann" 1950. All hard plastic with human hair wig. Rayon dress with ruffled skirt blends from pale blue into pale pink and back to blue. Tag: Wendy Ann/by Madame Alexander/All Rights Reserved.

21" "Maggie" #1500-1950. All hard plastic. Purple taffeta dress, cut in back to expose ruffled slip. Lavender suede shoes. Tag: white with blue script: Madame Alexander/New York/ All Rights Reserved. (Courtesy Elizabeth Montesano of Yesterday's Children)

14" "Amy" 1950. All hard plastic. All original. (Margaret). Note the unusual hands with molded very separate fingers. Tag: Louisa M. Alcott's/ Little Women/"Amy"/By Madame Alexander, etc. (Courtesy John Axe)

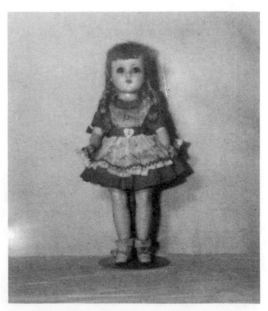

15" "Little Women" 1950, except Meg (far right) which is from the 1949 set. Left to right: Jo, Beth, Amy with a variation of material and 2 buttons missing from bodice. Marme, missing lace shawl and Meg from 1949. The four 1950 have large, open fingered hands. (Courtesy Jay Minter)

14" All hard plastic with rayon floss hair in pigtails. (Margaret). Original red dress with white pinafore. Letters are printed on pinafore in red. 1950. (Courtesy Sally Bethscheider)

15" "Meg" from the 1950 set of "Little Women." Gown is white with red print. (Courtesy Elizabeth Montesano of Yesterday's Children)

18" "Lovey-Dovey" Hard plastic head, cloth body and vinyl limbs. Pierced nostrils. May have originally been on a latex body. Marks: Alexander, on head. 1950. (Courtesy Mary Partridge)

1951

Betty. Same as Maggie. 14½" and 17½" in red rayon taffeta dress. Saran wig. Sold through Sears, Roebuck.

Margot Ballerina. (Margaret)

Alice In Wonderland. 15," 18" and 23." "Newtex-saran" wig in traditional Alice style, tied with hair ribbon. Dressed in blue taffeta as well as printed cottons and all with white lace trimmed organdy pinafore. (Maggie)

Alice In Wonderland. 15." Came with 13 piece trousseau. #247 Alice is 15" tall and came with 28 piece trousseau. Both these "Alices" were dressed in cotton print dresses with lace trimmed organdy pinafores. (Maggie)

Wendy Bride. 15," 18" and 23." Bridal gown trimmed with rhinestones. Long flowing veil of lace edged net with halo of white flowers. (Margaret)

Violet. 18." (Cissy) Walker, head turns. Extra joints, using the Madaline body to 1954.

Majorette. 14." (Margaret). Red and white wool, lined outfit.

Rosamund Bridesmaid. 15" and 18." Dressed in frothy gown of net, bound with satin and satin bodice. Two fluffy skirts cascade to her feet over an underdress to match. Trimmed with satin streamers and rosebuds. Her head dress is straw lace with rosette of pink rosebuds over each ear. Clothes came in assorted pastel shades. Inspired by book "Rosamund" by Maria Edgeworth. 1767-1849. (Maggie)

Nina Ballerina. 15," 19" and 23." Red rayon yarn wig. (Margaret)

Kathy. 15," 18" and 23." With pigtails. In pedal pushers of clan tartan, corduroy wesket over sheer white blouse and a Scotch tam with feather. Brown oxfords with roller skates. Also in two tone cotton color combinations and trimmed with rick-rack in contrasting shades. Beret of black velvet. Other various outfits. (Maggie)

Maggie Teenager. 15," 18" and 23." Came in three outfits. 1. Clan tartan skirt, white pique shirt and slippers to match. 2. Taffeta dress in assorted styles and colors with suede slipper to match. 3. Gaberdine shirtmaker type dresses of assorted colors with shoes to match.

Mary Rose Bride. 17." (Margaret)

Little Women. (3 Margaret and 2 Maggie)

Sonja Henie. 15," 18" and 23." Vinyl head with open/closed mouth. Light dimples. Hard plastic body and limbs. Came in two outfits: Short pink (very pale) satin skating costume with flowers and rhinestones over ruffled net underdress and satin panties. Flowers in hair. Long nylon stockings. White, high skating shoes. (ice). 2. White gaberdine skating costume trimmed with felt applique over a colored petticoat with contrasting jersey blouse and panties. White beret and high white skating shoes. Re-issue of doll along with star opening her own "Sonja Henie Ice Revue." (Madeline)

Clarabell. Clown from Howdy-Doody T.V. Show. 19." This same doll #49 was 29" tall and the #99 was 49" tall. (The last one is 4 feet, 3 inches tall.)

Alice. 18." Dressed as Little Girls From The Past. 4 outfits, all have extra long wigs. (Maggie)

Penny. 34." Teenager from a well known comic strip in the N.Y. Herald Tribune and syndicated throughout U.S.A. in 75 newspapers. Soft cloth body with vinyl stuffed head and limbs. "Newtex" wig is a pageboy. Assorted dresses and skirt/shirts designed to please the Boarding School and college girls. Open toed slippers and white socks. (This later was the Barbara Jane in a smaller size) #4280 Penny came in a 42" size.

Littlest Cherub. 9" Body and limbs of stuffed latex. Vinyl head. Dressed in a wide ribbon sash and bow, with a garland of flowers and flower halo. White wings. Ribbons were in assorted colors.

Slumbermate. 13" Sleeping baby with vinyl head and stuffed jersey body and limbs. Came in assorted pastel baby dresses.

Christening Baby. 11," 16" and 19." Cloth body, vinyl arms and legs with hard plastic head. Long christening dress with bonnet to match.

Sunbeam. 16," 19" and 23." Newborn infant. Cloth body with vinyl head and limbs. Dressed in diaper, shirt and booties and wrapped in pure wool shawl, tied with pink satin bow.

Bonnie. 11," 16" and 19." Cloth body with hard plastic head and vinyl limbs. Dressed in toddler type outfit of cotton combining plain and rosebud print with plain bonnet, trimmed with lace and rosebuds. Suede slippers. Came in assorted pastels. Glued on wig.

Bitsey. 11," 16," 19," 23" and 26." Cloth body with hard plastic head and vinyl limbs. Lace and rosebud trimmed permanent finish organdy dress and bonnet. Satin slippers to match. Glued on wig. (Bonnie)

Honeybun. 19," 23" and 26." Came in two outfits. Vinyl head with open/closed mouth and two upper teeth. Also in 1952.

Portraits. 14" Godey Lady in rose silk taffeta gown with peplums. White V shaped vest. Pearl bead button and braid trim. Lace trimmed matching poke bonnet with feather and flowers and black velvet ties.

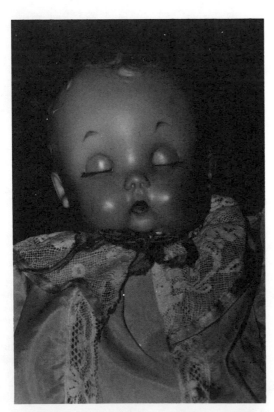

86

13" "Slumbermate" 1951. All soft stuffed kapok body and limbs. Excellent quality vinyl head with closed eyes and molded light brown hair. Open/closed mouth. Marks: Alexander, on head. (Courtesy Bessie Greeno)

18" "Maggie" All hard plastic. Original including red/white saddle shoes. This same doll sold as Betty in the 1951 Sears catalog. Marks: Alexander, on head. Tag: Madame Alexander, etc. (Courtesy Mandeville-Barkel Collection)

14" "Alice In Wonderland" All hard plastic with glued on blonde wig. Blue sleep eyes. Pale blue taffeta dress with white organdy pinafore. Marks: none. Tag: Madame Alexander etc. 1951. (Maggie face)

25" "Maggie Walker" 1951. All hard plastic walker, head turns. Blue sleep eyes. Original red satin dress. Shoes not original. Marks: Alexander on head. Tag: Maggie/Madame Alexander, etc. This 25" came with both the Maggie face and, as this one, the later to be Cissy face.

18" "Sonja Henie" Hard plastic body, arms and legs with early vinyl head. Open/closed mouth. Light cheek dimples. Original. Marks:- Alexander, on head. Tag: Madame Alexander, etc. 1951. (Madelaine face). Re-issue of doll, along with the star opening her own "Sonja Henie Ice Revue"

18" "Violet" All hard plastic walker, head turns. Jointed at elbows, wrists and knees (using Madeline body). Marks: Alexander, on head. Tag: Violet/By Madame Alexander, etc. 1951-1954. (Using later to be Cissy face). (Courtesy Roberta Lago)

18" "Alice" 1951. All hard plastic with glued on red wig. Marks: none. (Maggie face).

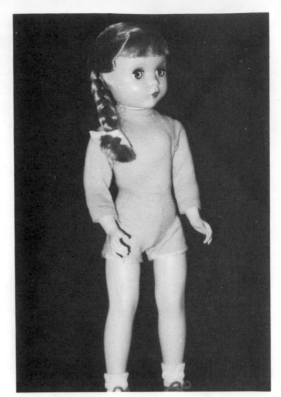

18" "Kathy" All hard plastic with glued on ash blonde wig. Blue sleep eyes. Original blue body suit. Rollers missing from shoe skates. Tag: Madame Alexander, etc. 1951. (Maggie face)

17" "Kathy" 1951. (Maggie face) All hard plastic with brown sleep eyes and blonde mohair wig. The outfit she wears is #2120 for Cissy and dates from 1957.

18" "Margot Ballerina" All hard plastic with blue sleep eyes. Hair in pageboy in back. Walker, head turns. Marks: Alexander, on head. Tag on outfit: Madame Alexander/All rights reserved. 1951.

15" Standing: "Meg" 1951 with reverse of print/plain of 1952 #1500. Sitting: "Marme" 1949. Hair braided over ears and top of head. Both all hard plastic. (Both Margaret). (Courtesy Elizabeth Montesano of Yesterday's Children)

14" Left: "Marme" in dark green, braids around head and wears gold button pin. 1951. Right: "Meg" in rose dress with green flowered apron. 1952. Both with Margaret face. (Courtesy Jay Minter)

14" "Jo" of The Little Women. These dolls with the wide spread fingers were used during 1950-1951. This one is from the 1951 set. (Maggie). Blue checked dress with bright blue apron with white trim. (Courtesy Jay Minter)

17" "Mary Rose Bride" All hard plastic. (Margaret). #1548-1951. Golden blonde hair and amber sleep eyes. Tagged dress: Madame Alexander/New York U.S.A./All Rights Reserved. This bridal wreath design was used again in 1958 with different design gown, for Elise. (Courtesy Jeannie Gregg)

17" "Sister of the Bride" (Bridesmaid). All hard plastic. (Maggie). Ca. 1951. Does not look it, but taffeta under the gold net is pale green. Tag in: Tene' Original. No information. (Courtesy Jeannie Gregg)

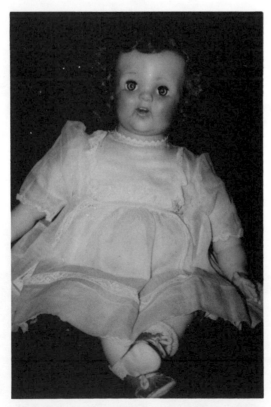

18" "Honeybun" Cloth body with vinyl limbs and head. Glued on saran wig, blue sleep eyes and open/closed mouth with two inserted upper teeth. Cryer in the back. Tag: Madame Alexander, etc. 1951. Organdy dress is yellow with white lace trim. (Courtesy **Bessie Carson**)

18" "Honeybun" 1951. Original coat and bonnet. Both are yellow with real fur trim on collars and cuffs. (Courtesy Bessie Carson)

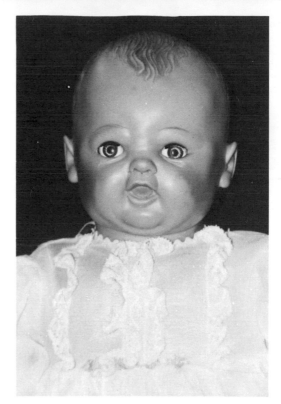

19" "Sunbeam" 1951. Early stuffed vinyl head, hands and legs. Cloth body. "Newborn" infant. This one is tagged Christening gown with matching bonnet. Came also just in diaper, shirt and booties and wrapped in wool blanket. Sleep eyes, open/closed mouth and molded hair. Marked Alexander, on head. (Courtesy Sharon Pressler)

Shows close-up of the face of Sunbeam newborn infant doll. (Courtesy Sharon Pressler)

1952

Tommy Bangs and Stuffy. Boy dolls. Tommy has the Maggie face and Stuffy, the Margaret face. They were Fashion Award winners of the New York Fashion Academy. These awards were given to doll costumes as well as lady and children's styles.

Madeline. 18" only. First fully jointed, hard plastic body. Extra joints included wrists, elbows, knees. Head of vinyl with open/closed mouth. (Sonja Henie, 1951 head). Dressed in organdy knee length dress with lace. Inspired by "Children's Classics" by same name by Ludwig Bemelmans.

Annabelle. 15," 18" and 23." From Kate Smith's T.V. program. Dressed in assorted pastel dresses with contrasting pull over sweaters with her name written across front. She is dressed to correspond with the little girl in Kate Smith's well loved book "Stories of Annabelle." (Maggie)

Maggie Walker. 15," 18" and 23." Walker, head turns as legs move. Dressed in flowered skirt with white blouse that has three rows of lace on short sleeves. Also was available in Trousseau case with large assortment of clothes.

Bride. 15," 18" and 23." Bridal gown of satin, lace trimmed. Lace edged veil-coronet. (Margaret)

Treena Ballerina. 15," 18" and 23." Nylon and tulle ballet costume trimmed with flowers on skirt, shoulders and in hair. (Margaret)

Snow White. 15." Pink and gold gown with gold sleeveless jacket. Ribbon through black hair. (Margaret)

Honeybun. Cloth and vinyl 18" and 22" baby. Repeat from 1951.

Little Women. 15." New outfits for 1952. Still three faces are Margaret and 2 are Maggie.

Little Men. 15." Taken from Louisa Mae Alcott's book, "Little Women." Dressed in period costumes. Two are Maggie and one Margaret.

Cynthia. 15," 18" and 23." Dressed in frilly knee length dress. Alexander's second black doll. (Margaret)

Rosebud. 16," 19," 23" and 25." Trademark 628,247-1952. Came in three outfits. 1. Dressed in redingote of dotted percale over white organdy sleeveless dress. Bonnet to match. 2. In imported lace trimmed organdy. Suede baby shoes. 3. In tailored coat and bonnet over lace trimmed organdy dress. All have cry boxes in cloth bodies and vinyl heads and limbs. The legs are straight, toddler type.

Bud. Little boy in 16," 19" and 25." Same doll as Rosebud. Dressed in overalls of white gaberdine and dotted shirt. Hat of gaberdine lined with cotton to match shirt.

Littlest Angel. 9." Latex with early vinyl head. Painted eyes.

Little Southern Girl and Boy. 10." Latex with vinyl heads. Painted eyes. Various outfits.

Dolly Dryper. 11." All vinyl baby with open mouth/nurser. Wears diaper panties, suede baby shoes and sun hat. Came with 7 piece layette.

Barbara Jane. 29." Cloth body with stuffed vinyl head and limbs. Dressed in assorted little girl dresses of polished cotton or organdy. All had open toed shoes. (Penny face)

Alice In Wonderland. 29." Same doll as above but in Alice style clothes and long blonde hair style.

McGuffey Ana. 29." Same doll as above but dressed in McGuffey style clothes. Curly banged hair style.

Penny. 29" and 31." Same doll as 1951 and Barbara Jane. This year has tightly curled hair style. Various little girl outfits.

John Powers Models. 18." All hard plastic. (Margaret, Maggie)

Louisa. 18." (Margaret)

13" "Treena Ballerina" All hard plastic with blue sleep eyes. Orange glued on wig. Tulle skirt, satin top and had flowers in hair. 1952. (Margaret face). (Courtesy Jay Minter)

15" "Treena Ballerina" All hard plastic. #1515 and #1518 (18"). 1952 (Maggie) Also used the Margaret doll, which is #1540 and 1840.

20" "Annabelle" All hard plastic. Blue sleep eyes/lashes. All original. 1952. (Courtesy Connie Chase)

15" "Annabelle" #1510-1952. All hard plastic. Brown sleep eyes, original dress and pull over sweater with name. From Kate Smith's T.V. program. Tag: Kate Smith's Annabelle/By Madame Alexander, etc. (Maggie face). (Courtesy Roberta Lago)

15" "Maggie Walker" All hard plastic walker, head turns. Brown sleep eyes. Outfit is #1515-1952. (Courtesy Roberta Lago)

15" "Maggie" All hard plastic, with a variation of skirt printed pattern. #1515-1952. (Courtesy Marge Meisinger)

14½" "Maggie Walker" in #1611-1952. Blue checked taffeta dress set with rhinestones on bodice. (Courtesy Phyllis Houston)

23" "Maggie Walker" 1952 (#2316). All hard plastic. White top with red/green plaid skirt. Wears tag: Fashion Award. (Courtesy Shirley Bertrand)

18" "Louisa" All hard plastic. 1952. (Margaret) (Courtesy Mary Partridge)

15" Blonde: "Amy" #1500-1952. Dress is pink cotton with floral bodice. "Marme" is from the 1950 set with large hands with individual fingers. (Courtesy Elizabeth Montesano of Yesterday's Children)

14" "Stuffy" of The Little Men. All hard plastic. Pants are white/black check and the jacket and cap are a delicate blue. (Maggie) 1952. (Courtesy Mandeville-Barkel Collection)

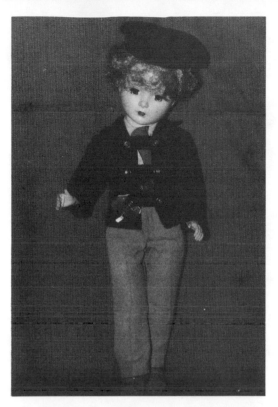

15" "Tommy Bangs" from the Little Men by Louisa May Alcott. (Margaret). All hard plastic. #1501-1952. (Courtesy Marge Meisinger)

15" "Nat" from the Little Men set. (Maggie). #1501-1952. All hard plastic. (Courtesy Marge Meisinger)

15" "Snow White" All hard plastic. Gown of pink and gold with gold jacket. Came in three sizes: 15," 18" and 23." 1952. (Margaret face). (Courtesy Roberta Lago)

17" "Madeline" All hard plastic with vinyl head. Blue sleep eyes, open/closed mouth and glued on wig. Jointed at elbow, wrists and knees. Original dress as shown in booklet "Madame Alexander Fashions for Madeline." Marks: Alexander on head. 1952.

29" "Barbara Jane" mold used for several different dolls. All stuffed vinyl arms, legs and head. Cloth body. Marks: Alexander, on head. 1952. (Courtesy Alma Carmichael)

29" "Alice In Wonderland" Cloth body with stuffed vinyl head and limbs. Blue sleep eyes. Original pale blue taffeta dress with white pinafore. Marks: Alexander, on head. Tag: Alice In Wonderland/by Madame Alexander. 1952. #2969 (Barbara Jane face). (Courtesy Mae Teters)

17" "Bride" #1550-1952. All hard plastic. (Margaret) Hair has been combed out and veil is missing. (Courtesy Evelyn Chisman)

22" "Rosebud" Cloth body with cryer. Vinyl head, arms and legs. Molded hair, blue sleep eyes. Marks: Alexander, on head. 1952 also had rooted hair.

17" "Rosebud" 1952 #3561. Cloth body with vinyl head and limbs. Red dynel wig. Blue sleep eyes. Marks: Alexander, on head. Not original clothes.

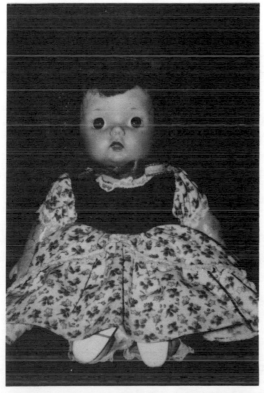

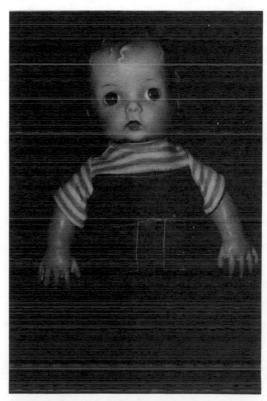

10" "Southern Girl" Latex body and limbs. Vinyl head with glued on wig and painted eyes. Original. Marks: Alexander, on head. Tag: Madame Alexander. 1952.

10" "Southern Boy" Latex one piece body and limbs. Vinyl head with molded hair. Painted eyes. Original. Marks: Alexander, on head. Madame Alexander, on tag. 1952.

11" "Bitsey" 1952. Cloth body with limbs of early vinyl. Head is hard plastic. Original and tagged. (Courtesy Sally Bethscheider)

1953

The highlight of this year was the drama of newly-crowned Queen Elizabeth in dolls. The scene depicts the Queen with her 6 attendants leaving Westminister abbey. The Queen is in embroidered gown, with the Imperial State Crown, real ermine and jewels. Ladies in Waiting are in silver gowns and tiaras. This group called "The Recessional" was donated, by Madame Alexander, to the Brooklyn Children's Museum. The Queen has the Margaret face, two attendants have the Maggie face, two the Margaret face and two have the yet to be released Cissy face.

Miss Flora McFlimsey. (new version). 15." This is the first use of the new Cissy mold outside of the Recessional dolls and Binnie Walker. From Mariana's book about a little Victorian doll. Hard plastic with vinyl head. Dressed in Victorian style short dress with long stockings, button shoes and hat with bow and flowers.

Little Women. Repeat from 1952. (3 Margaret, 2 Maggie)

Cynthia. Repeat from 1952. (Margaret)

Margot Ballerina. Repeat from 1952. (Margaret)

Rosamund Bridesmaid. Repeat from 1952. (Maggie)

Maggie Walker. 15," 18" and 22." Same doll as 1952. Came with assorted dress styles.

Madeline. 18." Same as 1952. Came in assorted style dreses and hats.

Wendy Bride. 15" and 18." Dressed in nylon tulle with veil to match, flowing from a starched brim. (Margaret)

Winsome Winnie Walker. 15," 18" and 23." Cissy head but has full hard plastic arms. Came in two outfits this year. 1. Taffeta dress under cloth coat with matching hat. Gloves. 2. Imported organdy dress trimmed with val lace, tucks and tiny pearl buttons. Assorted style bonnets. Trademark 645, 218-1953.

Peter Pan. 15." Dressed just as in the Disney film. (Maggie). From story written by James M. Barrie. (1904)

Wendy. 15." From Peter Pan. Dressed in blue satin. (Margaret)

Beau Arts Creations were the forerunners to the 21" Portraits. These are all 18" tall and they are all walkers.

#2025 Queen Elizabeth. In elaborate white brocade court gown with blue sash of the Garter Order. Jeweled tiara, earrings and bracelets. Long velvet robe cape with border of white fur cloth and silver braid. Long white gloves. (Margaret)

#2020B Princess Margaret Rose. Wears court gown of pink faille taffeta decorated with sequins. Her tiara and bracelet are jeweled and her earrings and necklace are pearls. Long white gloves. (Margaret)

#2020C Dressed for Opera. Gown of pale pink satin and a long brocaded satin coat of dove blue, trimmed in rhinestones. Sets in tiara, bracelet and earrings are also rhinestones. (Margaret)

#2020D Garden Party. Gown of aqua taffeta, draped with a stole of nylon net embroidered with flowers and jewels. Her tiara and bracelet are jeweled and her necklace of pearls. (Maggie)

#2020E Royal Evening. Gown of chartreuse taffeta trimmed with rosebuds and a big sash of forest green taffeta. Her tiara is gold and set with green stones. (Maggie)

#2020 Debutante. White satin ball gown and rich taffeta evening cape. Carries tiny muff covered wth roses. Hair is simply arranged with a single band of pearls. (Maggie)

The following are the 18" Glamour Girls of 1953. All are walkers.

#2001A Edwardian. Pink embossed cotton gown, black lace gloves with a bonnet that is black taffeta and lace, with pink ostrich feather. (Margaret)

#2001B Blue Danube. Long dress of soft blue with tiny pink rosebuds and green leaves accentuated with white val lace. White straw lace bonnet has tiny rosebuds tucked into her curls at each side. White gloves. (Margaret)

#2001 Picnic Day. Gown has green leaves on strawberry pink, a wide green sash with big bow. Trimmed with black val lace. Big straw hat with pink roses. (Maggie)

#2010A Godey Lady. Red taffeta gown and bonnet. Grey fur cloth cape stole. (Margaret)

#2010B Civil War. White taffeta dress with wide sash and big bow of red. Tiny red rosebuds and green leaves are sprinkled down the front of her gown and trim her picture hat of white horsehair braid. Her bodice and puff sleeves of nylon net are trimmed with ruffles of val lace. (Margaret)

#2010C Victorian. Gown of pale pink taffeta has a bodice of black velvet and her puff sleeves have bands of black. The full skirt has a garland of pink roses and streamers of black velvet and pink satin as its only trimming. Black straw lace bonnet is trimmed with pink rosebuds and big tulle bow. (Maggie)

#2020A Queen Elizabeth II. Same doll as #2025 but minus the cape. (Margaret)

Prince Phillip. Black Tux with watch chain. No hat. (Margaret)

Queen Mother. 17."(Margaret)

Lady Churchill. 18." (Margaret)

Sir Winston Churchill. 18." Same doll as Prince Phillip, only 18" and straighter hair. Wears hat. (Margaret)

Rosebud. Repeat of 1952.

Bud. Repeat of 1952.

Cry Dolly. All vinyl baby dressed in a sunsuit and matching bonnet of waffle pique trimmed with lace and rick-rack. Big white organdy bows. Booties. 14," 16," and 20." The 14" and 16" were also offered with a 12 piece layette.

Quiz-kin. 7½" (8"). Molded hair. Has two buttons in back to nod head "yes" or "no." They were available in the following outfits also. Trademark 646,343-1953.

Wendy Ann/Alexander-kins. 7½" (8"). Re-introduction of these miniature dolls. Came with 32 available outfits that included Peter Pan, Little Madaline, Little Southern Girl in pink organdy dress and pantaloons. Straw bonnet with feather and tiny flowers. Agatha in long dress of dark green with red flowers/green leaf trim on skirt and a lace straw bonnet with green feather. Others were: Bride and Groom, Little Godey, Little Melanie, Ballerina, Blue Danube, Victoria, Goya. All these are non-walkers and have straight legs.

Billy. 7½" Boy version of Wendy Ann.

14" "Queen Elizabeth II" In robe declared Queen. All hard plastic. (Margaret)

14" Back view of the robe of the newly crowned Queen.

"Prince Phillip" and "Queen Elizabeth" in red robe. All hard plastic. (Both Margaret)

"Queen Elizabeth" In purple robe. All hard plastic. (Margaret)

"Queen Elizabeth II" and six ladies in Waiting holding her train. (Margaret, Cissy and Maggie)

"Queen Mother" All hard plastic. (Margaret)

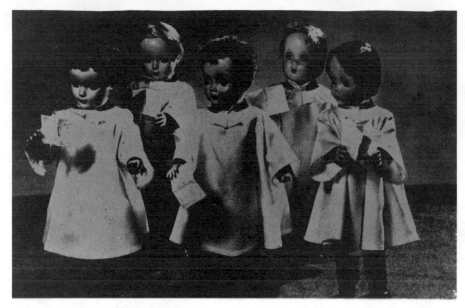

"Choir Boys" All hard plastic. (2 Margaret, 2
Maggie and one Cissy)

"Prince Phillip" and 8" "Prince Charles" All hard
plastic. (Margaret and Wendy Ann)

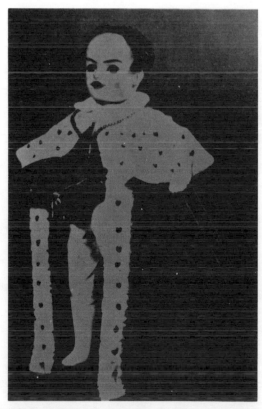

"Anthony Eden" All hard plastic. (Margaret
with heavily painted features)

18" "Queen Elizabeth" Hard plastic #2030A-1954 One of the Me and My Shadow Series. Matching 8" queen in color section. Also used in 1953. (Margaret) (Courtesy Mandeville-Barkel Collection)

18" "Prince Phillip—Sir Winston Churchill" 1953. All hard plastic with men's hair style. (Margaret). The Prince Phillip does not have a hat but hat is worn by the Sir Winston Churchill. (Courtesy Mary Partridge)

14" "Princess Margaret Rose" Gown is lavender. #2020B-1953. Tag: Princess Margaret Rose / Madame Alexander, etc. (Margaret face). (Courtesy Helen Faford)

14" "Princess Margaret Rose" 1953. All hard plastic. (Margaret). The gown is yellow with white lace trim. Natural straw hat. (Courtesy Mandeville-Barkel Collection)

15" "Wendy Bride" 1953. #1552. All hard plastic with blonde wig and blue sleep eyes. Net over satin gown, satin bodice and starched bridal cap. (Courtesy Roberta Lago)

17" "Queen Mother" Full lace gown with satin ribbon. Matching star and tiara. Special hairdo. (Margaret). (Courtesy Renie Culp)

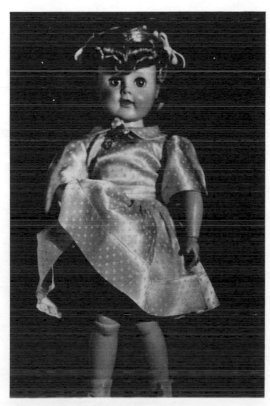

18" "Madeline" #1845 1953. Hard plastic with ball-like joints, including elbows, wrists and knees. Vinyl head with glued on wig. All original. Marks: Alexander, on head. Tag: 18" tall/ Madame Alexander, etc. This is an extra dress sold in 1953. (Courtesy Mandeville-Barkel Collection)

18" "Madeline" Hard plastic body with vinyl head. Open/closed mouth. Blue sleep eyes. Extra joints at elbows, wrists and knees. Original. 1953. (Courtesy Roberta Lago)

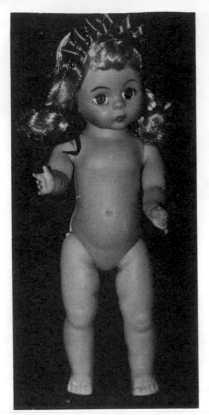

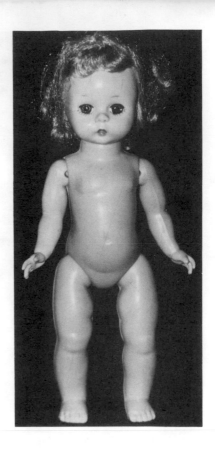

The 7½" and 8" doll on this page are shown clockwise from the first in 1953 to the current one: 1. Straight legs with deeper seams on feet, wrinkles at ankles and a darker tan color. The eyes are oval and the lips are dark red. 2. Straight leg walker. Seams deeper on feet, wrinkles at ankles, tan color that gets shiny and has a bisque look. Oval eyes and red lips. 3. Bend knee walker. Seams deeper on feet, tan color that gets the shiny bisque look. Oval eyes and red lips. 4. Last bend knee doll with pink skin tones, seam line deeper on sole of feet. 5. Current doll has powdery look to rigid plastic. Straight legs. Eyes rounder, higher cheek color, oranger lips. Seam line near edge of toes and seams not cleaned off through ears and neck. Gets shiny and deeper pink after being played with. All these dolls are marked Alex, on back. All have sleep eyes with molded lashes and painted lashes below the eyes.

INTERNATIONAL, AMERICANA
AND STORYBOOK DOLLS (7½"-8")

CURRENT AND AVAILABLE
Argentine Girl (571), was Tyrolean to 1973
Austria (598), was Tyrolean to 1973
Austria Boy (599)
Belgium (562)
Betsy Ross (431)
Bo Peep (483)
Brazil (573)
Canada (560)
China (572)
Czechoslovakia (564)
Denmark (569)
Finland (561)
France (590)
Geman (563)
Great Britain (1977)
Greece (565)
Gretel (454)
Hansel (453)
Hungary (597)
India (575)
Indonesia (579)
Irish (578)
Israel (568)
Italy (593)
Japan (570)
Mary, Mary (451)
Mexico (576)
Miss Muffet (452)
Norway (584)
Netherlands (591), was Dutch to 1973
Netherlands Boy (577), was Dutch to 1973
Poland (580)
Portugal (585)
Red Boy (440)
Red Riding Hood (482)
Rumania (586)
Russia (574)
Scarlett (425)
Scotland (596)
Spanish Girl (595)
Sweden (592)
Switzerland (594)
Thailand (567)
Turkey (587)
United States (559)
Yugoslavia (589)

DISCONTINUED DOLLS AND YEAR
African—1971
Amish Boy—1969
Amish Girl—1969
Argentine Boy—1966
Boliva—1966
Cowboy—1969
Cowgirl—1970
Ecuador—1966
English Guard—1968
Eskimo—1969
Hawaiian—1969
Greek Boy—1968
Indian Boy (Hiawatha)—1969
Indian Girl (Pocohantas)—1970
Korea—1970
mcGuffey Ana (American)—1965
Miss U.S.A.—1968
Morocco—1970
Peruvian Boy—1966
Priscilla—1970
Spanish Boy—1968
Vietnam—1969

8" "Wendy Ann" 1953. Straight legs. Yellow organdy, lace trimmed dress with attached pink slip. Lace trimmed panties. Patent shoes. Replaced hat. (Courtesy Mary Partridge)

8" "Agatha" Straight legs. 1953-54. Marks: Alex., on back. Tag: Agatha/of Little Women/ Madame Alexander. (Courtesy Mable Sherman)

8" "Peter Pan" Hard plastic with straight legs. Lamb's wool wig. Original tan and green outfit of felt. Original red feather from hat missing. Marks: Alex., on body. Tag: Alexanderkins/Madame Alexander. 1953. (Courtesy Daisy Houghtaling)

8" "Little Southern Girl" #305-1953. Pink organdy gown with straw hat with feathers. Straight legs. Marks: Alex., on body. Tag: Alexanderkins/Madame Alexander. (Courtesy Jane Thomas)

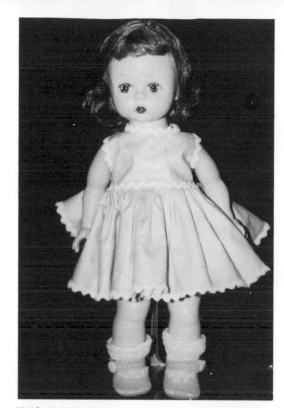

7½" "Wendy Ann" #509-1953. Pale blue soft cotton dress with appliqued rosettes and attached satin full slip. Straight leg, non walker. (Courtesy Jay Minter)

8" "Quiz-kin" All hard plastic with jointed knees. Has two buttons in back to make head answer yes or no. Marks: Alex. on back. Pastel dress with rick-rack trim. 1954. (Courtesy Jay Minter)

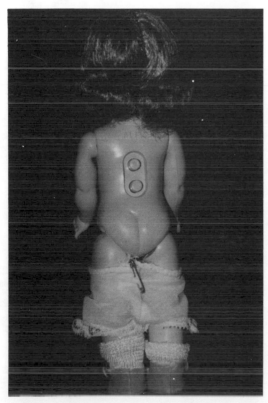

8" "Wendy Ann as Quiz Kid" Push buttons make head nod yes or no. 1953.

7½" "Wendy Ann" #388-1953. (Courtesy Jeannie Niswonger)

15" "Miss Flora McFlimsey" Hard plastic body (unjointed elbows) and vinyl head. (Uses Cissy mold). This doll is one of the very few Alexander made with a vinyl head. #1502-1953. Catalog reprint.

16" "Cry Dolly" All vinyl with molded hair, blue sleep eyes and open mouth/nurser. Excellent body molding. Marks: Alexander, on head. #671-1953. Same doll as Kathy in 1954, 1955 and 1956. Was Kathy Cry Doll in 1957.

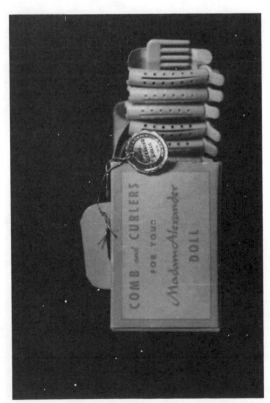

Shows the box that came with Alexander dolls of the 1950's, which included curlers and a comb. (Courtesy Phyllis Houston)

"Wendy Ann" in #459-1953-1954. Came in lavender, pink, blue and pale yellow. Taffeta with lace trim. (Courtesy Gloria Harris)

1954

Me and My Shadow Series. Portrait dolls (7) and Wendy Ann in matching outfits of four of them.

#2015 Blue Danube Waltz. 18." Gown of blue taffeta with side drapery of blue and gold striped taffeta. Gold coronet in hair, gold necklace and jeweled bracelets. (Margaret)

#2030A Queen Elizabeth. 18." White court gown with blue sash of the Garter and Star. White orlon ermine cape (short). Jeweled tiara, earrings and bracelets. Long white gloves. (Margaret)

#0030A Queen Elizabeth. 7½." In matching outfit except her robe is full length and in red.

#2030C. Victoria. 18." In costume of 1850's of slate blue faille taffeta with side panniers and bustle drapery etched with narrow white silk braid. Hat of starched white lace with roses and forget-me-nots, tied with fuschia pink ribbon. Fuschia velvet reticule. (Maggie)

#0030C Victoria. 7½" In tiny matching outfit.

#2036D Mary Louise. From Godey Period. Gown of fille taffeta the color of burnt sugar. Jacket and hat of olive green wool felt. Yellow kid gloves. (Cissy)

#0035D Cherie. 18" Dressed for the opera. Bouffant gown of heavy white satin with drapery, with pink roses. Full length coat of Goya pink taffeta (lined) and fastened with large bow. Rose trimmed satin bag and rosebuds in hair. (Maggie)

#2035F Agatha. In Edwardian gown of rose irridescent taffeta trimmed with braid, flowers and pleated tulle ruffles. Her tight basque ends in a drapery which falls in a short train in back. Ornate necklace, trimmed hat, white kid gloves and parasol. (Cissy)

#2035E Elaine. In garden dress of sky-blue organdy trimmed with rows of tiny val lace ruffles and stitching. The underdress is baby pink taffeta and under that a white taffeta hoop skirt. Puff sleeves and a round neck outlined in pearls and a big blue satin sash. Her picture hat is of white straw lace. (Cissy)

#0035E Elaine. 7½." Matching dress to above but has bunch of roses at waist in front and hat is "stiffer."

Binnie Walker. Trademark 663,863-1954. 15," 18" and 25." In three outfits. 1. Navy blue taffeta dress with white collar and cuffs. Coral pink velvet hat. Blue suede shoes and white kid gloves. 2. Taffeta dress under gaberdine coat. Leopard plush hat and muff. 3. Striped cotton dress with contrasting pinafore. Straw hat, black slippers and white gloves. Walker, head turns side to side. Also issued in two styles of trunks with trousseau. (later to be Cissy)

Margot Ballerina. Repeat from 1953 with change of ballet costume that came in various shades of pastels. (Margaret)

Sweet Violet. 18." Trademark 660,178-1954. Fully jointed, all hard plastic (knees, elbows and wrists). Two outfits. 1. In polished cotton dress with contrasting yoke and bonnet. White kid gloves, black shoes. 2. Pink taffeta dress and pink faille coat. Hat and bag of moss green velvet. Pink suede shoes. (Cissy-later)

Active Miss. Same as Sweet Violet.

Wendy Bride. 15" and 18." Nylon tulle over taffeta. Starched lace bonnet and long veil. (Margaret)

Story Princess. 15" and 18." From N.B.C. Television. Dressed in sky-blue taffeta, pink sash and a circlet of flowers in hair. White kid gloves. Story Princess was played by Arlene Dalton of Salt Lake City, Utah. (18" Cissy-later. 15" Margaret)

Flowergirl. 15," 18" and 25." Dressed in fluffy net and lace dress over taffeta, pink sash of satin and a circlet of flowers in hair. White kid gloves. (Cissy-later)

Mary Ellen. 31." Trademark 663,177-1954. Walker, turns head from side to side. Plastic with vinyl head. In three outfits. 1. Long party dress of nylon net over taffeta. Pink satin sash and slippers. Circlet of flowers in hair and white kid gloves. 2. Red coat of heavy pile fleece with brass buttons. Taffeta dress. Muff and hat of leopard plush. 3. Dress with pleated red taffeta skirt, fitted jacket of Middy blue wool felt with brass buttons and white collar. White French sailor beret with red pompom. White kid gloves.

Century of Fashions. 14" and 18." Dolls on market late 1954 into 1955. (Margaret, Maggie and Cissy)

Binnie Walker with braids. 15," 18" and 25." Same 1954 doll but wears striped cotton dress with velvet bodice and has braids. Black straw hat.

Kathy. 13," 15," 18" and 21." All vinyl baby. Open/mouth nurser. Offered in three outfits. 1. Cotton sunsuit, lace edged with sun bonnet to match. White felt sandals. 2. Taffeta bonnet and coat over matching taffeta sunsuit. White baby shoes and socks. 3. In permanent finish organdy dress trimmed with tiny pearl buttons, val lace and Swiss embroidery over taffet slip and panties. Double lace frilled bonnet, tied with pink ribbon. White kid baby shoes. All have molded hair.

Pinky. 13" and 17." Stuffed vinyl with vinyl head and jointed shoulders. Molded hair. Dressed in one piece pram suit of short pile fleece. Matching lace trimmed bonnet.

Christening Baby. 13." All vinyl with molded hair. Dressed in long christening gown of sheer organdy with bodice of imported Swiss embroidery. The bonnet and skirt are trimmed with val lace. She has long streamers and bonnet ties of white satin ribbon.

Bonnie. 16," 19" and 30." All vinyl baby. In two outfits. 1. one piece cotton romper with bodice and shoulder straps edged with lace. Felt sandals. 2. Dress of lace trimmed organdy over taffeta underwear. Satin sash and hairbow. White kid baby shoes.

Ruffles. Trademark 660,843. 21" Clown with bendable wire frame body and limbs. Felt and cloth.

Dryer Panty Baby. With special tagged plastic lined diapers. Uses Kathy Series dolls.

Inky. 14" Poodle. Wears hat and large bow at neck.

Alexander-kins. 7½" All straight leg walkers. Came in 45 different outfits including: Apple Annie of Broadway, Bride and Groom, Ice Skater, roller skater, Queen, Little Godey, Little Melanie, Cheri, Agatha, Mary Louise, Guardian Angel (trademark 660,842), Victoria dressed in long gown with green striped skirt, black bodice with net puff sleeves, pink and black braid trim. A contour black hat with large roses. Little Southern Girl is dressed in pink organza dress with pantaloons with blue ribbon trim. Sleeveless with lace trim at sleeve openings. Straw bonnet hat with attached flowers, ear level on both sides. Melanie. Blue net over blue taffeta underdress. Lace trimmed cap sleeves, lace at neck and one row lace near bottom of skirt. Straw hat with flowers inside brim. Madelaine, Bill, First Alexander-kin bent leg baby with molded hair and open mouth/nurser. Sold with trunk and trousseau.

In 1954 a large assortment of extra doll clothes, packaged separately, was sold. Madame Alexander offered 12 additional outfits and 4 hats for the 7½" (8") size, 15 outfits and 3 hats for the girl/lady dolls of 15," 18" and 25" sizes and 12 outfits and 3 bonnets for the babies. Also in 1954 a trademark was taken out on the name "Baby So Big" (660,177), but it was not used.

1954 Bible Characters. These were a series of dolls dressed from the Old Testament and used the 7½" (8") dolls.

This catalog reprint shows what must be the rarest of all the 7½"—8" hard plastic Wendy Alexanders. These are the eight "Bible Characters" of 1954. See Color section for David and his harp.

18" "Victoria" #2030C-1954. All hard plastic. (Maggie). Costume of 1850 is slate blue with white silk braid trim. Starched white lace hat with flowers. Fuschia pink velvet reticule. From the Me and My Shadow Series. (Courtesy Marge Meisinger)

15" "Story Princess" #1560-1954. Sky blue taffeta gown. (Margaret). Exact copy of one of the gowns worn by the Story Princess on the N.B.C. Howdy Doody and Perry Como Shows. Replaced tiara and wand is missing. (Courtesy Kathy Walter)

18" "Civil War" One of the Glamour Girls of 1954. This one is #2010B. White with red sash and flowers. White horsehair braid hat. Eyes are brown. (Margaret). (Courtesy Charmaine Shields)

18" "Active Miss" Same doll as Violet (Sweet Violet). Original. 1954. Marks: Alexander, on head. Tag: Madame Alexander, etc. (Later to be Cissy face)

18" "Binnie Walker" #1522-1954. Black and white stripe with yellow pinafore. Straw hat with black and white band. (Courtesy Virginia Vinton)

8" "Little Scarlett" #410-1954. (Courtesy Jeannie Niswonger)

8" Wendy Ann as "Little Melanie" #411-1954. (Courtesy Jeannie Niswonger)

8" "Little Southern Girl" 1954. Walker, straight legs. Pale blue organdy with straw bonnet with flowers. Marks: Alex., on back. Tag: Alexanderkins/Madame Alexander. (Courtesy Mable Sherman)

8" "Apple Annie" Straight legs. 1954. Red plaid gown and straw hat with daisies. Carries basket of apples. Marks: Alex., on back. Alexanderkins/Madame Alexander. (Courtesy Mable Sherman)

8" "Victoria" 1954. Walker with straight legs. Green stripes on white with pink/black trim. Flowers on black hat. (Courtesy Jane Thomas)

8" "Queen" from the Me and My Shadow Series. All hard plastic with jointed knees. White brocade with scarlet velvet robe and blue garter ribbon. #2030A. 1954. In 1955, this doll sold by itself and part of a series. Marks: Alex. on back. Tag: Alexander-kins/By Madame Alexander. (Courtesy Kay Shipp)

8" "Bill" All hard plastic. Bend knees. (Wendy face). 1954. (Courtesy Jay Minter)

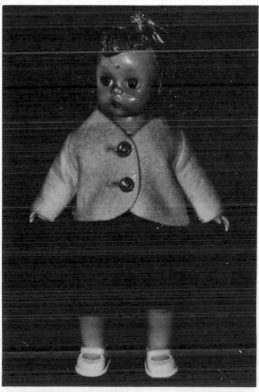

"Wendy Ann" #311-1954. Soft cotton check pink/ white with white pique top. Rick-rack and 3 pink button trim. Bend knees walker. (Courtesy Mary Partridge)

"Wendy Ann" #393-1954. Navy taffeta skirt, yellow jersey one piece body suit with felt white coat. Eagle on shoulder. Straight leg walker. Replaced shoes. (Courtesy Mary Partridge)

8" "Alexander-kins" #370-1954. Cotton with red and blue trim. Red straw hat. Tag: Alexander-kins/Reg. U.S. Pat. Off./N.Y. U.S.A. (Courtesy Mary Partridge)

8" "Wendy Ann" #474-1954. One piece with matching poke bonnet. Pink polished cotton but came in various colors. Straight leg walker. (Courtesy Jay Minter)

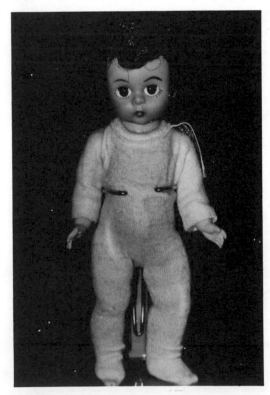

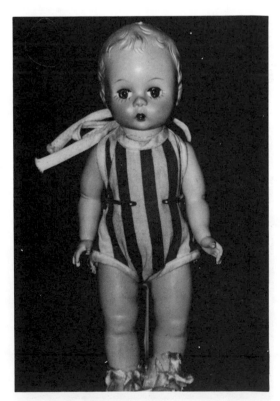

8" "Billie" In white flannel sleepers with feet. #364-1954. Straight leg, walker. (Courtesy Jay Minter)

7½" "Bill" #300-1953-1954. One piece striped romper sunsuit. Straight legs, non walker. Has molded hair and was used with and without wigs. Heavy hard plastic. (Courtesy Jay Minter)

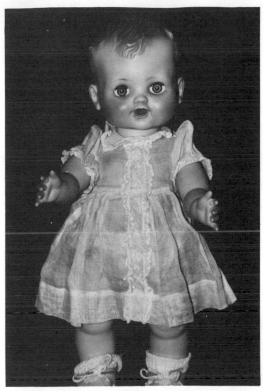

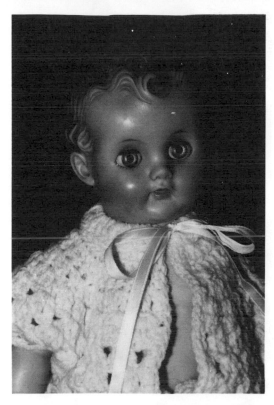

13" "Dryer Baby." This is the Kathy-1954 used as a special doll. All vinyl with open mouth/nurser. Dress is white organdy with lace trim, buttons down back. Matching bonnet missing. Tag on dress: Madame Alexander's/Dryper Baby Doll/Trademark. The doll wears plastic, lined regulation diaper. See following photo for tag. Also was issued as 11" Dolly Dryper with layette #459-1952. (Courtesy Jay Minter)

13" "Christening Baby" #3565-1954. All vinyl with one piece stuffed body and legs. Molded brown hair. Blue sleep eyes. Open/closed mouth. Not original. Marks: Alexander, on head. (Courtesy Margaret Weeks)

19" "Bonnie" Stuffed one piece vinyl body and legs. Vinyl arms and head. Rooted hair, blue sleep eyes. Open/closed mouth. Marks: Alexander, on head. 1954.

14" Hard plastic. Part of the 1954 "Fashions of a Century" series. This one is "1920." (Courtesy Mary Partridge)

15" "Marme" of Little Women. 1954. Bend knees. (Margaret). (Courtesy Phyllis Houston)

15" "Meg" of Little Women. 1954. Straight legs. (Margaret) (Courtesy Phyllis Houston)

1955

This was the first year that the Cissy was released, although the face had been used on the walkers of the previous years. 20" to 21." The new Cissy had a figure of a debutante, an adult figure, high heel feet and oversleeved, jointed elbowed arms. A walker. Trademark 686,168. Debutante Series (except Queen). The Cissy doll was used extensively in magazine ads, advertising Yardley of London.

#2095. Cissy in Summer Gown. 20." Gown of white organdy trimmed with rows of shirred val lace and red rosebuds. Large picture hat of white straw lace with bag and sash of red satin. Ruby ring.

#2094 Cissy. 20." Dressed in gown of heavy champagen slipper satin. Muff of matching nylon tulle with red roses. Necklace and earrings of rhinestones and topaz.

#2097 Cissy. 20." Gown of blue satin with rhinestones on bodice. Bracelet and three stone rhinestone ring. Carries ostrich feather fan. Coronet of flowers and jewels in hair.

#2099 Cissy. 20." As Queen Elizabeth. In court gown of white brocade with blue garter sash and star. Her tiara, earrings and bracelets are jeweled with rhinestones and rubies. Long white gloves.

#2098 Cissy. 20." Princess. Gold taffeta gown with matching short evening coat trimmed with gold braid. Wears emerald ring, gold hoop earrings. Carries hanky of white lace.

#2101 Cissy. 20." Bride. Gown of white brocade with pearls appliqued on bodice and skirt. Veil of white nylon tulle with coronet decorated with tiny blossoms, pearls and rhinestones. Bridal muff of tulle with blossoms. Pearl necklace.

#2100 Cissy. 20." Long torso gown of mauve taffeta with flared decolletage and huge bow of mauve, green and gold striped taffeta. Drop pearl earrings, wide rhinestone and gold bracelet.

#2091 Cissy. Offered in three street length dresses. 20." 1. Dress of black taffeta and lace over a frilly cancan petticoat of pink taffeta and nylon net. Black strap sandals. Pink hat of net and flowers. Rhinestone bracelet and fitted plastic handbag. 2. Red dress of silky cotton with red and white striped shirt, over cancan slip of white taffeta with nylon net ruffles. White straw hat. 3. Dress of navy taffeta with removable short jacket. Dress has a long torso, very full skirt, tiny sleeves and low neckline. Hat of straw is cornflower blue, trimmed with flowers and veil.

Wendy Bride. 15," 18" and 25." Gown of taffeta, puff sleeves and overskirt caught up with tiny flowers. Hard plastic with vinyl, jointed elbow arms. (Margaret)

Bridesmaid. 15," 18" and 25." Long gown of nylon tulle, trimmed with flowers, over taffeta with hoop petticoat. Has big sash, flowers circlet in hair and silver slippers. (Cissy)

Story Princess. 15." Sheer pink taffeta gown with bodice trimmed with sequins at the neckline. Large bouffant skirt with rosebuds in folds. Tiara of sequins. Carries wand. (Margaret)

Scarlett O'Hara. 20." (Cissy) Soft white cotton gown, lace down front and hem of skirt. Square neck with red ribbon trim. Straw hat with red streamers, red sash at waist.

Margot Ballerina. 15" and 18." Tutu of nylon tulle with bodice of taffeta with shoulder drape of tulle and flowers. Flesh colored nylon tights and pink slippers. Coronet of flowers in hair. Vinyl arms jointed at elbows and she has jointed knees. (Margaret). (Prima Ballerina Margot Fonteyn)

Skater's Waltz. 15" and 18." Bright pink skating skirt and matchin bonnet of wool felt over black jersey leotard trimmed with felt flowers and gold braid. White shoe skates. Jointed arms (vinyl) and jointed knees. (Cissy). (Walker legs only.)

Binnie. 15," 18" and 25." Bright red taffeta redingote, over simple white dress with red dots, trimmed with venise edging and pearl buttons. White straw lace hat with red box. Vinyl arms with jointed elbows and jointed knees. (Cissy)

Mary Ellen. 31." Plastic with vinyl head and arms. The arms are jointed at the elbows and the legs are jointed at the knees. In two outfits. 1. Long gown of aqua blue taffeta. Bonnet and wrist muff are matching tulle, trimmed with rosebuds. 2. In long Bridesmaid gown of yellow taffeta, trimmed with gold braid, applied flowers and rhinestones. A bandeau hat of taffeta with tiny flower clusters at each ear with gold mesh veil.

Binnie Walker. 25." Walker legs only. Vinyl arms joined at elbows and jointed knees. Wears long formal gown of pink satin. Overdress is caught up with tiny bouquets of rosebuds. Satin underdress with hoop. Rosebuds behind one ear. Pearl necklace. (Cissy)

Binnie Walker. 15," 18" and 25." Offered in three outfits, plus 18" size only in Midnight blue wool coat of wool felt with white collar and cuffs edged with lace and pearl buttons. Wears dress of taffeta over a hoop petticoat. Hat of blue felt with white bow. Also was offered in white metal trunk or red metal train case, in the 15" size only. With 12-piece trousseau. The other outfits this year are: 1. Dress of novelty weave cotton trimmed with lace and tiny pearl buttons. Cardigan of white jersey decorated with flowers and rhinestones. 2. Dress of taffeta with tiny checks and trimmed with four rows of braid at the hemline. Roll collar and big sash with rhinestones on bodice. Hoop petticoat, straw hat. Pigtail hairdo. 3. Pinafore of striped pique over polished cotton dress, trimmed with braid and tiny pearl buttons. Hoop petticoat. Hat of straw with box. (Cissy)

Bonnie. 16" and 19." Offered in additional three outfits. 1. (Various shades of color) Redingote of linen type fabric with matching bonnet, over dress of sheer organdy, lace trimmed. 2. Dress of organdy with large sash. Trimmed with lace and tiny silk flowers. Satin hair ribbon. (This one offered in four sizes: 14," 16," 19," 24.") 3. Coat and bonnet of flannel with wool and silver braid. Swiss organdy dress trimmed with lace.

Kathy. 15," 18" and 21." All vinyl baby. Molded hair. Came dressed in Swiss organdy dress and bonnet, a repeat of the taffeta coat and organdy dress of 1954 and in sunsuit and bonnet of checkered cottons of various colors. The 15" size also came in long christening robe of organdy and in trunk with trousseau.

Little Women. 15." Three have the Margaret face and two the Maggie face. Newly designed period costumes once again.

In 1955 there was extra wearing apparel which could be purchased separately, including 18 outfits/items for Cissy and two hats; 10 outfis and two hats for Wendy/Alexander-kins; 10 outfits for Binnie Walker.

Alexander-kins (Wendy). This is first year the 8" doll was offered in the Little Women outfits and these dolls have been used every year since and are still currently available. The following are some of the outfits this charming little doll was released in during 1955. These are straight leg walkers.

Curly-locks. Pale yellow taffeta with flowered pinafore, soft green bodice and quaint lace cap.

Bo Peep. Mauve taffeta dress with big fluffy panniers of rosebud print. Bonnet with flowers inside brim.

Gretel. Pink taffeta dress, printed cotton pinafore and bonnet.

Hansel. Suede peaked hat with black velvet trousers, white shirt and striped stockings.

Juliet. Brocade gown of overdress as shown in the Technicolor production of Romeo and Juliet, released by United Artists. Played by Olivia Hussey.

Romeo. Purple tights, gold boots and a jacket and hat trimmed in gold braid. Played by Leonard Whiting.

Red Riding Hood. White taffeta with red taffeta cape and hood. Carries basket.

Cinderella. Blue taffeta, silver trimmed and has silver tiara.

Scarlett O'Hara. Dress of flowered muslin, trimmed with braid and tiny bows. Puff sleeves of tulle and big picture hat.

Alice In Wonderland. Blue taffeta dress and pinafore with Swiss embroidery.

Little Godey Lady. Cerise taffeta gown and beaded black wool flet jacket. Matching hat trimmed with ostrich plume and rose.

Queen Elizabeth. Court gown of white brocade with scarlet velvet robe. Tiara and blue garter ribbon with star.

Lady in Waiting (to the Queen). Pink satin gown with side ornaments of tulle and flowers. Coronet and veil.

Baby Angel. Long white nylon tulle robe with white satin bodice and pink wings. Halo and harp of silver, flower trimmed.

Bill. Groom, in tux.

Wendy Bride. Gown of heavy white satin, Juliet cap of lace and nylon tulle bridal veil.

Wendy's Bridesmaid. Gown of petal pink nylon tulle, trimmed with flowers. Tiny flower cap.

The Best Man. White dinner jacket, black trousers, maroon tie and cummerbund.

Walking Her Dog. Blue checked cotton dress, white straw hat and red slippers. Tiny wire hair terrier.

Gardening. Checked gingham dress with plain pinafore with a big pocket.

Summer Morning. Bright colored cotton with braid and button trim. Sleeveless.

Marketing. Dress of checked cotton and pique. Carries tote bag.

Helping Mummy. Candy striped pinafore over navy taffeta dress.

Going to See Grandma. Mauve taffeta dress, nylon pinafore and straw hat.

Playing in the Garden. Over a checked dress and matching bonnet, she wears plain pinafore with three pockets for toys.

Waltzing. Long white organdy trimmed with two rows of ruffles edged in red. Carries red satin bag.

Highland Fling. Scarlet plaid gown with tartan sash and matching hat with feathers.

The Mombo. Striped gown with Spanish shawl. Gold earrings and a lace fan.

Rodeo. Cowgirl outfit of white suede cloth trimmed with fringe and felt applique. Big sombrero hat and boots.

Dude Rance. Denim levis with plaid shirt. Cowboy boots and sombrero hat.

Baby Clown. Two tone taffeta suit. Big neck ruff and clown hat. Came with tiny dog named Huggy.

Swimming. Suit of lace trimmed taffeta, matching beach hat. Sunglasses.

Play on the Beach. Denim playsuit, carries shovel.

Maypole Dance. Turquoise taffeta with tiny yoke of lace edged organdy. Flower circlet in hair.

Tennis. Shorts, T-shirt, tennis racket and sunglasses.

Roller Skating. Wide taffeta skirt worn over one piece jersey outfit. Beany cap with feather and roller skates.

Ballet. Tutu of white nylon tulle with satin bodice. Flowers i hair.

Drum Majorette. White and deep rose trim. Drum hat with gold trim. Gold boots and a button.

Matinee. White taffeta dress with pale blue coat of gaberdine. White felt bonnet with ostrict plume.

School. Checked coat of gaberdine, pique dress and red straw hat.

On Way to Beach. Polished cotton swim suit and matching coat. Sun hat, glasses and beach bag.

Rainy Day. Pink raincoat and bonnet, over blue polka dot dress. Blue rain boots.

On the Train. White wool felt jacket with matching beany cap over pleated plaid dress with white top.

Goes Visiting. Two outfits. 1. Baby blue wool felt jacket over white polished cotton dress with pleated skirt. Blue bonnet. 2. White wool jersey cardigan with pixie cap, worn over pink dress with pleated skirt. Flower applique on sweater.

Birthday Party. Mauve taffeta dress with pinafore trimmed with braid and flowers. Flower trimmed straw hat.

Tea Party. White organdy dress with red rick-rack trim. Straw hat with red berries.

Sunday School. White lace trimmed organdy dress with lace bonnet.

School Visitor's Day. Polished cotton dress, checked pinafore and straw hat with flowers.

School Day. Bright green dress, checked pinafore with ruffled hem. Green hat.

School Day. White pique with trim and top of dress and sleeves of print cotton. Straw hat with streamers.

School Day. Chartreuse cotton with flowered pinafore and straw hat.

School Day. Dress of pink and white with cerise pinafore. Spruce green hat.

Davy Crockett. Light brown trousers and jacket with tan fringe. Fur hat and black belt. Also girl in one piece outfit (skirt)

1955 was an outstanding year for these little 8" dolls, as was 1956. If a collector has only a few in her collection, she can consider herself fortunate. 1955 also saw two trademarks that were not used, 681,329, Dumplin and 686,167, Nickey.

18" "Cherie" #2031-1955. (Margaret). The Cherie of this year has the Maggie face. White with Goya pink taffeta opera coat with large bow. (Courtesy Charmaine Shields)

21" "Cissy as Queen Elizabeth II" #2099-1955. White brocade gown and silver tiara.

20" "Cissy-Scarlett Portrait" #2071-1955. White soft cotton gown with lace and red ribbon trim. Natural straw hat with red streamers. Wig is very dark brown. Tag: Cissy/Madame Alexander.

17" "Margot Ballerina" #1841-1955. All hard plastic. (Margaret). (Courtesy Carrie Perkins)

18" "Binnie Walker" Hard plastic with vinyl over-sleeve arms. Jointed elbows and knees. #1818-1955. (Later to be Cissy) Marks: Alexander, on head. Tag: Binnie Walker/Madame Alexander.

18" "Binnie Walker" #1856-1955. Red checked taffeta dress. Had navy blue coat with white collar and cuffs. Blue sleep eyes and blonde wig that is combination of glued on and rooted into skull cap. (Later to be Cissy) (Courtesy John Axe.

20" "Cissy" #2083-1955. Red jumper with red/white striped blouse. Had straw flat brimmed hat with red ribbon.

20" "Cissy" in #2091-1955. Black taffeta with narrow lace stole.

31" "Mary Ellen" All hard plastic walker, head turns. Glued on wig, sleep eyes. Pale pink taffeta dress, aqua coat and hat. Muff is artifical fur and neck-piece is real ermine. Marks: Mme. Alexander, on head. Dress and coat tag: Mary Ellen/Madame Alexander/Reg. U.S. Pat. Off. N.Y. U.S.A. Outfit #3163-1955. (Courtesy Phyllis Houston)

Shows close up of the face of Mary Ellen. The eyes look black but are actually an odd grey-brown.

31" "Mary Ellen" #3164-1955. Exclusive outfit made for Marshall Field. This same outfit also was used on #1518 Binnie Walker this same year. (Courtesy Marge Meisinger)

8" "Juliet and Romeo" Walkers, straight legs. He is in lavender and black with gold trim and she is in brocade white with rose trim. Marks: Alex., on backs. Alexander-kins/Madame Alexander. 1955. (Courtesy Jeannie Niswonger)

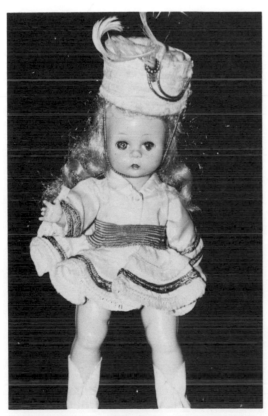

8" "Wendy Drum Majorette" One piece body suit. Detachable skirt. All white with rose trim. Rose striped vest missing and original boots were gold. #482-1955.

8" "Majorette" Shows missing vest from other photo. Boots are replaced and shows the variation of hat trim. 1955. (Courtesy Jeannie Niswonger)

8" "Cinderella" Walker, straight legs. Pale blue satin gown with silver trim and tiara. Marks: Alex., on body. Alexander-kins/Madame Alexander. 1955. (Courtesy Phyllis DeMent)

8" "Little Godey" Walker, straight legs. 1955. Rose taffeta with black beaded jacket. Black straw hat with feathers. Marks: Alex., on body. Alexander-kins/Madame Alexander. (Courtesy Phyllis DeMent)

8" "Alice In Wonderland" Walker, straight legs. Blue cotton dress with white cut out pinafore. Marks: Alex., on back. Alexander-kins/Madame Alexander. 1955. (Courtesy Ann Tuma)

8" "Wendy Ann" #457-1955. Sunday School dress of pink organdy with white lace trim on bodice and center of skirt. White lace bonnet is missing. Straight leg, walker. Replaced shoes. (Courtesy Jay Minter)

8" Early Little Red Riding Hood. #471-1955. The cape is red taffeta. (Courtesy Jeannie Niswonger)

8" "Dude Ranch" Walker, straight legs. 1955. Marks: Alex., on back. Alexander-kins/Madame Alexander. (Courtesy Jeannie Niswonger)

8" "Wendy" #475-1955. (Courtesy Jeannie Niswonger)

8" "Marme" of 1955. Shouldn't have hat on. Blue flowers with blue apron. (Courtesy Jay Minter)

8" "Jo" of Little Women. Jointed knees. Marks: Alex., on back. Tag: Alexander-kins/Jo. 1955. (Courtesy Kay Shipp)

8" "Wendy" #447-1955. Tea Party at Grandma's. (Courtesy Jeannie Niswonger)

8" "Wendy" #445-1955. (Courtesy Jeannie Niswonger)

8" "Wendy" #408-1955. (Courtesy Jeannie Niswonger)

"Wendy" Shown in #449-1955 rain set. (Courtesy Jeannie Niswonger)

"Wendy" #476-1955 **Waltz Gown.** White with red trim. (Courtesy Jeannie Niswonger)

"Wendy" #456-1955. Takes Dog for Walk. Dress is blue check with white organdy top, lace trim. Dog is tan with black "pipe cleaner" tail and legs. Straight leg, walker. Replaced straw hat. (Courtesy Virginia Jones)

8" "Davy Crockett" girl. 1955. Straight leg walker with red saran wig. Has separate jersey panties. Dress is one piece with green top and tan skirt that closes in the back. Tag: Madame Alexander's "Davy Crockett." (Courtesy Margaret Weeks)

8" "Wendy" as Davy Crockett. Red wig with yellow fleece cap. Replaced pants. Had matching suede cloth pants, wide black belt, long gun and tan slippers. 1955. (Courtesy Jay Minter)

15" "Beth" of Little Women. 1955. Bend knees. (Maggie). (Courtesy Phyllis Houston)

15" "Wendy Bride." All hard plastic. #1551-1955. (Margaret). Also came as blonde. Oyster white gown. Came in 18" and 25" sizes using the Cissy body with extra joints. (Courtesy Shirley Bertrand)

8" "Wendy" #464-1955. White dress with navy blue coat and white cuffs and collar. White hat. (Courtesy Gloria Harris)

1956

This year Cissy became the most prominent doll in the Alexander line. She was 20" tall and offered in the following "Cissy Fashion Parade."

#2035 Garden Party. Sheer organdy gown trimmed with rosebuds and a big organdy sash. Wide brimmed straw hat with baby rosebuds tied with veil.

#2025 Dancing Dress. Nylon tulle over dawn pink taffeta, ankle length gown. Skirt has unpressed pleats, bodice of lace. Corsage at waist, wide pink sash and flowers in her hair. Solitaire ring.

#2030 Bridesmaid. Gown of nylon tulle and silver threaded net the color of bluebells. Tiny hat with tulle and rosebud. Carries bouquet. Wears pearl necklace and solitaire ring.

#2040 Bride. Gown of tulle of finely pleated skirt. Lace bodice, satin sash pulled through loops of pearls. Medici cap of tulle with chapel length veil. Pearl necklace, solitaire ring.

#2042 Queen Elizabeth. White brocade gown over hoop skirt of taffeta. Blue sash of the Garter with star. Long white gloves, jeweled earrings and necklace.

#2036 Evening Out. Pink long torso gown in taffeta. Decolletage and diagonal side drapery held in place by jeweled ornaments. Pearl earrings, flowers in hair and evening bag.

#2041 Debutante Ball Gown. Ball gown of satin with cascading side drapery, over petticoat of taffeta. Shoulder shrug of orlon nutria is satin lined. Jeweled earrings and a solitaire ring.

#2043 The President's Ball. Black velvet and nylon tulle gown, tight fitting to the thighs. Flared at bottom. Lined with pink satin. Pink rosebuds at the deep flounce line.

Cissy was also offered in the following outfits:

Theatre dress of aqua taffeta with ivory satin coat, lined to match dress, fastened at neck with big bow.

Cocktail dress with long torso, made of taffeta and worn over a cancan petticoat, velvet bolero. Hat made of flowers with veil. Rhinestone bracelet and bag.

Classic dress of red dotted Swiss organdy, over white taffeta cancan petticoat. Straw hat with flowers and veil.

Traveling suit with circular skirt of black and white checked suiting, fully lined and worn over red cancan petticoat. Blouse of white pique. Bolero jacket, white straw hat with red roses. Wears jeweled bracelet, carries white gloves.

Afternoon Tea. Low waisted taffeta dress with low neckline, large puffed sleeves. Taffeta cancan petticoat. White tulle and straw hat.

Shopping dress of striped cotton (shirtwaist dress). Tiny velvet flower trimmed hat with nose veil. Dress is belted. Taffeta cancan petticoat.

Wendy Bride. 15" and 18." Nylon tulle in unpressed pleats. Underdress of taffeta and a satin sash. Tulle veil attached to Medici cap. Pearl necklace. (Cissy)

Margot Ballerina. 15" and 18." Tutu of nylon tulle over nylon tights and taffeta panties. Flowers at waist. Came in various pastel shades. (Cissy)

McGuffey Ana. 18" and 25." Velveteen jumper with nylon blouse and hoop petticoat. Bonnet matches jumper. High button shoes. Hair in braids. (Cissy)

The new 11½" (12") Lissy is a "Teenagae" doll with medium high heeled feet, small bosom, jointed elbows and knees and was issued in 1956 as a bride, bridesmaid, ballerina, along with 8 additional outfits. She was also issued with a nine-piece trousseau in a "Window" box package. Lissy is referred to as a "Sub-Deb" and Cissy's "Saucy younger sister" in the 1957 FAO Schwarz catalog.

Kathy. All vinyl baby with molded hair, open mouth/nurser, sleep eyes and cry box. 15," 19," 21," and 25" came dressed in romper of cotton, trimmed wiht Swiss embroidery. Matching bonnet. Barefoot sandals.

Kathy. 11," 15," 19," 21" and 25" with rooted hair. All vinyl baby. Came in same romper as described above.

Kathy. 11" and 15." Came in long christening dress of sheer organdy with wide flounce at bottom. The bodice and bonnet are trimmed with val lace and satin ribbon. Lace edged long white taffeta petticoat.

Kathy also came in three additional outfits: 1. Organdy dress trimmed with lace with flower medallions. 2. Pin dot organdy with matching bonnet and organdy pinafore. 3. Organdy dress and matching coat. These three have rooted hair. The 11" size was also issued in "window" box with 11 piece layette.

Little Women. Two have Maggie faces and three have Margaret face. 15" tall and newly designed clothes again.

Story Princess. 15" and 18." (Also in 8" size). From Perry Como and Howdy Doody shows. Gown of nylon tulle. Puff sleeves. Long white lace trimmed pantalettes and silver slippers. Silver tiara and carries wand. (Margaret)

In 1956 there were 36 items sold separately for the Cissy doll. These included lingerie, casual attire, sportswear, evening clothes, shoes, hosiery, millinery and furs. There were two trademarks taken out during 1956 that were not used: 21,491, Melinda and 16,683, Alexandra.

The 1956 line of Alexander-kins (Wendy) included 74 different outfits. Baby Genius was also introduced with 16 different outfits. The following are a few of the 8" Wendy outfits. Dolls now have jointed knees and are walkers with turning heads.

#563 Nurse. In white uniform with single band on top.

#631 Southern Belle. Blue and white striped gown with straw hat and flowers. This same outfit also came in pastel shades.

#633 Melanie. Forest green velvet gown, a hat of tulle, and carries matching parasol.

#632 Cousin Grace. Flowered silk gown with picture hat.

630 Cousin Karen. Summer gown of flowered cotton with blue velvet bodice. Straw hat with flowers in sides.

#622 Rose Fairy. Jeweled gown of pink tulle with velvet bodice cut like petals. Carries rose wand and has one rose in circle of leaves for a crown.

#577-615 Repeat of Bride and Groom

#602 Flower Girl. Satin gown with bell shaped circular skirt.

#621 Bridesmaid. Pale blue taffeta trimmed with pink rosebuds. Pink straw bandeau style hat, rosebuds at sides.

#631 Scarlett. Rosebud print muslin with picture hat of Milan straw. Carries parasol.

#623 Ball Gown. Gown of gold taffeta trimmed with yellow rosebuds. Gold tiara.

#606 First Long Dancing Dress. Made of white nylon tulle, velvet sash and hair ribbon.

#620 Garden Party. Bouffant gown of Swiss organdy. Straw hat with flowers and streamers.

#609 Little Women. All wear apron/pinafores. 3 are solid in color and 2 are flowered.

#610 French Flower Girl. One-piece dress with white organdy bodice and separate organdy apron. Flowered skirt. Red silk turban. Carries flower basket.

#698 Red Riding Hood. Long striped dress, cape and carries basket.

#590 Alice in Wonderland. Blue taffeta with white pinafore.

#579 Parlor Maid. Black taffeta maid's outfit with white organdy apron.

#564 Ballerina. Tutu of nylon tulle with satin bodice. Flowers circle hair.

#561 Pierrot Clown. Pink satin clown suit with tulle ruff at neck, matching tall pink peaked hat.

#616 McGuffey Ana. Plaid dress with white pinafore. Straw hat and pigtails.

#700 Blue Boy and Pinky. Exclusives for certain franchised stores.

Baby and Toddler Little Tiny Genius. All hard plastic.

The outfits for the 1956 Alexander-kins are too numerous to list, the remaining ones including school dresses, riding habit, swimsuits, ice and roller skating costumes, coats, raincoats, sailor dresses, sweaters, sportswear and pajamas.

18" "McGuffey Ana" #1879-1956 (Cissy) Alexander catalog reprint.

14½" "Story Princess" All hard plastic with green sleep eyes. Original. (Cissy face) 1956.

20" "Cissy" #2096-1956. Gold satin dress with matching opera coat with white taffeta lining. Black lack shawl ties around neck. Red hair pulled to top of head, from front.

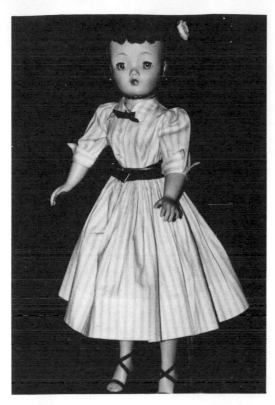

20" "Cissy" #2014-1956. Fine cotton, pink striped shirtwaist style dress with black contour vest and black velvet hat with flowers.

20" "Cissy" Gown is pale blue with blue dots, large pink rose at waist. Pearl necklace and earrings. This dress is tagged Cissy/Madame Alexander, etc. but, so far, is unidentified. Ca. 1956. (Courtesy Phyllis Houston)

20" "Cissy" #2025-1956. Pink lace bodice with unpleated tulle ankle length dress.

20" "Cissy" #2020-1956. This matching cape/coat and dress of satin came in various colors. The #2021 had a two tone color combination and a large bow tie.

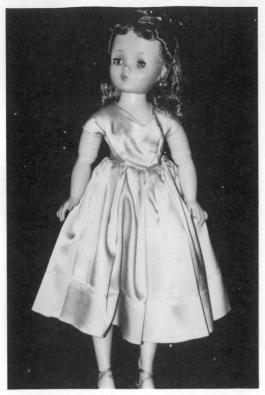

Shows the basic dress worn under #2020 and 2021-1956.

20" "Cissy" #2042-1956. The gown is black, lined in pink with flared net low skirt with rosebuds between the layers of net.

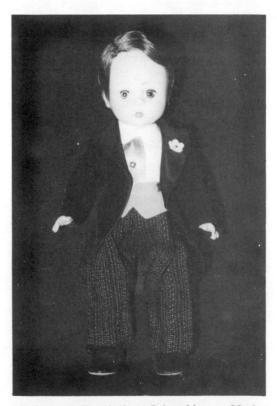

8" "June Wedding" (Wendy) #605-1956. Pink (came in other pastel colors, too) taffeta gown with flower trimmed straw hat. (Courtesy Anita Pacey)

8" "Groom" (Wendy face) Jointed knees. Marks: Alex., on back. There were earlier grooms but this one dates 1956. (Courtesy Kay Shipp)

8" "Southern Belle" Walker, straight legs. Blue striped dress with navy straw hat decorated with flowers. Marks: none on doll. Tag: Alexander-kins/By Madame Alexander. 1956. (Courtesy Jeannie Niswonger)

8" "French Flower Girl" (Wendy Ann) #610-1956 (Courtesy Jeannie Niswonger)

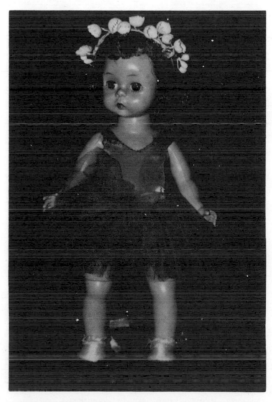

8" "Cousin Karen" Walker, jointed knees. Blue and pink flowered dress with white straw bonnet. Marks: Alex., on back. Alexander-kins/By Madame Alexander. 1956. (Courtesy Jane Thomas)

"Wendy" #564-1956. Ballerina with deep rose net and satin bodice. White Lillie of the Valley flowers at waist and circlet in hair. (Courtesy Kathleen Flowers Council)

"Wendy" #555-1956. Ice Skater. Pink one piece body suit. Deep green felt skirt and peaked bonnet with rose rick-rack trim and bonnet tie. White ice skates. (Courtesy Kathleen Flowers Council)

"Wendy" Alexander-kins in Sand Box #515-1956.

"Wendy" #541-1956. Beach set. Blue striped / flowered cotton swim suit. Beach coat and hat of white pique with blue trim. Blue felt beach bag. (Courtesy Kathleen Flowers Council)

"Wendy" #587-1956. Sunday School Dress. Palest blue (came in other pastels, also) taffeta dress edged in lace. Hat is white straw with rows of lace trim. (Courtesy Kathleen Flowers Council)

"Wendy" #582-1956. House Party. Polished cotton brown dress. Lime green pinafore. Green hat with tiny lavender/white flowers. Same flowers in tiny basket. Braids with matching lime green ribbons. (Courtesy Kathleen Flowers Council)

"Wendy" #580-1956. Sherbet orange gaberdine coat with black buttons and collar. Lined in pale blue taffeta that matches dress. Bonnet cap is orange with same blue lining. (Courtesy Kathleen Flowers Council)

"Wendy" #580. Without coat to show dress.

8" "Wendy" #556-1956. (Courtesy Jeannie Niswonger)

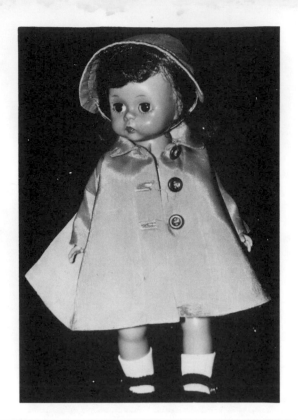

Pink jersey gown and pink dotted swiss robe for Wendy. 1956. #566. (Courtesy Kathleen Flowers Council)

8" "Wendy" in yellow rose printed dress and panties with yellow taffeta rain coat and bonnet. Lined in same material as dress. #572-1956. Boots missing. (Courtesy Mary Partridge)

"Wendy #346-1956. Aqua dress with lace trim. Bonnet missing. Bend knee walker. (Courtesy Mary Partridge)

"Wendy" #380-1956. Pink gaberdine coat over pink checked taffeta dress. Bend knee walker. (Courtesy Mary Partridge)

"Wendy" in beach outfit. #562-1956. (Courtesy Jeannie Niswonger)

8" "Wendy" #538-1956. Shown with wood Alexander dressing table. (Courtesy Jeannie Niswonger)

Chair is #63-1960 and Wendy is shown in dress #538-1956. (Courtesy Jeannie Niswonger)

"Wendy" #0530-1956. Pale lavender flowered dress with lace trim, matching bonnet and panties. (Courtesy Virginia Jones)

8" "Wendy" #584-1956. Blue checked dress that buttons down front. White organdy collar and cuffs. Came in various colors. (Courtesy Jay Minter)

8" "Wendy" in Roller Skating outfit. #502-1956. Jointed knee walker. Red felt skirt with gold waist band and metal heart. One piece, short sleeve jersey-cotton panties and top. Replaced shoes. Same hat as used with rompers. (Courtesy Jay Minter)

8" "Wendy" #606-1956. First long dancing dress. White nylon with green velvet sash with rosette and full cap sleeves. Jointed knee walker. (Courtesy Jay Minter)

8" "Wendy" #554-1956. Flowered print cotton with white rick-rack trim. Buttons down the back. (Courtesy Jay Minter)

21" Godey. Portrait doll of 1961. Uses the Cissy face and walker body but the Jacqueline one piece delicate arms.

21" Scarlett in red. Portrait doll of 1962. Uses the Jacqueline doll with straight, delicate arms and hands. Arms not jointed at elbow. (Courtesy Elizabeth Montesano of Yesterday's Children)

21" Queen. #2150-1965. Marks: Alexander/1961. (Courtesy Roberta Lago)

21" Coco Portrait Godey. #2063-1966. (Courtesy Elizabeth Montesano of Yesterday's Children)

21" Godey. #2195-1970. Marks: Alexander/1961. (Courtesy Roberta Lago)

21" Madame Pompadour. #2197-1970. Marks: Alexander/1961. (Courtesy Roberta Lago)

21" Renoir. #2184-1970. Marks: Alexander/1961. (Courtesy Roberta Lago)

21" Gainsborough. #2192-1972. Marks: Alexander/1961. (Courtesy Roberta Lago)

21" Renoir. #2190-1972. Marks: Alexander/1961. (Courtesy Roberta Lago)

21" Cornelia. #2191-1972. Marks: Alexander/1961. (Courtesy Roberta Lago)

21" Renoir. #2190-1973. Marks: Alexander/1961. (Courtesy Roberta Lago)

21" Melanie. #2295-1974. Marks: Alexander/1961. (Courtesy Roberta Lago)

11" Renoir. #1175-1968. (Courtesy Mary Partridge)

11" Godey. #1172-1969. (Courtesy Mary Partridge)

11" Renoirs. Left to right: #1175-1969, #1175-1968 and #1180-1970, which also came with striped skirt. These Portrettes were made using the Cissette doll. (Courtesy Roberta Lago)

11" Scarlett. #1174-1968, Melanie #1173-1969 and Scarlett #1174-1970. (Came with white and also black bands) (Courtesy Roberta Lago)

11" Melinda. Left: #1173-1969. Right: #1173-1968. (Courtesy Roberta Lago)

11" Godey. Left: #1172-1969. Right: #1172-1968. (Courtesy Roberta Lago)

11" Jenny Lind. #1171 1969. (Courtesy Roberta Lago)

11" Renoir. #1175-1969. (Courtesy Mary Partridge)

11" Melanie of 1970. (Cissette). (Courtesy Mary Partridge)

This is the Portrait Miniature Southern Belle of 1970. (Cissette). (Courtesy Mary Partridge)

8" Bride-1970 and Bill, the Groom-#421-1961. (Courtesy Roberta Lago)

8" Bolivia 1963 to 1965. Peruvian-1965 to 1966. Equador-1963 to 1965. (Courtesy Roberta Lago)

Wendy Ann Does The Mambo. #481-1955. (Courtesy Roberta Lago)

8" Pierrot Clown. #561-1956. (Courtesy Roberta Lago)

8" Little Lady (Maggie face). #1050-1960. (Courtesy Carrie Perkins)

148

8" Spanish Girl and Boy. Boy-1964 to 1968. Girl-1961 to date. (Courtesy Roberta Lago)

8" Argentine Boy and Girl. Boy-1965 only. Girl-1963 to 1965. (Courtesy Roberta Lago)

9" Littlest Angel. One piece latex body and limbs with early vinyl head. Painted eyes. 1952. Tags: on wings and gown: Madame Alexander, etc. Tag on red and white striped undershorts: G. Fox & Co./ Hartford, Conn. This doll may have been exclusively made for the G. Fox Dept. Store. (Courtesy Mandeville-Barkel Collection)

8" Colonial Girl. Same doll as the Priscella but with lighter dress and different basket of fruit. Part of the Americana group. 1962 to 1964. (Courtesy Roberta Lago)

8" Priscella. 1965 to 1970. In a light blue polished cotton dress and carrying a different basket of fruit, this doll was issued as Colonial Girl from 1962 to 1964 and part of the Americana group. (Courtesy Roberta Lago)

149

8" Betsy Ross. 1976-1975-1974. (Courtesy Roberta Lago)

8" Betsy Ross with a variation of print used in gown. Date unknown. (Courtesy Jeannie Gregg)

8" Parlour Maid. #579-1956. White organdy apron and lace cap worn over black taffeta uniform. Feather duster. Came both blonde and brunette. (Courtesy Gloria Harris)

8" David and his harp from the 1954 Bible series. (Courtesy Mandeville-Barkel Collection)

8" Tinkerbell. Same as 11" (Cissette) size except she wears white stockings and slippers. Tag reads: Tinker Bell/Walt Disney Prod./Madame Alexander. The tag on the 11" size reads: Tinker Bell/Madame Alexander. The label on the 8" on is paper. This doll came in box for 8" doll marked Tinker Bell #1110. (Courtesy Mandeville-Barkel Collection)

Rag dolls from 1932. Tags: Little Women/ "name"/Copyright Pending/By Madame Alexander, Ny, USA/. Left to right: Meg, Beth, Amy and Jo. (Courtesy Mandeville-Barkel Collection)

16" Alice in Wonderland. All cloth. Trademark #304,488 Aug. 14, 1930. Had various print and trim dresses. The earlier Alices had "googly" type eyes, wide open and to the side with long painted lashes around top of eyes. Very "ooh" mouth with a flat face. (Courtesy Carrie Perkins)

7½" Tiny Betty Peasant. 1936 to 1940. All composition. (Courtesy Carrie Perkins)

21" "Princess Flavia" All composition. Has hand
painted features with pale blue eyelids, painted
lashes in the corners. Clothing is exceptional,
even for Madame Alexander. Princess Flavia
was the heroine (played by Madaline Carroll) of
Prisoner of Zenda, a childhood classic. 1939.
Remade in 1946. Tags: Green clover leaf on arm
saying Madame Alexander. Tag sewn to front of
rayon ribbon: Madame Alexander/New York
U.S.A. Doll is unmarked. (Courtesy Elizabeth
Montesano of Yesterday's Children)

21" "Mary Louise" a Godey Lady. All composition Portrait of 1946. Tag: Madame Alexander/New York U.S.A. The original price tag says: Bullock's Wilshire W660/0C2/$75.00. The taffeta of the gown has faded from rich blue to a soft grey. The eyebrows, eyelids and lashes are hand painted. Others in this series were: Princess Flavia, Camille, Carmen, Victoria of 1850 and Marm Lisa inspired by book by Kate Douglas Wiggins (1856-1923)

21" Carmen (Opera-Geraldine Farrar). All composition with beautiful clothing and hand painted features. These 1946 dolls retailed for $75.00 and being so expensive for the times, it is assumed that there are not very many of them for today's collectors. (Courtesy Elizabeth Montesano of Yesterday's Children)

18" Juliet. All composition with blue sleep
eyes and honey blonde hair (Wendy Ann).
Pale lavender gown. Tag: Madame Alex-
ander/New York U.S.A. 1939. Exclusive
for Marshall Field.

10" Pre-Movie Scarlett. 1937 and 14"
Southern Girl, before movie-1938. All
composition. Gone With the Wind was released in 1939. (Courtesy Roberta Lago)

14" W.A.A.C. and Soldier. 1942. All com-
positioon. (Both Wendy Ann). She is
tagged W.A.A.C./Madame Alexander and
he is tagged: Madame Alexander, etc.
(Courtesy Mandeville-Barkel Collection)

15" Flora McFlimsey. All composition and
original. Brown sleep eyes. Freckles.
(Courtesy Elizabeth Montesano of Yesterday's Children)

14½" Sleeping Beauty. 1940. All composition. (Courtesy Mary Partridge)

The 1944 Wedding Party. All composition.
(Wendy Ann). Left is Bridesmaid in pink
and yellow. Front one in blue is Maid of
Honor. (Courtesy Elizabeth Montesano of
Yesterday's Children)

11" Scarlett O'Hara. 1941. All compo-
sition. Tagged. Scarlett O'Hara/Madame
Alexander, etc. (Courtesy Mandeville-
Barkel Collection)

28" Princess Elizabeth. 1937. All composition. Mohair wig. Tag: Princess Eliza-
beth/Madame Alexander, etc. Also marked same on head. (Courtesy Mandeville-
Barkel Collection)

15" Peter Pan. #1505-1953 and Wendy #1506-1953. (Maggie and Margaret). (Courtesy Carrie Perkins)

13" Wendy Ann. 1937. All composition. Molded, painted hair. Original riding outfit. Tag: Wendy Ann/Madame Alexander, etc. (Courtesy Mandeville-Barkel Collection)

11" McGuffey Ana. 1938. All composition. Marked head and dress. Head: Princess Elizabeth. Straw hat missing. (Courtesy Mary Partridge)

14" Jeannie Walker. #1680-1942. Original except hat. Walker mechanism registered, completely new for the times as far known never copied. (Courtesy Mary Partridge)

30" Mimi. #3030-1961. (Courtesy Roberta Lago)

14" Dr. DeFoe along with set of 7½" Dionne babies in an original basket with original basket. 1936. (Courtesy Mandeville-Barkel Collection)

17" Princess Margaret Rose. 1946. (Margaret). All hard plastic. (Courtesy Roberta Lago)

15" Karen. 1948-1949. All hard plastic. (Margaret). Tag: Madame Alexander, etc. /All Rights Reserved. Head is marked: Alex. (Courtesy Elizabeth Montesano of Yesterday's Children)

14" "1900" Part of the 1954 "Fashions of a Century" series. (Margaret). (Courtesy Mary Partridge)

16" Sleeping Beauty. #1895-1959. 18" Prince Charming of 1950. (Courtesy Roberta Lago)

14" Cinderella and Prince Charming of 1950. (Courtesy Carrie Perkins)

15" Wendy Ann. #1855-1950. All hard plastic. (Margaret). Tag: Madame Alexander, etc. Head marked Alex. (Courtesy Elizabeth Montesano of Yesterday's Children)

15" Cynthia. #1530-1952. (Courtesy Roberta Lago)

163

15" Disney's Snow White. 1952. #1535.
(Courtesy Carrie Perkins)

18" Lady Churchill. 1953. All hard plastic.
(Margaret). Gown of same color and
material as opera coat. (Courtesy Sandy
Rankow)

18" Garden Party. Part of the Glamour
Girls series. Walkers. All hard plastic.
#2001C-1953. (Margaret). Has wired hoop
skirt. (Courtesy Elizabeth Montesano of
Yesterday's Children)

10" Jacqueline. Dressed in #887-1962.
(Courtesy Mandeville-Barkel Collection)

18" Annabelle. #1810-1952. All hard plastic. (Maggie). From Kate Smith's TV Show. (Courtesy Mandeville-Barkel Collection)

This Cissy was redressed by Virginia Vinton and is shown to show what talent of dressing can do for a doll that has no clothes of her own. Virginia dressed her as Louisa Boren, Seattle's first bride. Married on Jan. 23, 1853 to David T. Denny, she was known as the "Sweetbriar Bride" as wherever they lived, she planted a rose gathered from the family garden in Cherry Grove, Illinois, prior to the eight month covered wagon journey to Seattle.

18" Story Princess. #1892-1956. (Courtesy Roberta Lago)

29" Penny. 1952. Same doll as Barbara Jane but has large painted eyes. Cloth body with stuffed vinyl straight legs and arms. The slightly larger doll of 1951 had a pageboy hair style. (Courtesy Mary Partridge)

15" Set of Little Women. All hard plastic.
(Two Maggie and three Margaret). Left to
right: Jo, Meg, Marme, Beth and Amy.
(Courtesy Mandeville-Barkel Collection)

15" Set of Little Women using both the
Margaret and Maggie dolls. Shown here
with one of the Little Men, "Stuffy" 1952.
(Courtesy Mandeville-Barkel Collection)

20" Cissy. Modeling #2041-1956. Cissy fur coat in back and the matching set is for Cissette. (Courtesy Elizabeth Montesano of Yesterday's Children)

20" Cissy in #2021-1956. Aqua Theatre outfit. Red head with tiny forehead curls. (Courtesy Elizabeth Montesano of Yesterday's Children)

20" Cissy. Standing: #2142-1958 and sitting is #2120-1957. (Courtesy Elizabeth Montesano of Yesterday's Children)

21" Queen Elizabeth. 1960. This is only other known doll used with the 1959 Sleeping Beauty mold but there may be others. (Courtesy Roberta Lago)

12" Left to right: Rozy #1130-1969, Suzy #1150-1970, Janie 1965, Lucinda #1135-1969 and Fredrick of Sound of Music #1107-1965. (Courtesy Roberta Lago)

President's Ladies. See individual photos in black and white section for 1976. (Courtesy Roberta Lago)

8" "Wendy" #555-1956. Red striped cotton with red rick-rack trim. Buttons down the back. (Courtesy Jay Minter)

8" "Little Tiny Genius" Toddler. All hard plastic with straight legs. #750-1956. (Courtesy Jeannie Niswonger)

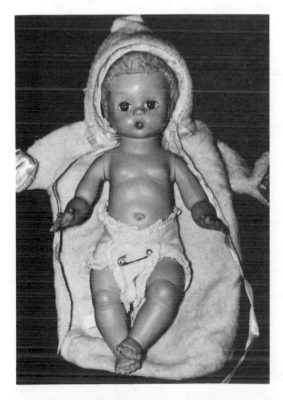

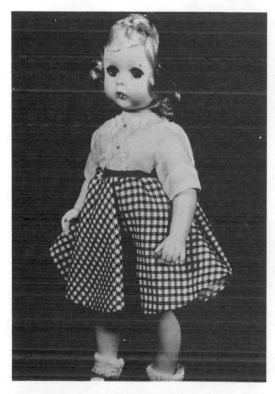

"Little Genius" 1956. Pink sacque of flannel with satin lining. (Courtesy Mary Partridge)

"Lissy" is shown in #1226-1956. (Courtesy Mary Partridge)

Outfit #1242-1956 is shown on the later Lissy that takes wigs and was sold as **Pamela**. (Courtesy Jeannie Niswonger)

12" "Lissy" With extra joints at elbows and knees. **This skirt and top date 1956.** (Courtesy Roberta Lago)

15" "Amy" of Little Women. **1956. Bend knees.** (Courtesy Phyllis Houston)

15" "Jo" of the Little Women. **Straight legs.** (Maggie) 1956. (Courtesy Phyllis Houston)

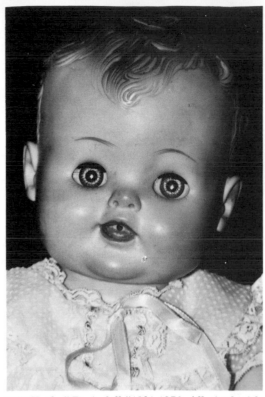

25" "Kathy" Basic doll #4801-1956. All vinyl with deeply molded hair. Blue sleep eyes. Open mouth/nurser. Large, wide spread fingers. Marks: Alexander, on head. (Courtesy Pearl Clasby)

11" "Kathy" #2446-1956. All vinyl and this 11" size has very large round eyes. Open mouth / nurser. Marked Alexander on head. Tag:Kathy/ Madame Alexander. (Courtesy Marie Ernst)

1957

The Cissy doll (20" to 21") once again commands attention this year and a new doll has been introduced, the Elise with vinyl jointed elbows, jointed ankles. The body and heads are of hard plastic. Lissy is still available and is issued in various outfits and has 12 different outfits available. There are also 12 different outfits available for the Elise.

Cissy Models Formal Gowns were the main dolls this year.

#2173 Black velvet cut on princess lines, with cape stole of orlon ermine, fastened with corsage of roses. Pearl necklace and earrings. Rhinestone bracelet. Long black gloves.

#2171 Queen. Gold brocade court gown. Gold tiara with jewels. Jeweled earrings and bracelets. Pearl necklace. Blue shash of the Garter with star. Long white gloves.

#2176 Gainsboro. Long taffeta gown and large picture hat trimmed with flowers. Pearl necklace and solitaire ring.

#2170 Bride. Nylon tulle with double train of white satin. Chapel length veil attached to coronet of flowers. Satin bodice with imported satin applique. Long white gloves. Pearl necklace, earrings and solitaire ring.

#2175 Lady Hamilton. Very large skirted gown with nylon half slip with wide ruffles of nylon lace. Draped bodice and skirt are trimmed with pink roses. Large picture hat.

#2160 Garden Party. Gown of dotted nylon net worn over pink taffeta. Large picture hat of horsehair braid and trimmed with flowers. Wide satin sash hangs to floor in back. Pearl necklace, rhinestone earrings and solitaire.

#2174 Elegance. Purple velvet gown with long tight fitting torso with a wide flare of layers of lilac nylon tulle. Decolletage is lined with pink satin and there is a large bunch of pink roses at skirtline. Rhinestone dress clip, earrings and bracelet.

#2172 Opera. Lace print gown of heavy faille with circular skirt, fully lined. Velvet sash, caught at waistline with corsage of roses. Cape stole of orlon ermine, satin lined.

The 1957 Cissy was offered in six outfits, plus 12 extra outfits, two hats, a matching muff, bonnet and stole of orlon, and accessories. Also offered was chrome plated clothes rack. The following outfits were sold on the dolls:

#2143 Afternoon Gown. Knee length dress of taffeta with a removable jacket and flower trimmed hat to match. Carries handbag. Wears matching bracelet and ring with pearl earrings and necklace.

#2141 Afternoon Dress. Navy taffeta with shoulder cape of pleated organdy. White gloves and hat of white straw trimmed with white flowers. Wears watch, circled with brilliants, a matching bracelet and pearl drop earrings.

#2120 Afternoon Dress. Yellow gold material with flowers printed all over. Big straw hat with flowers. Cameo pin center of neckline. Pearl bracelet with matching earrings.

#2130 Dressmaker. Polished cotton dress trimmed with shirred lace. Large picture hat. Earrings of gold set pearls.

#2110 Shopping dress. Taffeta dress with sleeves of polka dot cotton, hat of white straw with bent down brim.

#2114 Summer Morning. Cotton skirt, tailored shirt of striped cotton. Straw hat. Chatelaine watch on chain attached to skirt.

Elise is 16½" tall, all hard plastic with jointed vinyl arms and has jointed ankles. She is covered by Trademark #26,910. 1957. Besides the extra outfits offered for her this year, she came dressed in the following:

Bride. The gown is of nylon tulle with matching chapel length veil and coronet of flowers.

Ballerina. Tutu of nylon tulle, attached to a bodice of satin, trimmed with flowers. Long tights and ballet slippers.

Bridesmaid or Party Gown. Dotted nylon net over wide petticoats. Pink satin sash. Square neckline outlined with lace. Carries basket of flowers. Pearl necklace and matching bracelet.

Model. Checked taffeta with puff sleeves of lace trimmed nylon and little girl collar. Hat is flower trimmed. Nylon lace petticoat.

Going Visiting. Chocolate brown velvet coat, lined in pink taffeta, worn over pink taffeta dress. Cocoa brown hat trimmed with pink roses.

Jumper. Cocoa brown, shirt of shell pink crepe with bow at neck. Cocoa brown hat and golden charm bracelet.

Dumplin' Baby. 23½". Cloth body with hard plastic head, arms and legs. Denim overalls dotted cotton shirt and sun bonnet.

Dumplin' Baby. Dressed in organdy trimmed with feather stitching and lace. Taffeta underwear. Bonnet is mass of tiny lace ruffles, tied with satin bow.

Kathy Cry-Dolly. All vinyl baby that wets, cries tears and has molded hair. 11" tall and dressed in long christening gown with two rows of inset wide lace on skirt.

Kathy Cry-Doll. 11," 15," 18," 21." All vinyl baby with molded hair. Drinks and cries tears. Dressed in lace trimmed organdy with taffeta underwear. Bonnet of shirred lace ruffles.

Kathy Cry-Dolly. With molded hair and dressed in checked romper with yoke of tucked batiste, matching sun bonnet.

Kathy Cry-Dolly. With rooted hair, wearing organdy dress, lace trimmed over taffeta underwear. Shirred lace bonnet.

Little Women. Using the 11½" (12") Lissy doll. All newly designed outfits. These dolls, made with Lissy, were used until 1968.

1957 introduced the Cissette doll covered by Trademark #26,911 (1957). Cissette is all hard plastic with high heels and a porcelain-like finish. She is 10" tall, jointed at knees, shoulders, hips and neck. The clothing and accessory items for this doll are too numerous to list, so we have listed the main ones only.

#961 Gainsboro. Gown of blue taffeta with matching sash. Tiny pink rosebuds on puffed sleeves. Picture hat with roses and jewelry.

#971. Queen Elizabeth II. Gold brocade gown with blue sash of the Garter. Jeweled earrings and bracelet. Pearl necklace. Gold threaded coronet.

#975 Lady Hamilton. Gown of pink silk gauze, trimmed with roses. Shoulder drapery caught at the waistline in back, then cascades down to form short train. Large picture hat, jeweled earrings and bracelet.

#973 Regal. Black velvet gown over pink lace petticoat. Orlon ermine stole with corsage of roses. Rhinestone earrings and bracelet. Hair is in upsweep.

#905 Toreador pants. Velvet, sheer lace blouse fastened with pearls. Pearl drop earrings. Chiffon sash with big side pouf.

#974 Theatre. Sheath gown with bouffant overskirt of dotted nylon tulle. Tiny roses at long torso line. All in black. Pearl necklace, jeweled bracelet and earrings.

#979 Dancing. Ankle length gown of gold tulle. Draped decolletage trimmed with pink harebells. Pearl earrings and bracelet.

#960 Bridesmaid. Gown of sheer dotted nylon tulle. Picture hat of horsehair braid with flowers. Satin sash and corsage of rosebuds attached to sash. Pearl jewelry.

#980 Bride. White tulle and lace. Tulle veil with flower wreath.

#970 Bride. White tulle with pile of flowers to hold short veil of tulle.

#914 Ballerina. Layers and layers of nylon tulle attached to bodice of satin and trimmed with flowers. Coronet of flowers.

In addition to the above, Cissette came dressed in 22 different outfits that included dresses, matched dresses and coats, bathing suits, bermuda shorts, robe and nightie, coat (plush) with hood, corduroy coat with hood, felt coat and hat, skirt and blouse and reversible coat and hat. Also this year there was offered brass furniture for the 8" and 10" dolls. It had no sharp edges and all items had ball feet. Included in this group: bed with foam mattress, vanity set, side chair with velvet cushion, arm chair with velvet cushion, and table and two chairs with velvet cushions.

This year (1957) saw an outstanding group of the Alexanderkins (Wendy) dolls, headed by the Wedding Party. These were jointed knee walkers.

#410 Bride. Dressed in nylon tulle over satin. Short nylon tulle veil.

#377 Bridegroom. Dressed in formal morning clothes.

#408 Bridesmaid. Pink nylon gown with large picture hat tied with tulle.

#398 Flowergirl. Dressed in blue and wearing Watteau bonnet of lace.

#411 Little Minister. In full clerical robes.

#395 First Communion. Knee length white dress with tulle veil.

#399 Graduation Gown.

#376 First Long Party Dress. Gown of pink organdy with white embossed flowers.

#363 Nurse. Repeat from 1956.

#435 Aunt Pitty-Pat. Combination of checked and plain taffeta, hat with veil, parasol and jeweled drop earrings. (Played by Laura Hope Crews in movie, Gone With The Wind)

#431 Scarlett O'Hara. Gown of white organdy trimmed with two tiers of lace. Hat with flowers.

#434 Aunt Agatha. Antebellum gown with velvet bodice, feather trimmed hat.

#432 Cousin Grace. Nylon tulle gown with two rows lace and flower clusters near hem. Large picture hat with flowers. Jewel on black ribbon around neck.

#409 Little Women. Different outfits from 1956. Meg in lavender dress with striped pinafore with matching hairbow. Jo in bright blue taffeta with red/white print pinafore. Marme print dress with black taffeta tea apron. Beth in pink checked dress with lace trimmed pinafore. Matching hairbow. Amy in blue polished cotton and pink pinafore.

#433 Nana-governess. Skirt and blouse of the Gibson Girl type.

#347 Bobby. The boy next door. Navy short pants, white wool felt sports jacket with brass buttons. Navy cap.

#397 Prince Charles of England. Two piece blue suit, white shirt and oxfords. Blue billed cap.

#396 Princess Anne. White lace dress with ribbon trimmed hat.

#373B Bill. Riding outfits of brown corduroy breeches, tailored shirt and brown helmet cap. Riding crop.

There were 28 additonal dresses, riding habit, roller skating outfit, ballerina, snow suit, coat of orlon, car coat and slacks, raincoat, play sets, ice skating outfit, swimming suit and sunsuit. One special issue was 388E, the Cherry Twins. One was blonde and one brunette. Each came dressed in white organdy dress embroidered with cherries and cherry red hat. Little Genius came dressed in a christening gown, and has nine dresses, sunsuit, two piece creeper suit. This was an all vinyl baby. Open mouth/nurser. Molded hair.

During 1957 the following trademarks were taken out and not used this year: #40,994, Robin. #40933, Kelly. #26,523, Princess Caroline.

Fairy Princess. 21" Wears gown and tiara. (Cissy).

1956-1957 and 1958 were big years for Cissy as she was used on the advertising of Yardley of London Cosmetics firm. They ran full page color ads showing Cissy using or along with their products. It was in 1957 that Coty issued the Fairy Princess line with cologne, dusting powder, bath mitt, lipstick and refill, bubble bath and hand care set. All was designed for the 4 to 12 year olds, and released along with the doll.

20" "Cissy" In dress that is green, trimmed with pink sask and roses. The dress has printed in roses. Tag: Cissy/by Madame Alexander, etc. Extra-1957. (Courtesy Kathryn Fain)

20" "Cissy" #2110-1957. Red taffeta with red polka dot cotton sleeves, collar and bow. Wears two different type shoes by mistake.

21" "Cissy" in extra dress sold in 1957. Dress is for the basic #2100 doll of 1957. Blue flowered print very soft, fine cotton with lace trim at neck and sleeves and red rick-rack trim on skirt. Bodice trimmed with rhinestones. Wide leatherette belt missing. (Courtesy Virginia Jones)

174

20" "Cissy" in navy blue dress with small cape. #2140-1957. (Courtesy Kathy Walter)

20" "Cissy" Original green net over satin gown. Tag: Cissy/Madame Alexander, etc. Gown unidentifed. Ca. 1957. (Courtesy Evelyn Chisman)

20" "Cissy" in extra outfit sold for the #2100 basic doll—1957. (Courtesy Charmaine Shields)

16" "Elise" Hard plastic with vinyl over-sleeve arms and jointed at elbows. Original. 1957. (Courtesy Jay Minter)

16½" "Elise" in Ballerina outfit. #1635-1957. (Courtesy Mary Partridge)

16½" "Elise Bride" Organdy with white net. Pearl earrings. #1650-1957. (Courtesy Jeannie Gregg)

12" "Lissy" Jointed at elbows and knees. This is one of the extra outfits that could be purchased in 1957. Tag: Lissy/By Madame Alexander. (Courtesy Kay Shipp)

12" "Lissy" in outfit #1151-1957. Had wide white quaker collar. Tag: Lissy/by Madame Alexander.

12" "Meg" of Little Women. (Lissy). 1957. (Courtesy Jeannie Niswonger)

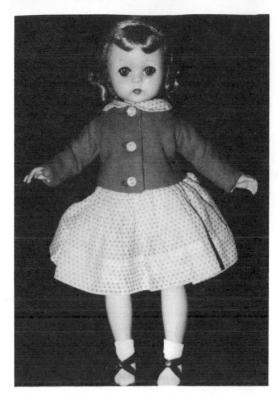

12" "Lissy" in #1234-1956-1957. Pin dot organdy dress and wool cardigan sweater. Extra joints at elbows and knees. Tag: Lissy/By Madame Alexander. Courtesy Kay Shipp).

12" "Lissy" in Bridesmaid gown of tulle. #1161-1957. Had tulle hat tied with wide tulle sash. Tag: Lissy/By Madame Alexander.

12" "Lissy Bride" #160 and "Lissy Bridesmaid" #1161. Both 1957. (Courtesy Roberta Lago)

10½" "Cissette" #916-1957. Navy taffeta with puff sleeves, sash and inset pleat in back are dotted organdy. White straw cloche hat. (Courtesy Lois Harbert)

10½" "Cissette Ballerina" #0914-1957. The flowers go up across shoulders. Flowers missing from hair. (Courtesy Gloria Harris)

10" "Cissette Queen" Gold brocade, blue banner ribbon and replaced tiara. #971-1957. (Courtesy Mary Partridge)

10" "Cissette" in #973-1957. (Courtesy Jeannie Niswonger)

10" "Cissette" in #940-1957. (Courtesy Charmaine Shields)

10" "Cissette" #0970-1957. White with red and blue trim. (Courtesy Mary Partridge)

10" "Cissette" #805-1957. One piece yellow striped topless sunsuit with rows of lace at back. Rick-rack trim on suit and matching skirt. Matching bonnet. (Courtesy Mary Partridge)

10" "Cissette" in extra dress—1957. Navy/white cotton with white trim. (Courtesy Mary Partridge)

10" "Cissette" All hard plastic shown in original white/navy reversible coat and hat. #0931-1957. (Courtesy Anita Pacey)

10" "Cissette" This is one of the extra dresses sold for the basic Cissette #801-1957. The doll (note the 3 stone rhinestone earrings) was originally dressed in ballgown-1956. (Courtesy Kathy Walter)

10" "Cissette" #0924-1957. (Courtesy Jeannie Niswonger)

10" "Cissette" All hard plastic. Glued on wig. Blue sleep eyes/molded lashes. Jointed knees. High heel feet. In gown and robe #0922-1957. Marks: Mme. Alexander, on back. Tag: Cissette/Madame Alexander, etc.

10" "Cissette" in pink nightie #0921-1957. (Courtesy Kathy Walter)

10" "Cissette" #973-1957. Black velvet with fur cape. (Courtesy Jeannie Niswonger)

10" "Cissette" #941-1957. Navy taffeta. (Courtesy Jeannie Niswonger)

Metal table and chair set with velvet cushions are #91-1957. Shirt and blouse outfit on left Cissette is #819-1958 and dress on right Cissette is #910-1957. (Courtesy Jeannie Niswonger)

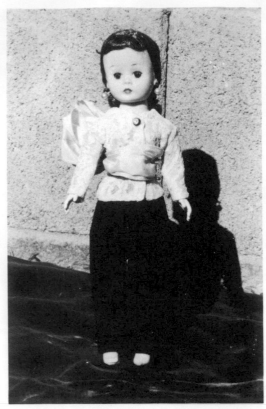

10½" "Cissette" #905-1957. Toreador pants of velvet that are black. The blouse is sheer lace and white. The taffeta bow is yellow. (Courtesy Lois Harbert)

This 1957 extra nightgown was sold for the basic #1100 Lissy doll. Shown on later doll called Pamela that takes wigs. (Lissy) (Courtesy Jeannie Niswonger)

The metal bed is #90-1957 with a variation of the spread (Came in various prints and styles) (Courtesy Jeannie Niswonger)

"Bill and Wendy" Shown with 1957 Alexander
furniture of all wood. She is #331-1960 and he is
#319-1960. (Courtesy Jeannie Niswonger)

8" "Prince Charles and Princess Ann" #395 and
#394-1957. (Courtesy Jeannie Niswonger)

8" "Billy & Wendy" Marks: Alex., on backs.
Alexander-kins/By Madame Alexander. 1957.
(Courtesy Kay Shipp)

8" "Prince Charles" #397-1957. Same doll as Billy #567-1958. (Courtesy Jeannie Niswonger)

"Wendy" #340-1957. (Courtesy Jeannie Niswonger)

8" "Aunt Agatha" (Wendy). Jointed knees. Marks: Alex., on back. Tag: Alexander-kins/by Madame Alexander. 1957. (Courtesy Kay Shipp)

"Wendy Bride" #410-1956-1957. Used in the Wedding Party of 1957. (Courtesy Kathleen Flowers Council)

"Wendy" #358-1957. Pink check cotton dress with lace and button trim. Bend knee walker. (Courtesy Mary Partridge)

8" "Wendy" #372-1957. With basic yellow cotton dress and panties with aqua polka dot taffeta rain coat and matching bonnet. Jointed knees. (Courtesy Mary Partridge)

12" "Marme" All hard plastic. (Lissy) 1957.

8" "Wendy" #373-1957. (Courtesy Jeannie Niswonger)

8" "Little Genius" Vinyl with hard plastic head. Open mouth/nurser. Caracul hair glued on. #246-1957. Bonnet missing. (Courtesy Roberta Lago)

"Little Genius" #265-1957. White organdy dress with pink trim. Pink gaberdine coat and bonnet. (Courtesy Mary Partridge)

9" "Bitsey and Butch" #2716 and 2717-1957. All vinyl. (Courtesy Jeannie Niswonger)

22" "Dumplin Baby" Cloth body with vinyl limbs. Hard plastic head. Glued on mohair wig. Blue sleep eyes/lashes. This one has replacement body. Marks: Alexander, on head. #7205-1957.

15" "Kathy Cry Dolly" #4510-1957. All vinyl with rooted hair. Open mouth/nurser. Marks: Alexander, on head. Childhood doll of Kathleen Flowers Council.

8" "Wendy" Dressed in two piece satin pajamas. #366-1957. Jointed knee, walker. Pale blue with roses. (Courtesy Jay Minter)

Shows Cissette sitting at vanity set. #75 1957. (Courtesy Jeannie Niswonger)

1958

Cissy is once again used as Portraits, wearing gowns of classic enchantment.

#2282 Tulle over satin flowery gown. Straw picture hat trimmed with roses.

#2280 Bride in lace dress embroidered with bridal wreath pattern. Full length veil of tulle attached with coronet of flowers.

#2252 Cocktail dress of satin that is calf length. Bouffant stole of tulle and short gloves.

#2285 Red taffeta gown, sheer tulle stole with dots.

#2281 Queen. In gold brocade, gold tiara with jewels, long white gloves.

#2283 Silk Ball Gown. With pink camellias print, long cape stole of velvet, lined to match gown. Flowers in hair, with gold veil.

Cissy was also offered with 12 additional outfits, 5 hats and accessories, plus she came dressed in a shirtmaker dress of print nylon with rhinestone buttons and tiny ruffles of lace. A sheath of velvet with side drapery, large picture hat and gloves. Chemise dress of sheer wool, buttoned down the front and lined in taffeta, hat and bag. Cotton print shirtmaker dress and hat tied with tulle. Another printed cotton with large straw hat and polished cotton with large picture hat tied with tulle.

Kelly. (with a 1957 Trademark). Rigid vinyl body and limbs with vinyl head. She is jointed and strung. She was issued in five different outfits. Came in 16" and 22" sizes.

Edith, the Lonely Doll. 16" and 22." This is the same doll as Kelly with hair in ponytail. From the book by Dare Wright, featured in Life Magazine.

Elise. 16½" had 12 additional outfits this year along with many accessories. (She was called Sweet 16 doll in FAO Schwarz catalog this year.) She was also issued in the following outfits:
Lucy Bride. Sheer tulle embroidered with wreath design. Full length tulle veil attached with coronet of flowers.
Shadow print nylon with satin sash and corsage of roses. Large picture hat with roses.
Net trimmed with roses over satin. Long wide stole of dotted net.
Ballerina. Repeat of 1957.
Shirtmaker dress of shadow nylon, trimmed in lace. Large straw hat.
Dark cotton with white pin dots. Straw hat with veil tie.

Lissy. Offered this year as Bride, ballerina and in a party dress and in a cotton dress with pinafore. She also had 10 extra outfits, three hats and various accessories. 12" tall, with jointed knees and elbows.

Kathy Cry Dolly. All vinyl drink and wet baby came in 11," 15," 18," 21," and 25" sizes. The 11" also came in window box with layette. She was issued with molded hair and rooted hair in all sizes.

Lovey-Dove. All vinyl baby with cryer. Closed mouth and rooted hair. Came in two organdy dresses and a sunsuit with matching bonnet.

Dumplin' Baby. Cloth body and hard plastic head and limbs. 23½." Dressed in an organdy dress and checked bib overalls, matching bonnet and pastel blouse.

The Little Women were put out in two sizes this year (1958). One set used the Lissy doll and was 12" tall. The other set used the 8" Wendy Ann doll with different outfits than were used in 1957: Jo in polished cotton with white organdy blouse. Meg with blue striped pinafore. Amy in lace trimmed print. Beth in checked cotton and Marme in dress of plaid taffeta with solid taffeta apron and fichu of organdy.

Cissette was offered in 12 different dresses, two ball gowns, bride, Queen, slacks and jackets, swim suit with matching skirt, velvet pants and lace blouse, raincoat, white coat and fur hat, and 10 additional extra outfits, plus hats and accessories.

The Alexander-kins (Wendy) were issued as bride (with groom), bridesmaid, in party dress, plus 11 other dresses, ballerina, ice skater, riding habit, cabana outfit. Billy in blue flannel suit with short pants, white shirt and eton cap.

The all vinyl Baby Genius was released in 5 dresses, a christening gown and two romper suits. Trademark #49,804 was taken out for "Cuddles" and not used this year.

20" "Queen" #2042-1958. (Cissy). Ash blonde wig, blue sleep eyes. Gown is gold brocade with blue ribbon sash and gold tiara. Marks: Alexander, on head. Tag: Cissy/Madame Alexander.

20" "Cissy" #2213-1958. Pale blue dotted Swiss. (Courtesy Roberta Lago)

20" "Cissy" #2284-1958. Called One Enchanted Evening. Gown and gloves are black. (Courtesy Charmaine Shields)

21" "Cissy" In an extra dress sold for the #2200 basic doll in 1958. Called "Summer Breeze." Very pale lavender with lace at sleeves.

16½" "Elise Bride" #1750-1958. Extra joints at elbows (vinyl arms), knees and ankles. Marks: Mme./Alexander, on back. Alexander, on head.

15" "Elise Ballerina" With variation of outfit. Flower trim with flowers and ribbons in hair. 1958-1959. (Courtesy Amy Zwickle)

16½" "Elise" Dressed in extra outfit for basic doll 1958. (Courtesy Charmaine Shields)

12" "Lissy" In yellow organdy dress that was sold separately in 1958. (Courtesy Mary Partridge)

10" "Cissette" In white/pink gown and pink velvet cape. Original. #873-1958. (Courtesy Anita Pacey)

10" "Cissette" All hard plastic. Dress from 1958. White with red flowers.

10" "Cissette" In extra dress that could be purchased in 1958.

10" "Cissette" #825-1958. (Courtesy Jeannie Niswonger)

10" "Cissette" In extra dress—1958. Red cotton with lace trim. (Courtesy Mary Partridge)

10" "Cissette" In extra dress—1958. Pink striped cotton with white collar and cuffs. (Courtesy Mary Partridge)

10" "Cissette" #813-1958. Pink dress with lace and rhinestones. Horsebraid hat. (Courtesy Mary Partridge)

10" "Cissette" As Bridesmaid in #852-1958. The chaise is wood and dates from 1957. (Courtesy Jeannie Niswonger)

10" "Cissette" #853-1958. (Courtesy Jeannie Niswonger)

10" "Cissette" #0918-1958. Flowers replaced as are shoes. (Courtesy Jeannie Niswonger)

"Wendy" #540-1958. Skater's outfit. Flower trimmed felt skirt. (Courtesy Lillianne Cook)

"Wendy" #540-1958. Shows the variation of colors and flower decorations. (Courtesy Jeannie Niswonger)

8" "Wendy" as Jo of Little Women. One in back is from 1958 and one in front is #381-1963, and a walker. (Courtesy Jay Minter)

8" "Wendy" #583-1958. Bridesmaid. Dress came in pastel shades with small roses. Flower trimmed straw hat. (Courtesy Jay Minter)

8" "Little Ice Queen" 1958. All hard plastic with jointed knees. Original velveteen outfit with real fur trim. Metal tiara. (Courtesy Connie Chase)

25" "Kathy" 1958. All vinyl, heavy baby with only slightly bent baby legs. Large brown sleep eyes, open mouth/nurser. Rooted hair. Not original. Arms are jointed above the elbows. Marks: Mme/Alexander/1958, in circle on head. (Courtesy Anita Pacey)

15" "Edith, The Lonely Doll" Same doll as Mary-Bel with hair pulled into ponytail. Came with brown and blue eyes. Marks: Mme. Alexander, in a circle. 1958 underneath. Came in checked dress with ¾ length sleeves and white apron.

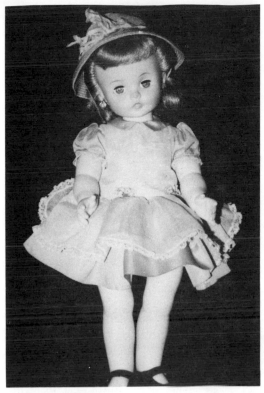

16" "Kelly" #1512-1958. Same doll as Mary-Bel, with jointed waist. Original. Marks: Madame Alexander, in circle/19, upside down 58. Mme/ 1958/Alexander, in circle on back. (Courtesy Margaret Weeks)

15" "Kathy Tears" All vinyl with brown sleep eyes. Open mouth/nurser. Rooted hair. Original pink pleated nylon, lace trimmed dress. Satin sash. Nylon tulle bonnet. Marks: Mme. Alexander, 1958, on head. Tag: Kathy/Madame Alexander, etc. (Courtesy Linda Krattli)

1959

21" Cissy was released in three outfits. 1. Bride with pleated nylon tulle over two underskirts, bodice of lace and puff sleeves. Coronet of flowers and veil to floor. 2. Knee length dress of satin with matching stole and hat of flowers and tulle. Handbag set with pearls. 3. Gold lace street length skirt with wool jersey emerald green blouse.

Elise was issued in five outfits. 1. Bride. Same as the Cissy. 2. Bridesmaid. Pleated nylon with flowers on the bodice and flared, pleated sleeves. Sash of velvet ribbon, large picture hat. 3. Street length sheer nylon sprinkled with pastel flowers, velvet sash and straw hat with dotted veil. 4. Ballerina in layers and layers of gold net. Bodice of gold cloth has a deep yoke with sequins matching her tiara. Pink tights and gold ballet slippers. 5. Skirt of printed sateen with lace trimmed nylon blouse. Taffeta belt. Straw hat with flowers. Elise is 16½" tall.

Shari Lewis. Star of television came in two sizes. 21" and 14." The 21" size used the Cissy body. She came in three outfits: 1. Skirt of satin and blouse of rayon jersey. Wide contour belt of gold, crystal necklace, pearl earrings, rhinestone watch and solitaire ring. Flower trimmed hat. 2. Short evening gown of gold lace, fully lined with satin skirt. Taffeta belt, waist corsage of roses, gold bead necklace with matching bracelet and solitaire ring. Pearl earrings. 3. Dress and coat of heavy slipper satin and fastened at neck with rose. Pearl jewelry and evening bag. There were additional Shari Lewis outfits that we do not have information on.

Sleeping Beauty. One of the most outstanding dolls created by Alexander Doll Co. and only outranked by Coco. Came in two sizes with the 16½" size using the Elise body and 21" using the Cissy body. Gown of soft blue satin trimmed with gold. Gold tiara with rhinestone stars, gold brocade net floor length cape. Rhinestone necklace and ring.

Marybel, The Doll Who Gets Well. 16" (Kelly face). All vinyl with brown eyes and blonde rooted hair. Came in shorty pink satin pajamas and case that holds casts, crutches, gauze, etc.

Kelly. 12," 16" and 22." Released in five outfits. Three were party dresses and one with simple pinafore, the other being a contrast of striped cotton.

Edith, The Lonely Doll. 16" and 22" (Kelly face). Dressed in checked gingham and pinafore. Edith is from books by Dare Wright.

Kathleen. 23." Trademark 72,404 (1959). All vinyl toddler. Open mouth/nurser. Came with molded as well as rooted hair but the rooted hair version offered in 27" size only. Came in three outfits, a sunsuit with matching bonnet, a polka dot coatdress of polished cotton and a lace trimmed nylon party dress.

Kathy Tears. 11," 15," 17," 19," 23" and 26" came in four outfits. Two romper suits with matching bonnets and two pleated nylon dresses with bonnets of nylon tulle ruffles. The 17" size also came packed with baby swing, which had an aluminum frame and swing of cotton denim. Doll in two piece romper suit.Kathy Tears came with molded as well as rooted hair in all sizes except the 11" size. The 11" size was released in a christening gown of swiss embroidery and matching bonnet.

Cissette. 10" came in eight outfits this year and all could be bought separately. She came as bride; bridesmaid in long gown of pleated nylon, with large picture hat. Queen in white brocade; in a party dress of pink satin with dotted tulle stole. As ballerina in gold net. Street length dress of lace. Cotton dress with bertha collar of val lace and ribbon ties at collar. Straw hat with flowers. In checked sheer nylon dress.

The Alexander-kins (Wendy). Came with various outfits all of which could be bought separately. Bride with pleated nylon. Flower girl in long gown of nylon pleated tulle. Organdy dress with pinafore in two variations, both with straw hats. Pleated skirt with white shirt and beanie. Leotards and pinafore. Plain and striped cotton combined in same dress with straw hat. Billy in short pants, white shirt and visor cap.

Baby Genius. 8." Came in four outfits that could also be bought separately. Dress of nylon, one of dotted cotton, romper and matching coat and a christening outfit.

1959 was a great year for additional outfits put out for all size dolls, adult and babies. The tags on the clothes generally just have the size of the doll they would fit rather than the name of the doll.

Little Women came in two sizes, the 12" using the Lissy face and the 8" using the Wendy face. Once again there were new costume designs.

16½" "Elise" Including hat, #1816-1959. Printed sateen skirt with nylon blouse. Taffeta belt. (Courtesy Charmaine Shields)

21" "Sleeping Beauty" Hard plastic body and limbs, with vinyl unjointed arms. Blue sleep eyes and high heel feet. Hard plastic head. #2195-1959. Marks: Alexander, on head. Tag: Madame Alexander/Presents/Walt Disney's/Authentic/Sleeping Beauty.

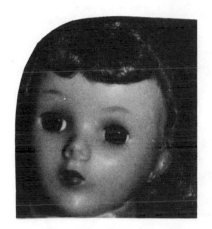

14" "Shari Lewis" #1432-1959. (Courtesy Carrie Perkins)

10" "Cissette" Dress #790-1959-63. Tag: Cissette/Madame Alexander.

10" "Cissette Ballerina" #713-1959. Gold net and lined body suit with sequin trim. Had sequin tiara. Replaced leotards.

8" "Billy and Wendy" #420 and #432-1959. (Courtesy Jeannie Niswonger)

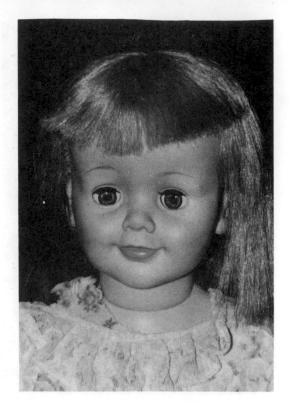

30" "Betty" Plastic and vinyl Flirty, sleep eyes. Head sockets into neck making posable head. Marks: Alexander, 1959.

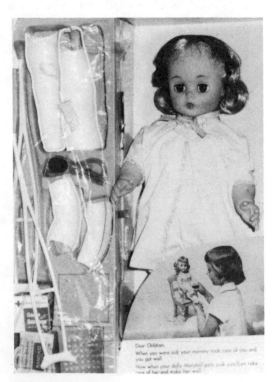

16" "Mary Bel—The Doll That Gets Well" #1670-1959. Rigid vinyl body and limbs with vinyl head and rooted hair. Brown sleep eyes/lashes. Open/closed mouth. Jointed waist. Also used as Edith, the Lonely Doll and Pollyana. Marks: Mme. Alexander, in circle with 1958 (Upside 2-5)

198

15" "Elise Ballerina" Jointed ankles, knees and elbows. #1810-1959. Gold net skirt, gold lame bodice that is sequin trimmed. Sequin tiara. (Courtesy Roberta Lago)

8" "Wendy" #446-1959. In robe. Pink check cotton with white lace trim. (Courtesy Jay Minter)

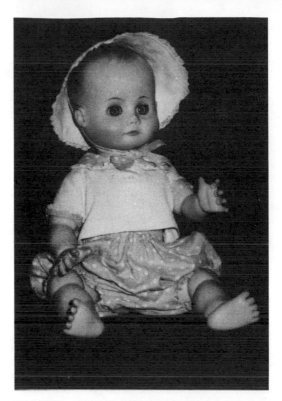

15" "Kathy Tears" #3805-1959. All vinyl with painted hair, sleep eyes and open mouth/nurser. Marks: Mme (1958) Alexander, in circle on head. Tag: Kathy Madame Alexander.

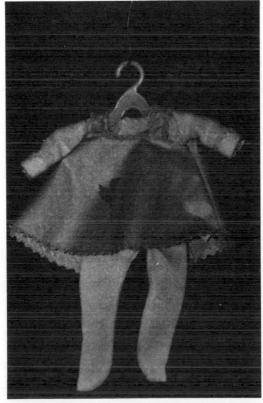

Extra outfit for "Little Genius" #100-1959. White one piece with pink cotton top. (Courtesy Virginia Jones)

1960

Joanie. Plastic with vinyl head. Flirting eyes with long lashes. 36" size. Came in four outfits. 1. Cotton dress trimmed with white braid and pearl buttons, with sash tied in back. Walker, if moved forward by pressing one leg forward and then heel to toe fashion. 2. Lace trimmed organdy with pinafore tied with satin sash to match hair ribbon. Walker. 3. Pinafore of red polished cotton over white organdy dress. Walker. 4. Nurse in white with white nurse pinafore, wears nurse's cap and watch on chest.

Betty. 30." Plastic with vinyl head. Flirting eyes and long lashes. Walker by moving legs. Came in three outfits. 1. Swiss organdy dress trimmed in val lace, organdy sash tied in back. 2. Soft cotton dress with lace edged organdy collar and big sash. 3. Cotton dress with lace edged organdy collar and big sash. 3. Cotton dress with white blouse front trimmed with buttons and folds of blue. Roses of braid around hem.

Elise. Still jointed at knees, ankle and elbow. Came in three outfits. 1. Ball gowns of cornflower blue pleated nylon tulle trimmed with rosebuds and rhinestones. Coronet of flowers in hair. Jewelry. 2. Bride with gown of soft satin with full, lined skirt. Bodice has a wide lace bertha sprinkled with sequins and crystal beads. Wide satin cascade to floor. Full length tulle veil attached to coronet of flowers 3. Ballerina in pink nylon tulle tutu with satin bodice with rosebuds and rhinestones. Coronet of flowers and nylon tights.

Queen. 21." Offered with royal trousseau in 24" metal trunk through FAO Schwarz. (Sleeping Beauty of 1959).

Maggie Mixup. 16½." This one year used the Elise body with vinyl arms and jointed ankles. Came in three outfits. 1. Checked cotton skirt with straps, a white cotton blouse with lace trim, long black tights and straw hat. 2. Party dress of soft cotton with organdy top, sash and flower trimmed·hat. 3. Long tailored slacks with white jersey blouse and multi-colored sash. Straw hat.

Kathy Tears. With new face. This year this all vinyl baby is much fatter and has a "heavy" fat, chubby body with all fingers of the left hand curled. Cryer, open mouth/nurser and cries tears. Came in woven check cotton romper suit and dress coat of woven check cotton worn over the romper suit. Came with molded as well as rooted hair. Three sizes, 11," 17" and 19." The 11" and 17" also came in case with 8 piece layette. All three sizes also came in a sheer organdy dress trimmed with lace, having a matching bonnet.

Cherub. 12," 26." All vinyl newborn baby. Open mouth/nurser. Both sizes were offered in organdy dress with lace hem and matching bonnet, in bunting with a wide flaring satin lined shawl collar, tied with a satin bow. Doll wears diaper and flannel sacque. Both sizes were also offered with dress of pleated cotton with lace edged yoke. The 12" size only was released wearing a diaper in a satin bound flannel sacque and wrapped in a fringed shawl. Also in long organdy christening gown and bonnet. The 12" doll was also packaged dressed in rosebud print flannel wrapper and matching diaper and came in lace and taffeta covered cradle. Tiny pillow of lace trimmed taffeta. Also coverlet of taffeta on one side and rosebud print flannel on other.

Genius Baby. 21," 30." Plastic body with vinyl head and limbs. Open mouth/nurser. Flirting eyes with lashes. Cryer. Came in romper suit, organdy dress and matching bonnet, and chambray dress with matching hood bonnet.

Timmie Toddler. 23," 30." Cryer and walker. Plastic and vinyl. Flirting eyes. Open mouth. (Same face as Genius Baby.) Came in three outfits that included a checked cotton romper type suit under a braid trimmed pinafore tied with a bow in back. Also striped cotton romper type suit that tied in back and a cotton dress trimmed with buttons, bias folds on top, sash tie.

Marybel, The Doll That Gets Well. 16." Same as the 1959 model in case, but this year there is also a trousseau that includes dress, petticoat, satin housecoat, slippers and socks.

Queen. 21." Using the 1959 Sleeping Beauty Doll. Gown is pale gold with red sash that crosses from right to left.

Little Women (Lissy Face). 12." Completely different costumes with this the first year that the Marme has an apron without a top.

Little Lady. 8." Hard plastic, walker. Cotton gown with pinafore and long pantalets. High buttoned shoes. Came in gift box that is a shadow box frame also. Box also includes a packet of bubble bath, one bottle toilet water and one of perfume.

Pollyanna. 16" and 22." Rigid vinyl with vinyl head. (Marybel face). Pigtails and blue eyes. Came in two outfits: 1. Dress of polished cotton, trimmed with braid. Hat with flowers. High button shoes. 2. Polished cotton dress with pinafore of braid trimmed cotton print. High button shoes. The 1960 movie starred Haley Mills as Pollyanna. From the book by Eleanor (Hodgman) Porter (1868-1920).

Maggie Mixup. 8." Smiling mouth, freckles and straight red-gold hair. All hard plastic. Came in checked dress, pinafore and straw hat, pleated skirt with straps, white jersey sweater with sailor cap to match. Also plaid, pleated skirt, white pique blouse, beanie hat and roller skates attached to brown oxfords. The fourth outfit was a two-piece set of beach pajamas of cotton. Striped pants.

Wendy/Alexander-kins. 8." Came in cotton dress with frilly printed pinafore and straw hat. Cotton dress, sleeveless and trimmed with band of flowered ribbon at bottom. Polished cotton dress with organdy top trimmed with lace and hat. Candy striped cotton dress and straw hat. As a bride in nylon tulle with wide satin sash. Ballerina in pink tutu with satin bodice. Riding outfit. Pleated checked skirt, white blouse and straw hat. Bill came in matching materials. Checked short pants, white shirt and cap that matched pants.

Little Genius. 8." All vinyl baby came in four different dresses, a christening gown, overalls, leotards and jumper dress and in the carrying case, dressed in sunsuit, with a 9-piece layette.

Cissette. 10." All hard plastic with jointed knees. Walker. This year's Queen and Bride are repeats from 1959. She also was issued in a gown of gold cloth with long gold net stole fastened with a corsage of flowers to match flowers in hair. Ballerina with layers of nylon tulle attached to satin bodice, trimmed with flowers.

Sleeping Beauty. 10." Disneyland. Using the Cissette. Blue taffeta or satin gown with gold net cape and on bodice.

During 1960 a Trademark 91,220 for Baby Dimples was taken out and not used.

15" "Elise" #1735-1960. All hard plastic with vinyl oversleeve arms. Extra joints at elbows, knees and ankles. Blue sleep eyes and pierced ears. Marks: Alexander, on head. (Courtesy Mary Partridge)

"Cissy" #25-164. Daytime polished cotton dress in olive green with pink organdy sleeves and figures. Pink organdy sash. Sold FAO Schwarz. 1960.

16½" "Maggie Mixup" In outfit 1811-1960. (Courtesy Carrie Perkins)

15" "Maggie Mix-up" Hard plastic and vinyl with orangish straight hair. Freckles. In #1813-1960. (Courtesy Jay Minter)

16" "Pollyana" #1530-1960. Same doll as Mary-Bel. Marks: Mme/Alexander, in circle/1958. The 5 in the date is reversed. Tag: Pollyana/By Madame Alexander. 1960. (Courtesy Virginia Jones)

12" "Marme" of Little Women (Lissy) 1960. A few years had this variation of apron, some had row of rick-rack around hem. White organdy shwal missing. (Courtesy Jeannie Niswonger)

10" "Sleeping Beauty" (Cissette) All hard plastic with jointed knees. Tag: Disney's Sleeping Beauty/By Madame Alexander. Disneyland exclusive since 1960. Re-issued in 1972. The later doll has straight legs. (Courtesy Virginia Jones)

10" "Cissette Ballerina" #813-1960. All hard plastic with high heel feet and jointed knees. Pierced ears. Marks: Mme. Alexander, on head. Tag: Cissette/By Madame Alexander. Pink with flower trim. (Courtesy Lillianne Cook)

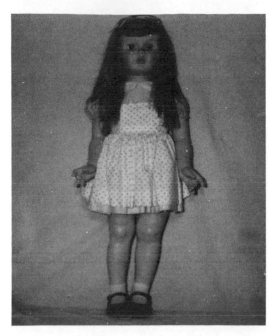

36" "Janie" #3513-1960. All plastic with vinyl head. Rooted hair and blue sleep eyes. (Courtesy Sally Bethscheider)

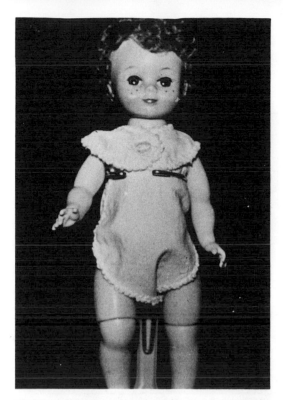

8" "Butch" All hard plastic walker with bendable knees. (Maggie Mix-up) Carrot red lamb's wool wig, green sleep eyes. Freckles. Not original. 1960. (Courtesy Jeannie Gregg)

8" "Maggie Mix-up" With blue eyes and original clothes. Tagged: Maggie/By Madame Alexandder, etc. 1960. (Courtesy Jay Minter)

8" "Little Lady" In aqua blue and white with blue and rose apron. (Maggie face) Walker and made in So-Lite rigid plastic. #1050-1960. Came in this frame along with toiletries. (Courtesy Amy Zwickle)

8" "Maggie Mix-up" All hard plastic with straight orange hair, green sleep eyes and freckles. Marks: Alex., on back. This Maggie face was used for some of the Internationals. Also came with blue eyes. 1960.

21" "Genius Baby" #6720-1960. Same doll used as Timmie. Plastic body with vinyl, posable arms, legs and head. Rooted blonde hair. Blue flirty eyes/lashes. Open mouth/nurser. Marks: Alexander/1960.

15" "Kathy Tears" #2710-1960. All vinyl. Rooted blonde hair. Blue sleep eyes/lashes. Open mouth /nurser. Cries tears. Marks: Alexander/1960. Not original.

12" "Cherub" #2668-1960 and 1961 only. All vinyl with much body detail. Socket head strung by rubber band to legs that have iron hooks. Blue sleep eyes/molded lashes. Toes curled under and all fingers separate. Open mouth/nurser. Marks: Alexander Doll Co., on head. Alexander Doll Co./1960, on back. (Courtesy Elizabeth Montesano of Yesterday's Children)

1961

Kitten. 24." Cloth body and vinyl head and limbs baby. Rooted hair. Kitten came in shirt, diaper and nylon tricot wrapper, an organdy dress, a batiste, lace trimmed dress, and a shortie dress with matching pants. (Trademark 115, 569.)

Scarlett O'Hara. 21." Taffeta dress with braid trim and matching short coat and bonnet. Lace mitts and velvet reticule. (Cissy)

Melanie. 21." Slipper satin with overdress of lace. Godey hairstyle. (Cissy)

Queen Elizabeth. 21." Gold brocade gown, sash of the Garter and jewels. Also, 3 piece brocade, short coat costume. Pill box hat of tulle. (Cissy)

Jacqueline. 21." White satin ball gown with matching long coat. This is entirely new head but using the Cissy body. The mold mark is 1961 and the Alexander Company used this very beautiful head from 1965 to date for the Portrait Series and even the Portraits of 1976 still have the mold mark of 1961.

Caroline. 15." All vinyl with rooted hair. Came in dotted Swiss dress, 3-piece play suit of corduroy, organdy/lace dress and several separate outfits could be purchased for her: 2-piece pajamas of flowered tricot or flannel, party dress of flower sprinkled nylon, a pique dress and leotards with short pique dress with contrasting collar.

Timmie Toddler. 23." Does not have flirting eyes. Rigid vinyl with vinyl head. Walks when led. Came in polished cotton romper style suit with large sash tie and a striped polished cotton pinafore over a romper of plain cotton.

Betty. 30." In dress with lined short jacket to match. White straw hat with flowers.

Joanie. 36." In nurse uniform. This cap differs from 1960 in that it is plain white and the 1960 has a black stripe.

Maggie Mixup. 17." Using the Elise body with extra joints at elbows and ankles. Red-gold hair, freckles and green eyes. Dressed in skirt and blouse with rick-rack trim and worn over leotards and taffeta petticoat. Flower trimmed straw hat and golden heart necklace. Also dress in long slacks with pockets, a cardigan and hat.

Pollyanna. 16," 22." Taffeta jumper dress over trimmed, beading and embroidered lingerie. Ribbon trimmed straw hat. Has pigtails. (Marybel)

Mary Sunshine. 15." Pale blonde ponytail pulled to top of head. Dressed in Swiss embroidery, lace trimmed dress with cap sleeves. (Caroline)

Elise. 17." Bride in tulle with floor length veil. Bridesmaid gown of tulled with satin sash, corsage and hat of horsehair braid. Ballerina in tutu of tulle with taffeta bodice. Hair is upswept into a topknot of curls with coronet of flowers. Long tights.

Mimi. 30." Trademark 115,567. Flirting eyes, rigid vinyl with vinyl head. Jointed in 12 places. Came in tyrolean outfit of felt suspender skirt with appliqued flowers, a 2-piece tennis outfit, slacks and striped top with straw hat and in a long gown of tulle ruffles over taffeta petticoat with lace trimmed

pantallettes and hat to match dress. Plaid skirt, red top—ala Scots. Separate outfits also available.

Madeleine. 18." Trademark renewal 118,540. Rigid vinyl with vinyl head. Has extra joints at knees, wrist, elbow. Dressed in pantalettes and tulle ruffled long dress with matching bonnet. High button shoes.

Marybel, The Doll That Gets Well. Repeat of 1959-60, but without the extra clothes of 1960.

Little Women. 12." Lissy face. Two have change of costume and three are repeats of 1960.

Kathy Tears. 12," 16," 19." All vinyl baby. Dressed in romper trimmed with lace, organdy dress and polished cotton with organdy sleeves. The 12" size also came in box with 7-piece layette, and a suitcase with an 11-piece layette.

Cherub. 12." All vinyl baby. Repeat of 1960 in christening outfit.

Genius Baby. 21." All vinyl. Came with either brown or blue eyes and in romper of woven checked cotton. Does not have flirting eyes.

Chatterbox. 24." Trademarks 116,182. Plastic and vinyl. Talker, says nine complete sentences. Dressed in pique, pleated in front and buttons down the back; also in romper of flower print cotton.

Margot. 10." Trademark 115,568. This is the Cissette doll with special hairdo that is very formal and elegant. Came dressed in gold sheath gown under long matching coat, a calf length satin gown with stole, a silver ball gown with rhinestone shoulder straps, a white satin gown with sequin trim and long matching cloak and an off-the-shoulder gown of satin in lilac with bodice outlined in sequins. Also in a black satin pants and overblouse set.

Wendy/Alexander kins/Little Women set has two repeats from 1960 and three with newly designed costumes. Amy wears blue with organdy pinafore; Jo is dressed in polished cotton; Marme is in taffeta with taffeta apron; Meg is in striped cotton and lace edged pinafore and Beth is in checked cotton with Swiss embroidery pinafore.

Wendy came dressed in nylon flower print dress, satin and tulle ballerina outfit, organdy dress and straw hat, nurse with baby, as bride alone, with Bill as groom, and in a special group called Americana. These four Wendys were as follows: 1. Charity in blue cotton dress with white organdy blouse and straw hat with stripes on the upright section. 2. Faith was dressed in a plaid dress, white organdy blouse and navy straw hat. 3. Amanda is dressed in polished gold cotton with organdy ruffles at hem and sleeve edges and has flower trimmed black straw hat. 4. Lucy came in striped cotton with organdy vestee and poke bonnet. Wendy Ann was also offered through FAO Schwarz in wicker sewing basket with outfits ready to sew (exclusive).

Wendy in National Costumes: #491—Dutch; #493—Italian; #492—Swedish; #495—Spanish; #490—French; #494—Swiss; and 496—Scots Lass.

Baby Genius. 8." All vinyl baby, open mouth/nurser. Came in organdy dress with cardigan sweater and hood, polished cotton romper with matching bonnet, play suit and hat (the outfit came with chair-rocker), and had extra clothes that included three dresses, gown and coat and bonnet. She was also dressed in a long christening gown.

Maggie Mixup. 8." Red-gold straight hair and freckles with green eyes. Was dressed in overalls, shirt and sun hat, ice skating outfit, cotton dress edged with lace, school dress of checked cotton, pleated skirt and blouse with roller skates and striped leotards with pinafore having a red heart. One special costume was Maggie as an angel. She has blue satin gown with silver wings and a starred crown. This Maggie has blue eyes.

Cissette. 10." Was issued as: Queen, repeat of 1960. Ballerina is repeat of 1960. A dancing gown of satin over tulle trimmed with rosebuds, having a pearl bracelet and earrings. As Fairy Princess in heavenly ruffled tulle trimmed wiht rosebuds and with hair piled on top of head. She also came with sunsuit, another sunsuit with removable skirt and in a polished cotton dress with pique blouse and flower trimmed hat.

Separate outfits were sold for all the dolls made by Alexander Doll Company; for example, this year there were the following for Chatterbox: a ruffled party dress, a coat trimmed with braid, candy striped pajamas and terry cloth robe and a pleated front, cotton dress. For Marybel, Polly-anna and Lonely Doll, a pique coat trimmed with braid, flowered nylon dress, candy striped pajamas and nylon dress with rows of val lace. For Elise and Maggie Mixup, a shirt-maker dress of polished cotton, a 2-piece set with pleated skirt, woven checked cotton blouse and sleeveless cardigan of pique, a polished cotton sleeveless dress trimmed with lace, and a lace trimmed nightie of nylon sheer and bed jacket of lace tied with ribbon.

During 1961, the following Trademarks were taken out and not used: 133,041 for Bobbie; 133,042 for Lambkin.

This is the 1961 Portrait "Scarlett" using the Cissy doll. The outfit is blue satin taffeta with black trim. She wears a tiny watch pin. #2240-1961. (Courtesy Charmaine Shields)

1961 Portrait "Melanie" using the Cissy doll. Gown is deep blue with white lace jacket. #2235-1961. (Courtesy Charmaine Shields)

21" "Jacqueline" and 14" "Caroline" in pink 2 piece outfit. Both dated 1961. (Courtesy Roberta Lago)

21" "Jacqueline" #2135-1961. Cissy body. Original. Marks: Alexander/1961, on head. Tag: Jacqueline/Madame Alexander, etc. (Courtesy Mandeville-Barkel Collection)

10" "Margot" All hard plastic with blue sleep eyes. (Cissette) Pale pink lips. Dark brunette hair piled on head. Dressed in an original silver gown. 1961-0965. (Courtesy Amy Zwickle)

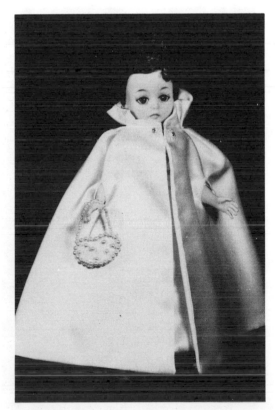

9" "Margot" In white gown and cape. (Cissette) #925-1961. (Courtesy Lillianne Cook)

9" "Margot" Dressed in an original lavender dress. (Cissette). Has blonde hair. #920-1961. (Courtesy Anita Paccy)

10½" "Iceland" A few of the Cissettes like this one were "Tried" dressed in International costumes. They were not as successful as the 8" size. All original in really fine quality clothes. 1961. (Courtesy Lillianne Cook)

8" "French" All hard plastic. Jointed knees. Walker, head turns. Marks: Alex., on back. Tag: French/By Madame Alexander. 1961.

8" "Meg" of the 1961 set of Little Women, using the Lissy doll. Gown is pink checked and pinafore apron is white. (Courtesy Marge Meisinger)

8" "Wendy" #423-1961. (Courtesy Jeannie Niswonger)

8" "Maggie Mixup" #611-1961. (Courtesy Roberta Lago)

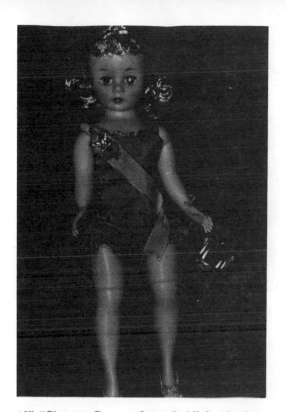

10" "Cissette Beauty Queen" All hard plastic with jointed knees. Bluish grey one piece suit. Yellow gold band with eagle emblem. Gold Cup. 1961. (Courtesy Jay Minter)

10" "Cissette" #0719-1961 Floss flocked organdy with wide lace trim collar. Replaced hat. (Courtesy Mary Partridge)

8" "Maggie Mix-up Angel" Walker, jointed knees. Has blue eyes and freckles. Gown is pale blue taffeta with silver trim. 1961. Marks: Alex., on back. Maggie/By Madame Alexander, on tag. (Courtesy Jeannie Niswonger)

8" "Nurse" #363-1961. Baby is all plastic with tiny sleep eyes. Marks: Alex., on back. Tag: Alexander-kins/By Madame Alexander. (Courtesy Anita Pacey)

8" "Faith, Americana" Walker, jointed knees. Red plaid with insert and sleeves of organdy. Navy hat with red ribbon trim. Marks: Alex., on back. Americana/Created by Madame Alexander. 1961. (Courtesy of Jane Thomas)

8" "Amanda, Americana" Walker, jointed knees. Gold polished cotton with white organdy ruffle. Black trim and hat. Marks: Alex., on body. Tag: Americana/By Madame Alexander. (Courtesy Jane Thomas)

8" "Switzerland" #394, 494 and 794. 1961 to date. (Courtesy Faye Iaquinto)

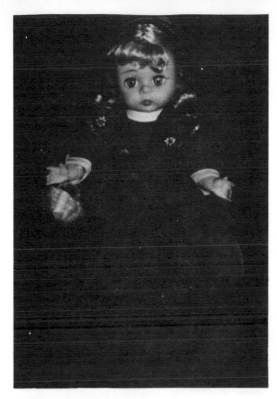

8" "Sweden" #392, 492 and 792. 1961 to date. (Courtesy Faye Iaquinto)

8" "Italian" 1961 to date. Variation of original costume. The first hats were dark. This one used in 1969 and again in 1973 to date. (Courtesy Marie Ernst)

8" "Italian" 1961 to date. Original costume but had dark hat to 1969. In 1969 the hat went to the fold type for one year, then this one in 1970-1971 and 1972. Returned to fold down style in 1973 to date (with costume variation) (Courtesy Jay Minter)

8" "Scotland" All hard plastic with straight legs. Green sleep eyes. 1961 to date. This one 1974 and currently available. (Courtesy Marie Ernst)

8" "Spanish" (Wendy) Glued on black wig, brown sleep eyes/lashes. Some came with two tiers on gown instead of three. Marks: Alex., on back. Tag: Spanish/Madame Alexander, etc. 1961 to date.

14" "Caroline" #49-5 separates—1961. Bright pink 2 piece set. (Courtesy Jay Minter)

14" "Caroline" All vinyl with rooted blonde hair. Blue sleep eyes. Open/closed mouth. Marks: Alexander/1961, on head. Alex. 1959/13, on back. Tag: Caroline/Madame Alexander, etc. 2 piece corduroy pink set with matching bonnet. (Courtesy Margaret Weeks)

15" "Caroline" Both 1961. Outfit on left is a pink two piece suit #4930 and right dress is blue with lace trim #4925. (Courtesy Shirley Bertrand)

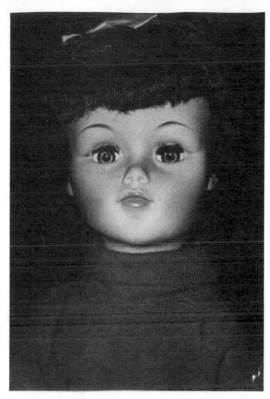

31" "Mimi" Plastic and vinyl with extra joints at elbows, wrists, knees, ankles and waist. Marks: Alexander/1961. (Courtesy Jay Minter)

23" "Chatterbox" Plastic body and legs. Vinyl arms and head. Blue sleep eyes/lashes. Open mouth/dry nurser. Push button in stomach makes her talk. Battery operated with changeable records. Marks: Mme/1961/Alexander, on head. #79-12-1961.

The wooden clothes rack is #50-1961 and gown on doll is #484-9161 with the long gown hanging in rack is #483-1961. (Courtesy Jeanie Niswonger)

8" "Baby Genius" In christening gown. #235-1961. (Courtesy Jeannie Niswonger)

1962

Jacqueline. 21." (Cissy body). It was during 1962 that a special request was made direct from Pierre Salinger, Press Secretary for the White House, that the Alexander Doll Company refrain from any reference to the First Lady in any advertising. The following costumes were offered for the Jacqueline and are tagged with her name. After this year, the Jacqueline doll was dropped from the line, until 1965, when re-introduced as the Portrait Series.

#2125. Gold ball gown of brocade with flaring side panels of satin. Pearl necklace, rhinestone earrings and ring.

#2140. Another gold brocade gonw but with fuller skirt than one above, worn with full length, lined evening coat of satin.

#2117. Riding clothes in brown tones. This outfit is the one that collectors seem to desire the most, and the one that commands highest prices.

#2130. Silver and white brocade evening gown with matching short jacket. It must be remembered that the Jacqueline doll has always had brown eyes and one curl on forehead.

Besides the above, there were six additional outfits that could be purchased separately, including street suits and clothes and lingerie.

It must be remembered that the "Jacqueline" has always been used for the Portrait Series, except in 1966, when the Coco was made. These dolls, right through to 1976 and 1977, are all marked with the same mold information. All will be dated 1961.

Jacqueline. 10." (Cissette). All hard plastic. Brown eyes and blue eyes were used. A large assortment of clothes were available for this 10" size, and all are tagged Jacqueline. A few of these are listed: 1. Two-piece suit and nylon blouse, hat matches suit. 2. Satin evening gown with matching full length stole. 3. Pink satin ball gown with evening bag. 4. Long coat over matching sheath dress with pillbox hat of tulle. 5. Slacks, sweater, with matching hat and lined leater jacket.

Caroline. 15." There were six additional outfits, plus pajamas, gowns and lingerie. Also the following: 1. Checked cotton dress with lace trimmed organdy collar. 2. Riding clothes of suede-like material and cocoa brown and beige. 3. Lace trimmed organdy dress with band of colored embroidery at waist, with big organdy tie.

Queen Elizabeth II of England. 21." (Cissy). Gold brocade gown with Sash of the Order of Bath. This sash runs from the left to the right. Single loop tiara with one double loop in center front.

Miss Judy. 21." (Jacqueline). Offered by FAO Schwarz in 100th Anniversary catalog in 24" metal trunk with extra clothes and accessories.

Elise. 17." Still with extra joints and jointed at the ankle. She came as Bride with tall coronet holding veil that is floor length and as a Ballerina with nylon tulle tutu and bodice of sequins. Wears a crownlike coronet.

Melinda. 16" and 22." Vinyl with a jointed waist. Open/closed mouth. Long, almost white hair with full bangs. Dressed in ruffled dress of pin dot cotton, trimmed with lace and white straw hat. Her other outfit was a party dress of lace edged organdy with red velveteen bodice and flower trimmed hat.

Bunny. 18." (Melinda face). Came in one size. Plastic and vinyl and no jointed waist. Has short hair style and bangs. Came in a dotted swiss dress trimmed with an organdy ruffle at hem, a Peter Pan collar and puffed sleeves. Also, a coat that buttons down the front, made of pique and has a matching bonnet. Coat is worn over a white pique dress. There were three additional dresses, a coat set, and a robe and nightie set available as well.

Smarty. 12." One size. Made of plastic and vinyl with toddler type legs that stand "pigeon-toed." This doll was released in six outfits and had four additional dresses and a gown and nightie. Trademark 138,929.

Sweetie Walker. 23." Plastic and vinyl. Will walk if led by hand. Trademark 138,927. Came dressed in rose printed, ruffled dress with puffed sleeves of organdy that is lace edged. Also, a polished pique coat over a dotted swiss dress.

Artie. 12" boy version of Smarty. Offered in FAO Schwarz 100th Anniversary catalog.

Sweetie Baby. 22." Plastic and vinyl, bent leg baby. Was dressed in a checked cotton dress with white organdy yoke. Also, lace trimmed organdy dress with matching bonnet.

Kitten. 14," 18," 24." Cloth body with vinyl head and limbs. Outfits are repeat of 1961. The 14" was also available in a long christening gown and packaged in a case with 8-piece layette. Five additional items were available.

Lively Kitten. 14" and 18." Cloth body with vinyl head and limbs. Large knob in back, when wound it made doll move its head, body, arms and legs. Dressed in same outfits as Kitten of 1961-1962.

Tommy. 12." (Lissy). Offered in FAO Schwarz 100th Anniversary catalog.

Katie. 12." (Lissy). Offered in FAO Schwarz 100th Anniversary catalog.

Kathy Tears. 16." All vinyl baby that has open mouth/nurser feature and cries tears. Came in checked gingham with puffed sleeves and trimmed with lace. Also, in an organdy dress and wool sacque sweater and matching bonnet.

Hello Baby. 22." (Kathy face) Trademark 138,928. Cloth body with vinyl head and limbs. Knob in back makes her raise her hand and she bends her head down. Came with telephone and receiver fits into right hand. Dressed in a cotton dress.

Dearest. 12" only. All vinyl, chubby baby. Open mouth/nurser. Came in two-piece dotted cotton creeper outfit and wool sacque sweater. Also, a simple lace edged cotton dress. She was also offered packaged with lace trimmed pillow and wearing a lace trimmed creeper outfit.

Little Women. 12." (Lissy). Repeat of clothes from 1961, except Marme now has a white bonnet and an apron (not taffeta), with cutout embroidery.

Little Women. 8." (Wendy). Repeat of 1961.

Marybel. Repeat of 1961.

Pamela. 12." Hard plastic with vinyl head that has "velour" strip over the top to attach wigs. She came in case, dressed in ballet outfit and had additional party costumes, nightie, lingerie and accessories that included three wigs.

Cissette. 10." This year she was released in a dance gown with yards of nylon tulle having the skirt made up of tight ruffles and she has an elaborate hairdo. She came as a Bride with tall coronet attached to floor length veil. She came dressed as queen in gold brocade; Ballerina with flowers in hair and the special costume of Gibson Girl in lined velvet skirt, shirtwaist, and hat trimmed with feathers and veil. She also had extra clothes that were available, including two ball gowns, a two-piece suit, two street dresses, slacks and top, and nightie and robe.

Wendy-Alexander-kins. 8." Basic doll #300 came in lace trimmed panties and shoes and sox. There were six additional outfits available that included nightie and robe, a two-piece sports set, and dresses. She came boxed in the following:
#355. Wendy in riding clothes of corduroy trousers, tan boots, white shirt and brown cap. Carries riding crop.
#358. Plaid pleated skirt, white sweater, cap and roller skates.
#363. Nurse in a striped nurse's uniform and white apron and cap. Tiny plastic baby, jointed and with sleep eyes (marked Hong Kong) with her, is dressed in lace dress and cap.
#353. Organdy party dress trimmed in lace. Hair pulled into top ponytail and tied with flowers.

The Internationals were joined by storybook dolls: Bo Peep and Red Riding Hood. The Internationals this year included: Tyrolean Girl (398), Tyrolean Boy (399), French (390), Spanish Girl (395), Scottish (396), Dutch (391), Hungarian (397), Swedish (392), Colonial Girl (389), McGuffey Ana (388), Swiss (394), Bo Peep (383), Italy (393) and Red Riding Hood (382).

During 1962, the Trademark for Cissy was renewed: 144,219.

Cissette was issued in "Special" costumes that included Klondike Kate, Diamond Lil, Barbary Coast, Gold Rush, Gibson, and Frankie & Johnny.

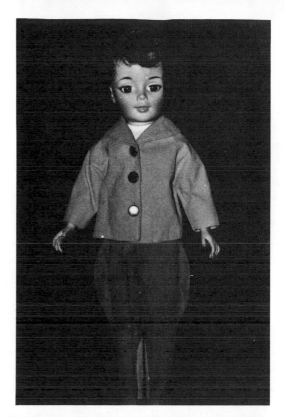

21" "Jacqueline" #2117-1962. Marks: Alexander 1961, on head.

This is from the FAO Schwarz catalog of 1962. Shows 21" "Judy" (Jacqueline) in 24" metal trunk. Doll and trunk full of clothes sold for $75.00. (Courtesy Marge Meisinger)

21" "Jacqueline" Wears pink tulle evening dress with single shoulderstrap. Original 1962. (Courtesy Phyllis Houston)

215

The 1962 Marshall Field catalog shows 21" "Jackie" (Jacqueline) with exclusive wardrobe. Her gown is white brocade, deep rose sash and side panels. Pretend white fur cape and additional wardrobe in trunk. This 1962 ensemble cost $65.00. (Courtesy Marge Meisinger)

21" "Queen Elizabeth II" 1962. (Cissy) The gown is gold brocade #2180. The sash is the Order of the Bath and there is a variation of the crown. (Courtesy Charmaine Shields)

10" "Jacqueline" #885-1962. Pink satin gown. (Courtesy Jeannie Niswonger)

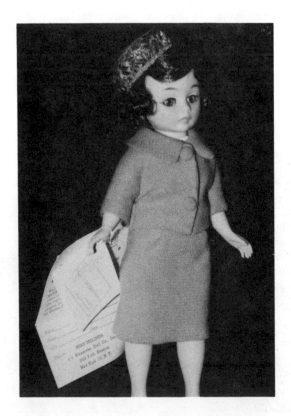

10" "Jacqueline" All hard plastic with glued on brown wig. (Cissette face) Blue sleep eyes, blue eyeshadow. Jointed knees. Marks: Mme/Alexander, on back. #894-1962. 2 piece blue outfit and hat.

10" "Jacqueline" This outfit is #865-1962 on Jacqueline (Margot eye make-up) and is #0731-1963 for Cissette. (Courtesy Jeannie Niswonger)

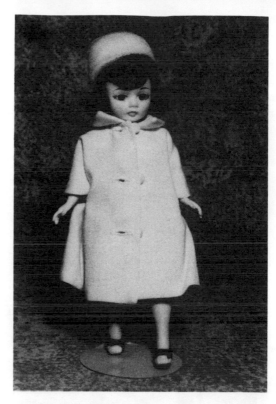

10" "Jacqueline" Dressed in coat and hat. #895-1962. (Courtesy Jeannie Niswonger)

10" "Cissette" #745-1962. Dance gown of nylon tulle. The 1963 gown did not have the rosebuds on skirt. (Courtesy Jeannie Niswonger)

11" "Gibson Girl" #760-1962. (Cissette) Has striped blouse and feathers on hat. (Courtesy Roberta Lago)

10" "Cissette Bride" #755-1962. Glued on wig. (Courtesy Lillianne Cook)

10" "Cissette Ballerina" #735-1962. Came in pastel colors. Marks: Mme/Alexander, on back. Tag: Cissette/By Madame Alexander.

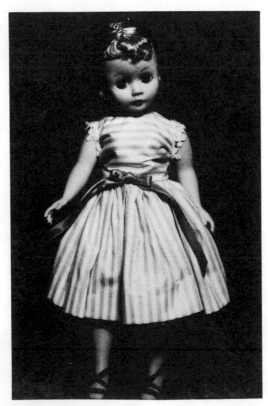

10" "Cissette" In an extra packaged dress of 1962. (Courtesy Jeannie Niswonger)

12" "Katie and Tommy" The special 1962, FAO Schwarz Anniversary (100th) dolls. Uses the Lissy doll. Both are all hard plastic. Catalog reprint.

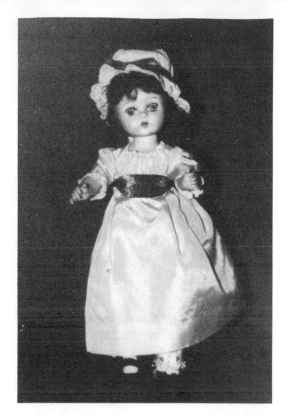

This is "Katie" made for FAO Schwarz 1962 100th Anniversary. (Courtesy Marge Meisinger)

14" "Caroline" #1305-1962. Pink and white dress with lace trim. (Courtesy Jay Minter)

14" "Caroline" In pajamas that are striped white/blue. Extra—1962. (Courtesy Sandy Rankow)

16" "Melinda" Plastic body with jointed waist. Rigid vinyl arms and legs. Vinyl head with brown sleep eyes/lashes. Open/closed mouth with two painted upper teeth. Marks: Alexander/1962, on head. #1512-1962.

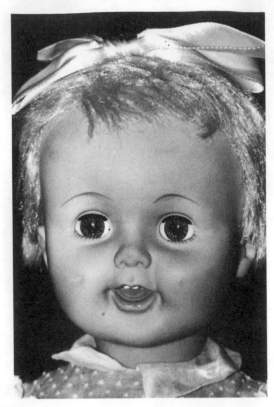

18" "Bunny" #1805. Plastic body and legs. Vinyl head and arms. Blue sleep eyes/lashes. Open/closed mouth with two upper teeth. Original blue dotted swiss dress with white trim and sleeves. Marks: Alexander/1962, on head.

8" "Scots Lass" With Maggie face. Walker, jointed knees. Green/red plaid. Marks: Alex., on back. Tag: Scots Lass/Madame Alexander. 1962. This doll begins in 1961 to 1963. Ones tagged: Scottish run from 1964 to date. (Courtesy Jane Thomas)

8" "Hungarian" Jointed knee walker. Marks: Alex., on back. Tag: Hungarian/Madame Alexander. #397-1962. This one was purchased in 1966.

8" "Tyrolean Girl" Bend knees. In 1974 became Austria. Was Tyrolean 1962-1973. This is #798-1964. (Courtesy Jay Minter)

8" "Bo Peep" Jointed knees. Marks: Alex., on back. Tag: Bo Peep/By Madame Alexander. #483-1962. This one was purchased in 1965.

Blonde "Maggie Mixup" Shown in the #398 Tyrolean girl dress of 1962. (Courtesy Jeannie Niswonger)

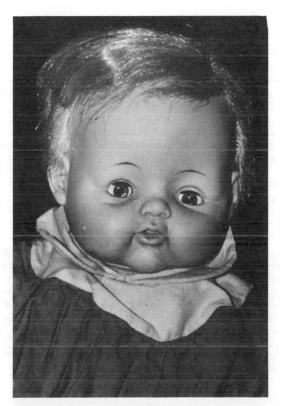

18" "Mama Kitten" Cloth with vinyl head and limbs. Knob in back makes doll move. Cryer. Marks: Alexander 1962, on head. Tag: Mama Kitten/By Madame Alexander. (Courtesy B. Monzelluzzi)

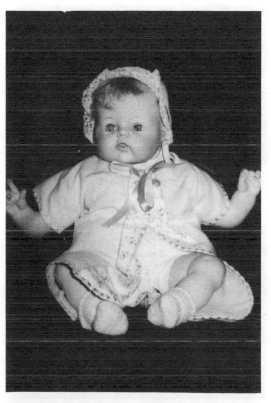

14" "Kitten" Cloth body with vinyl arms, legs and head. Rooted white hair, blue sleep eyes/molded lashes. Open/closed mouth. All toes curled under on left foot. Marks: Alexander 1961 on head. Tag: Kitten/By Madame Alexander #3611-1962.

221

12" "Smarty" Orange/red rooted hair. Blue sleep eyes. Open/closed mouth. Marks: Alexander/1962, on head. Tag: Smarty/Madame Alexander. #1155-1963.

17" "Elise Ballerina" #1740-1962. From the angle of the camera makes this doll appear to look very much like a Miss Ginny by Vogue but she is a standard Elise. (Courtesy Renie Culp)

10"' "Cissette" Shown in dress #0707-1962 which is a green/burnt orange print and hanging is #0706-1962 which is blue and white striped.

1963

Huggums. Trademark 165,403. Lively Huggums, 7295. 25" size only. Cloth body and legs with vinyl head and arms. Dressed in corduroy overalls with wool jersey shirt. Knob on back makes body and head move. Also available in one piece suit of nylon tricot.

Little Huggums. 12." All cloth body with vinyl head. Rooted hair. Came dressed in various colored lace trimmed cotton dresses and various colored suits of nylon tricot.

Kitten. 14," 18," 25." Same doll as 1962 but with outfit changes. This year she is released in a batiste dress with lace trimmed sleeve edges and a bib, although extra clothes were available.

Lively Kitten. 14" and 18." Same doll as 1962 but different clothes. In batiste trimmed with three rows of lace at the bottom, lace edged sleeves and bib. The other outfit this year is a dress of Swiss organdy, trimmed with embroidery and lace with bonnet having rows of shirred lace. Satin ties. This same dress was available on the 25" Kitten (non-moving).

Smarty Group. Plastic and vinyl. 12." Same as 1962. Two boys and two girls.

Katie. 12." Same doll as Smarty but a colored version.

The Little Shavers. Trademark 165,401. All vinyl babies

with "balled" jointes so that they swivel in all directions. 12." Painted eyes to the side. All came dressed in one piece or two piece outfits. (5).

Honey-Bea. 12." All vinyl baby. Open mouth/nurser. Sleep eyes. Cries tears. Came in flowered case with 13-piece layette and also in a window box with 9-piece layette. Also came in lace trimmed panties with bib to match, a long gown of batiste buttoned down the front, a christening gown of organdy and a nylon tricot sacque trimmed with rosebuds.

Mama Kitten. Same as Lively Kitten but also cries "Mama" until she is picked up. Various outfits.

Marybel. 16." Repeat of 1962.

Little Women. 12." (Lissy). Repeat of 1962.

Lissy. 12." In Classic Group: 1. Southern Belle in taffeta long dress with pantalettes, long curls and hat trimmed with feathers. 2. Scarlett O'Hara in green taffeta with matching bonnet. 3. McGuffey Anna in red velvet suit with circular skirt. Deep pile fur-like hat, coat collar and mittens. Patent leather slippers and buttoned gaiters. Hair in pigtails. Alice In Wonderland in pale blue with white pinafore. Long blonde wig.

Funny. 18." All checked gingham, yarn hair and dress decorated with patches.

Muffin. 14." Cloth doll with saphire color eyes. In dress and bonnet. Yarn hair.

Alexander-kins (Wendy). Internationals: Italy (393), Spanish (395), Dutch (391), Sweden (392), Swiss (394), Scots Lass (396-Maggie face), French (390), Ecuador (387), Tyrolean Girl (398), Tyrolean Boy (399), Hungarian (397), Bolivia (386). Others: Goya's Red Boy (760), Red Riding Hood (382), Colonial Girl (389), American Girl (388), Southern Belle (385), Bo Peep (383).

Wendy. 8." Also came as Ballerina, Bride with Groom, Nurse with baby, and Cousin Marie in dotted dress with a deep ruffle at hem and rick-rack trim and with curled brim straw hat. Also as Cousin Mary, dressed in organdy dress with three rows of lace at hem and flowered bonnet hat.

Little Women. 8." Two have had costume changes. The other three remain the same as 1962.

Wendy had extra outfits available and these included a coat and beret, two organdy dresses, a pleated skirt, jacket and hat, robe and two piece pajamas and a riding outfit.

Cissette. 10." This year came as Queen, Bride with three rows of lace at hemline, Ballerina, Gibson Girl (with plain blouse and flowers on hat).

Dearest. 12." Same doll as 1962. Came dressed in long gown of batiste, edged with lace and buttoned down the front. Also came with own pillow and dressed in same gown as above.

Melinda. 14" and 16." Also 22." The 16" and 22" dolls have swivel waists only. Same doll as 1962. Repeat of one outfit: Organdy dress with red velvet bodice and straw hat trimmed with flowers. She was also available in the following three outfits: 1. Below the knee party dress of organdy with rows of lace. The 14" size only: Lyers of pleated

nylon tulle ballet tutu with flowers in her hair. The 14" and 16" sizes also calme in a checked gingham dress with tucked skirt and a big sash.

Queen Elizabeth II of England. 18." Repeat of 1962 but with Elise body with jointed ankles instead of the Cissy doll.

Elise Bride. 18." Mauve taffeta gown with two deep ruffles, long sleeves with white straw hat trimmed with flowers and veil. Carries reticule and wears cameo brooch.

Scarlett Elise. 18." Black hair with full bangs. Organdy trimmed with vertical rows of lace. Very large straw picture hat; both hat and skirt are trimmed with roses.

Ballerina Elise. 18." Nylon layered tutu, trimmed with flowers. Wreath of flowers in hair.

Elise. 18." She was also offered in the following three outfits, plus many extra outfits were available: 1. Brocade ball gown with full length opera coat of satin and bandeau of roses in hair. 2. Checked shirt and shorts with a wrap-around skirt of corduroy, fully lined in taffeta. 3. Riding outfit with boots and cap.

Pamela. 12." Repeat of 1962 doll in case with 16-piece trousseau, plus a case with 14-piece trousseau and a window box with 8-piece trousseau. All have changeable wigs.

Cissette Special. In window box with 10 piece trousseau, consisting of cotton dress, velvet dress, chemise, panties, tulle hat, shoes, stockings, pearl necklace and earrings, pearl evening bag and 3 interchangeable wigs.

Littlest Kitten. 8." All vinyl baby. Sleep eyes and closed mouth. Came in various outfits that included christening gown, organdy and cotton dresses, 2-piece play suits, rompers and coat with a matching bonnet.

During 1963, the Trademark for "Quintie" was renewed, 117,593.

10" "Cissette" #790-1963 with three changeable wigs. 10 piece trousseau in window box. Listed in 1963 Alexander catalog. (Courtesy Mandeville-Barkel Collection)

10½" "Cissette" #790-1963. Came in window box with wigs. This is an extra dress in pack and tulle hat. Dress is deep rose, hat is white with matching rose. (Courtesy Carrie Perkins)

10" "Cissette" Came packaged with set of three wigs. #790-1963. Gown is #740-1963. (Courtesy Jeannie Niswonger)

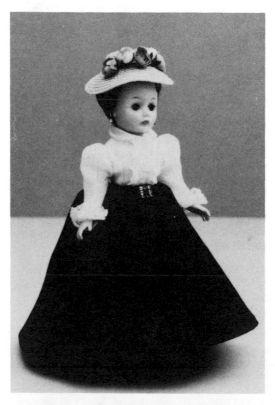

10" "Cissette Gibson Girl" #760-1963. This one has a plain blouse and flowers on the hat. (Courtesy Roberta Lago)

10" "Scarlett" of the Classic's Group #1256-1963. (Lissy). (Courtesy Jeannie Niswonger)

12" "Lissy" Alice In Wonderland #1257-1963. All hard plastic. All original. Marks: none. Tag: Lissy/By Madame Alexander. (Courtesy Mandeville-Barkel Collection)

12" Lissy-faced Jo of Little Women. 1963. Blue gown with white flowers and red apron. (Courtesy Marge Meisinger)

12" Lissy" As Jo of Little Women with a pattern variation of gown. (Courtesy Jeannie Niswonger)

12" "Pamela" 1963. Has three wigs and came in trunk with extra clothes. (Lissy). The later Pamela is plastic and vinyl where this one is all hard plastic. Dressed in a Lissy outfit. (Courtesy Roberta Lago)

18" "Renoir" #1765-1963. (Vinyl head Elise). Hard plastic body and legs with vinyl head and arms. Jointed knees and elbows. Glued on brown wig. Marks: Mme/Alexander/1958 (backward 1928), on head. Tag: Elise/Madame Alexander.

12" "Smarty Ballerina" 1963. (Courtesy Mary Partridge)

14" "Melinda Ballerina" Pale pink with rhinestones on bodice and lower skirt. Replaced slippers. Marks: Alexander, 1963, on head. #1410-1963. (Courtesy Phyllis Houston)

8" "Wendy" as Southern Belle. #385-1963. (Courtesy Lillianne Cook)

8" "Edith, The Lonely Doll" From book of same name. 1963 although the larger Edith was made in 1958-59. Pink checked dress with white apron. (Courtesy Jeannie Niswonger)

8" "Wendy" In riding outfit. #0441-1963. (Courtesy Lillianne Cook)

8" "Meg" #381-1963. Little Women. Knees jointed. (Courtesy Jay Minter)

8" "Wendy" In white/red dress. 1963. (Courtesy Anita Pacey)

8" "Red Riding Hood" #382-1963. (This one is later doll). Marks: Alex., on back. Tag: Red Riding Hood/By Madame Alexander.

10" "Cisette" Shown in "Square Dancing" #0720-1963. (Courtesy Jeannie Niswonger)

11" "Smarty and Baby" All original. Baby marked Hong Kong and has sleep eyes. 1963. (Courtesy Jay Minter)

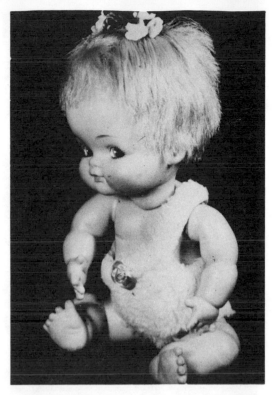

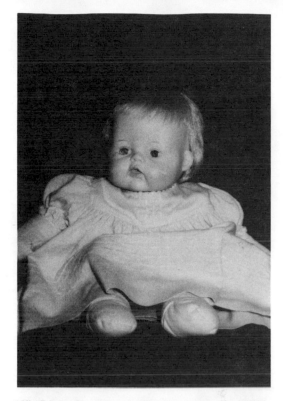

12" "Little Shaver" #2932-1963. (Courtesy Mary Partridge)

12" "Little Huggums" With rooted hair. #3810-1963. The rooted hair version came out one year ahead of painted hair ones. Marks: Alexander/ 1963, on head. This doll was also put out for many years and all are marked same.

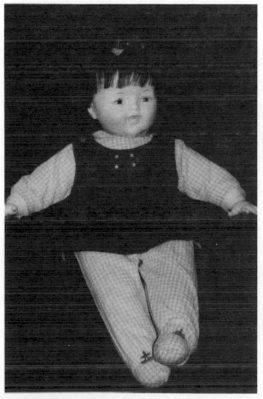

15" "Honey Bea" All vinyl with rooted hair, blue sleep eyes/lashes and open mouth/nurser. Crossed baby legs. Posable head. Marks: Alexander Doll Co./1965, on head. (#4710-1963.

25" "Big Huggums" Cloth with vinyl head and gauntlet hands. Painted blue eyes. #7813-1963. Also came as Lively Huggums with knob in back to make doll move. Marks: Alexander Doll Co. Inc., on head.

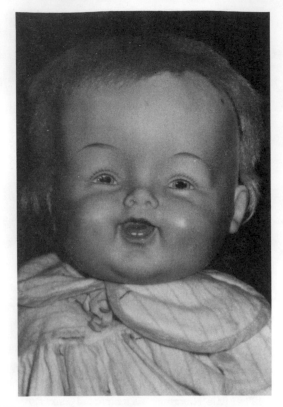

25" "Lively Huggums" Cloth with gauntlet vinyl hands. Vinyl head with rooted hair. Painted eyes. Open/closed mouth with molded tongue and two painted lower teeth. Knob in back to make body move. #7925-1963. Marks: Alexander Doll Co. Inc., on head. Tag: Lively Huggums/By Madame Alexander.

8" "Littlest Kitten" All vinyl with blue sleep eyes/molded lashes. 1963. (Courtesy Mary Partridge)

1964

Brenda Starr. 12." Comic strip carried in 135 newspapers in U.S. Came in two boxes, with one having an extra wig, although the doll's hair was not removable. Came in four dresses, bathing suit, sheath and coat, sheath and cape, and also in a ball gown and as a bride.

Janie. 12." Used the Smarty body. Came in five outfits: 1. White pique with red sleeves and trim. 2. Tucked organdy with lace and embroidery. 3. Cotton dress with lace sleeves and collar, appliqued rose. 4. Navy coat and hat. 5. White linen dress with applique.

Binnie. 18." Plastic with vinyl head. Came in two outfits: 1. White pique dress with red sleeves. Carries purse. 2. Blue cotton trimmed with white braid dress with tiny red appliqued strawberries.

Marybel. Repeat from 1963.

Elise Bride. 18." Has short veil and layers of lace on skirt. Still jointed at the ankles.

Elise Ballerina. 18." Nylon tulle tutu, trimmed with flowers and has flowers in hair.

Sugar Darlin'. 14," 18," 24." Trademark 187,709. Same body as used for Kitten in 1963. All three sizes came in cotton dress with organdy and lace trim and in an organdy dress with colored embroidery trim and lace tier bonnet. The 14"

size uses the Lively Kitten body with a music box and came in either organdy dress or tricot robe. The 18" size has the moving body and cries "mama" until picked up. She also came in either organdy dress or tricot robe.

Dearest. 12." This year comes in window box dressed in 2-piece sleep set and has 7-piece layette.

Sugar Tears. 12." Same doll as Honey-Bea, 1963, and renamed. Posable joints, open mouth/nurser and cries tears. Dressed in romper and striped T-shirt. Also came in window box with 7-piece layette.

Huggums. 25." Cloth body and legs. Vinyl arms and head. Rooted hair. Dressed in 2-piece pram suit of nylon tricot trimmed with lace and appliqued flowers. Matching bonnet.

Little Huggums. 12." All cloth with vinyl head. Came with both rooted and molded hair.

The Little Shavers. 12." Painted eyes to the side. One boy and four girls.

Funny. 18." Cloth doll repeat from 1963. Trademark 195,046 taken out this year.

Muffin. 14." Cloth doll repeat from 1963.

Wendy/Alexander-kins. 8." Basic doll came in bloomers, socks and slippers. She had various outfits available such as a 2-piece suit, terry beach costume, 6 dresses, nightie and robe and also came dressed as a nurse, ballerina, bride, in an organdy party dress with pinafore.

Alexander-kins (Wendy Ann). 8." Internationals: Polish (780), Spanish Boy (779), Spanish Girl (795), Swiss (794), Bolivia (786), Ecuador (787), Dutch Girl (791), Dutch Boy (77), Tyrolean Boy (799), Tyrolean Girl (798), Italian (793), Scottish (796), Mexican (776), Swedish (792), Irish (778), French (790), and, Others: Colonial (789) and American Girl (788).

Littlest Kitten. 8." All vinyl with closed mouth. Came in various outfits with extra clothes available.

Little Women. 12." (Lissy). Same costumes as 1963.

Little Women. 8." (Wendy) Same costumes as 1963.

Quintuplets. 7." Came boxed 5 to set. Collectors call them the Fisher Quints.

1964 also saw Trademarks (apparently unused) 186,989 for Petti-Tots and 202,345 for Alexander Rag Time Dolls.

12" "Brenda Starr" In 1964 outfit. (Courtesy Jay Minter)

12" "Brenda Star" Hard plastic body and legs. Outside jointed hips. Jointed knees. Very tiny feet. Vinyl arms and head. Rooted red-orange hair with one long lock on top. #910-1964. Marks: Alexander/1964, on head. Alexander, on back. Tag: Brenda Starr/By Madame Alexander.

12" "Lissy" as "Amy" from the 1965 set of Little Women. Dress is yellow dotted with white and white sleeves with tiny lace trim at neck. (Courtesy Marge Meisinger)

231

12" "Beth" of Little Women from the 1964 group. (Courtesy Jeannie Niswonger)

"Wendy" #625-1964, but is shown on a 1953 doll. Red dress with white sweater and rick-rack trim.

8" "Dutch Boy" Bend knees. 1964. Changed to #577-1974 to Netherlands Boy. (Courtesy Jay Minter)

8" "Irish" With different shawl. Bend knees. #788-1964. (Courtesy Jay Minter)

8" "Irish" #778. 1964 to date. (Courtesy Marie Ernst)

8" "Mexico" #776-1964 to date. Bend knee issue. (Courtesy Kathryn Fain)

8" "Polish" #780-1964 to date. (Courtesy Faye Iaquinto)

8" "Wendy" In pink polished cotton dress of 1964. (Courtesy Anita Pacey)

"Wendy" #624-1964. Blue nightie with pink robe with blue/rose flowers and lace trimmed. Bend knee walker. (Courtesy Mary Partridge)

12" "Janie" Plastic with vinyl arms and head. Rooted blonde hair and blue sleep eyes/lashes. Posable head. #1170-1964. Marks: Alexander/1964, on head. Tag: Janie/By Madame Alexander.

12" "Janie" Original. Marks: Alexander/1964, on head. Tag: Janie/Madame Alexander.

8" "Bride" #670-1964. (Courtesy Anita Pacey)

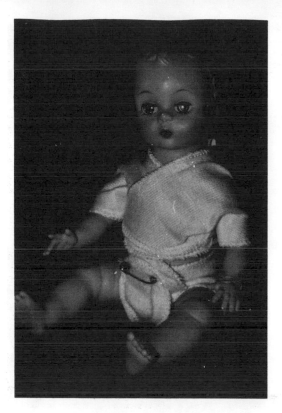

7" "Quintuplets" Vinyl with hard plastic heads (Little Genius face). Open mouth/nurser. Called "Fisher" Quints by collectors. Tags: Mfg. of the Original Quintuplets/By Madame Alexander. 1964. (Courtesy Jay Minter)

Shows close up of one of the "Quints" Molded hair and sleep eyes. (Courtesy Virginia Jones)

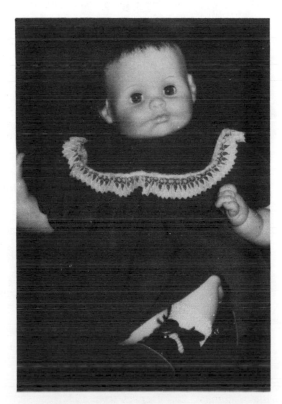

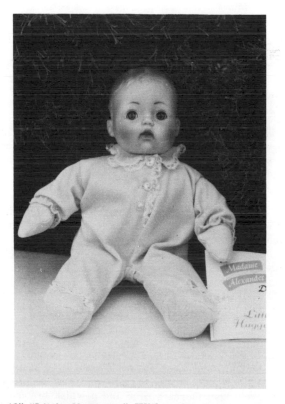

14" "Sugar Darlin'" Cloth with vinyl head and limbs. Blue sleep eyes/lashes. Rooted brown hair. Closed, smile mouth. #3525 1964. Original. Marks: Alexander/1964, on head. Tag: Sugar Darlin'/By Madame Alexander.

12" "Little Huggums" With painted hair. All cloth with vinyl head. Blue sleep eyes/molded lashes. Open/closed mouth. Marks: Alexander, on head. #3705-1964. Issued many years and all are marked same. (Courtesy Kathryn Fain)

17" "Binny" Plastic body with vinyl head and limbs. #1815-1964. Marks: 1964 Alexander, on head. (Courtesy Mary Partridge)

1965

Portraits. This is the first year for the portraits with the Jacqueline face and it must be remembered that all have the mold year of 1961, no matter if they were made for 1965 or 1976. This first year: Bride (#2151); Scarlett (#2152); Southern Belle (#2155); Renoir (#2154); Godey (#2153), and Queen (#2150).

Yolanda. 12." This is the Brenda Starr of 1964 with name change. She came in three outfits: 1. Turquoise satin formal with sequin trim. Sequins in hair. 2. Bride with tiers of ruffled lace. 3. Pink bouffant full pleated tulle formal with satin jeweled bodice.

Mary Ann. 14." Plastic and vinyl. Came in three outfits: 1. White pique jumper dress attached to red pleated skirt. 2. Scotch plaid pleated skirt, white sweater and hat. Red mittens, scarf and boots. 3. Ballerina tulle tutu and sequin bodice.

Orphant Annie. 14." Trademark 216,468. Mary Ann face. From poem by James Whitcomb Riley, "Little Orphant Annie." Dressed in brown calico print dress with lace edged organdy apron. Carries brown suede pocketbook. Black and white two button high top shoes. Freckles. Also came packed in window bow with extra wardrobe that consisted of green and white checked gingham dress with lace and braid trim, white organdy lace edged slip, pink and white dotted Swiss lace edged morning robe and a whisk broom.

Marybel. 16." Repeat from 1964.

Little Women. 12." (Lissy). All have newly designed costumes.

Polly. 17." All vinyl. Came in ten outfits this year: two different brides, a two-piece suit, ballerina outfit, four ball gowns and two street length dresses.

Leslie. 17." Polly face. Black version of Polly. This doll has mistakenly been referred to as Leslie Uggams and was not ever intended to represent the singer. The doll was on the marked before Miss Uggums became popular. This year, the doll was released in the two street length dresses and two ball gowns the same as Polly's.

Sitting Pretty. 18." Jersey covered foam body with vinyl gauntlet hands and vinyl head. Smiling mouth, closed. Wired body and limbs can be posed in any position. Dressed in full skirted cotton dress over white eyelet trimmed slip and lace trimmed panties.

Little Shavers. 12." Repeat from 1964.

Patty. 18." Melinda face. Laughing with open/closed mouth. Shoulder length blonde hair. Came in two outfits: 1. Turquoise blue organdy with lace ruffled trim over matching taffeta lace trimmed slip and panties. 2. Pink linen dress, fully lined. Blue applique tulip trim.

Janie. 12." Has four different outfits this year: 1. Pink organdy lace ruffled party dress. 2. Yellow pin dotted ruffled cotton dress with green satin ribbon detail on dress. Pigtails tied with green ribbon. 3. Red A-line cotton dress, appliqued tulip flower trim. 4. Ballerina pleated tulle tutu and sequin bodice.

Katie. 12." Smarty face. Black doll of plastic and vinyl. Toddler legs. Came in two outfits: Turquoise cotton dress with applique and pink organdy lace-trimmed party dress.

The Sound of Music Dolls. 11" Gretel (Janie face), 14" Louisa (Mary Ann face), 11" Frederick (Janie face), 17" Maria (Polly face), 14" Brigitta (Mary Ann face), 14" Liesl (Mary Ann face) and 11" Marta (Janie face).

Sweet Tears. 9," 14," 16." All vinyl, open mouth/nurser. Came in lace trimmed cotton dress, organdy dress on organdy covered pillow, and in two sizes (9" and 14") in christening gown with matching cap. These two sizes also came in window box package with layette.

Baby Ellen. 9," 14," 16." (Sweet Tears). Black version. 1. Came in striped cotton dress, laced trimmed. 2. Plain cotton, lace trimmed dresses and also a window box package with layette.

Pussy Cat. 14," 20," 24." Trademark 214,466. Cloth body. This doll was illustrated by Eloise Wilkins. All sizes came in pin checked polished cotton dress, white batiste dress, and pink organdy dress with matching bonnet. The 14" and 20" sizes also were available in batiste dresses with pleated front.

Lively Pussy Cat. 20." Cloth body and limbs same as Lively Kitten. Moves and cries "mama" until picked up.

Little Huggums. Repeat from 1964.

Big Huggusm. 25." Repeat from 1964.

Huggums, brother and sister. 25." Sister is dressed in white pique pinafore over pink and white pin dotted polished cotton, with ruffle trim and bonnet. Brother is in pin dotted polished cotton overalls with white pique long sleeved shirt.

Butch and Bitsey. 12." Cloth bodies and vinyl head and limbs. Brother Butch is dressed in short pants and jersey shirts of various materials and colors. Sister Bitsey is in pleated suspender skirt over jersey top in various materials and colors.

Funny. 18" cloth doll. Repeat from 1964.

Muffin. 14" cloth doll. Repeat from 1964.

Wendy. 8" Came this year in nurse's uniform, riding outfit, as ballerina, in organdy party dress, in cotton dress and as bride with tiers of ruffles. FAO Schwarz has special Wendy as Southern Belle in long white taffeta gown, trimmed with ruffles around hem, lace and rosebuds. Large straw hat with ribbon streamers.

Internationals: 8." Swedish (792), Tyrolean Boy (799), Brazil (773), Tyrolean Girl (798), Russian (774), Peruvian Boy (770), Mexican (776), Spanish Girl (795), French (790), Spanish Boy (779), Greek Boy (769), Italian (793), Israeli (768), Irish (778), Hungarian (797), Scottish (796), Argentine Boy (772), Swiss (794), Argentine Girl (771), Ecuador (787), India (775), Polish (780), Bolivia (786), Dutch Girl (791), Ducth Boy (777), Others: Miss Muffet (752), Scarlett (785), Mary, Mary (751), Bo Peep (783), Red Riding Hood (782), McGuffey (788), and Priscilla (789).

Little Women. 8." (Wendy face). All had costume changes.

Mary Ellen Playmate. 17." (Polly) for Marshall Field.

During the year of 1965, Trademark for Scarlett O'Hara 216,467 was taken out. This was a renewal. Another renewal was 214,466 for McGuffey Ana. Trademark 233,855 for Baby Eloise was taken out and not used.

17" "Maria" Of Sound of Music. (Elise) 1965. (Courtesy Jeannie Gregg)

17" "Maria" Of Sound of Music. (Elise). Variation of costume and date is unknown as this bodice with the full flowered apron from picture to left is the outfit that is shown in all the catalogs. (Courtesy Marge Meisinger)

13" Left: "Louise" In pink, green and white and right: "Brigetta" in Red, black and white. Large Sound of Music. 1965. (Mary Ann). (Courtesy Jay Minter)

11" Left to right: "Marta," "Fredrick" and "Gretel" of the large Sound of Music. 1965. (All Janie). (Courtesy Jay Minter)

13" "Liesl" Green with white stripes. 1965. Large Sound of Music. (Mary Ann). (Courtesy Jay Minter)

This is a "large" set of the Sound of Music dolls and shows the variation of some of the costumes. (Courtsy Jeannie Gregg)

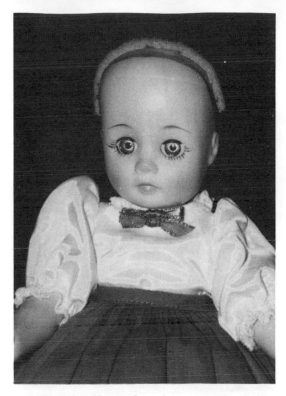

12" "Pamela" Plastic and vinyl. Blue sleep eyes. Came with change of clothes and wigs that attach with a velour strip. The first Pamela's with wigs used the Lissy doll and date from 1962 (#1200), this one used in 1965. She was called Alice in FAO Schwarz catalog. (Courtesy Jay Minter)

12" "Pamela" Shows the velour strip that holds the wigs to head.

This set is the #1291-1965 sold through FAO Schwarz and is Pamela with wigs. (Courtesy Jeannie Niswonger)

14" "Orphant Annie" #1480-1965. (Mary Ann) Inspired by poem "Little Orphant Annie" by James Whitcomb Riley. Has freckles. Brown calico printed dress, lace edged organdy apron and brown suede pocketbook. Also came in window box package with extra wardrobe bonnet brown print dress, green and white checked gingham dress and other items of clothing. (Courtesy Betty Motsinger)

239

12" "Jo" Little Women. #1225-1963-1964. With variation of print. This one is 1965. (Lissy). Bright red apron with blue and white print dress/organdy sleeves. (Courtesy Elizabeth Montesano of Yesterday's Children)

This shows the early Portraits (21" Jacqueline) using the Cissy body. All these Portraits will be marked 1961 even if issued in 1976 or 1977.

17" "Polly" #1724-1965.

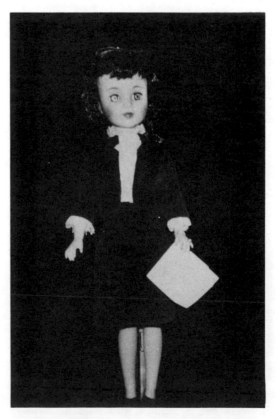

17" "Polly" #1731-1965. The suit is red. (Courtesy Roberta Lago)

17" "Polly" #1722-1965. (Courtesy Roberta Lago)

17" "Polly" In orange and white dress of 1965. (Courtesy Jay Minter)

17" "Polly Ballerina" Tulle with sequin covered satin bodice. #1731-1965.

17" "Mary Ellen Playmate" Exclusively made and dressed for the Marshall-Field Company. 1965. Tag reads: "Mary Ellen Playmate" (Polly). (Courtesy Marge Meisinger)

"Wendy" #0621-1965. (Courtesy Jeannie Nis-wonger)

8" "Israeli" #768-1965 to date. (Courtesy Faye Iaquinto)

8" "Peruvian Boy" #770-1965. Jointed knees. (Wendy face). Marks: Alex., on back. Peruvian Boy/By Madame Alexander, on tag. (Courtesy Virginia Jones)

242

8" "Miss Muffet" #752-1965. (Courtesy Jay Minter)

8" "Greek Boy" #769-1965 to 1968. Jointed knees.

8" "Argentine Girl" #771-1965 to 1972. (Courtesy Jay Minter)

8" "Mary, Mary" #751-1965. (Courtesy Jay Minter)

8" "Mary, Mary" #751-1965. Jointed knees. Variation of print. (Courtesy Jay Minter)

8" "Amish Boy" #779-1965 to 1969. (Courtesy Jay Minter)

8" "Argentine Boy" 1965. #762. (Courtesy Connie Chase)

8" "Russian" #774-1965 to date. Jointed knees. (Courtesy Marie Ernst)

8" "Brazil" Jointed knees. Glued on earrings. Orange scarf with fruit on top, gold sandals. Earlier Brazil had a hat with fruit attached. 1965 to date.

8" "Argentine" #771-1972 to date. Bend knee issue. (Courtesy Kathryn Fain)

8" "India" Two different in that the skin tones on one is "White." 1965 to date. (Courtesy Connie Chase)

8" "Wendy Ballerina" #620-1965. (Courtesy Jeannie Niswonger)

8" "Alexander-kins" (Wendy) #622-1965.

8" "Wendy" Dressed in #679-1965. White organdy with attached slip, rows of lace with tiny embroidered flowers on bodice. Jointed knees, non walker. (Courtesy Jay Minter)

13" "Sweet Tears" #3717-1965. All vinyl with rooted hair. Black, brown and blue eyes. **Open mouth/nurser. Marks: Alexander/1965 on head.** Original. (Courtesy Kathryn Fain)

12" "Janie" #1121-1965. (Courtesy Roberta Lago)

12" "Janie Ballerina" #1124-1965. Pink tulled with sequined satin bodice.

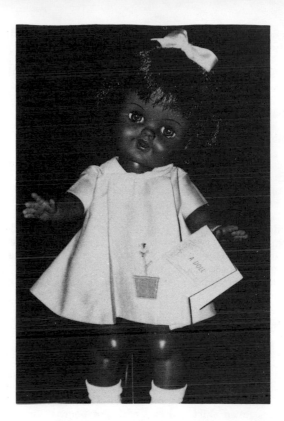

12" "Janie" Plastic and vinyl with rooted black hair. Blue sleep eyes. Freckles. #1122-1965. Marks: Alexander/1964. Tag: Janie/Created by/Madame Alexander.

12" "Katie" Black version of Smarty. 1965. Marks: Alexander 1964, on head. (Courtesy Jay Minter)

15" "Pussy Cat" Cloth body, vinyl head and limbs. Rooted hair and blue sleep eyes/lashes. Closed mouth. Cryer. Marks: Alexander/1965, on head. This doll was made for many years and all are marked the same. #3520-1965. (Courtesy Kathryn Fain)

1966

There was an increase of cloth dolls this year and along with Funny, 18," and Muffin, 14," there was 19" Muffin, Patchity Pam and Patchity Pepper, boy and girl and both 15" tall. Also, Good Little Girl, Bad Little Girl from the book of the same name, illustrated by Eloise Wilkin. Good Little Girl is dressed in pink and Bad Little Girl in blue. Both are 16."

Gidget. 14" (Mary Ann face). Plastic and vinyl. "All American" teenager. Dark hair is in full bangs and pulled into twin ponytails over the ears. Came in three outfits; a whtie dress with two rows of buttons down the front and double rows of trim at neck, sleeve and waist. Also in a jumper and sweater and in a long flowered dress with flowers in her hair.

Little Granny. 14." (Mary Ann face). Plastic and vinyl. Came in two outfits. A floral print dress with dark hair and a pin dot and a lace trimmed dress with white hair and glasses.

Leslie. 17." (Polly face). Came in cotton dress with wide lace trim and shawl collar, as a ballerina, a bride, and in formal with rows of lace on bodice and lace cap sleeves.

Elise. 17." Wears same outfits as Leslie.

Coco. 20." Soft plastic and vinyl. An entirely "new" face and used just for the year of 1966. The waist is jointed and legs, along with lower torso are molded in one piece. Large expressive eyes. Came in five outfits. 1. Silk printed sheath. 2.

Pin striped sheath with sleeves and neck trimmed with ruffled organdy. 3. Slim skirt with short cotton orange jacket with mandarin ties. 4. Full length black and white jersey jump suit with yellow satin ankle length coat. 5. Pink brocade sheath ball gown trimmed with pink marabou.

Sound of Music dolls. Repeat of 1965.

Orphant Annie. 14." Repeat of 1965.

Alice In Wonderland. 14." (Mary Ann face) Plastic and vinyl with shoulder length blonde hair tied with ribbon. Pale blue cotton dress edged with white braid and with a white apron over her dress. Long white stockings and black shoes.

Cinderella. 12." (Lissy face). Came in two outfits: Pale blue satin ball gown trimmed with lace, rosebuds and sequins. Wears tiara. Also dressed in a scullery maid outfit of a moss green full cotton skirt, mathcing kerchief, bright orange apron and carries a broom. Both these outfits and the doll were also available in a window box set.

Little Huggums. 12." Repeat from 1965.

Huggums. 25." Repeat from 1965.

Butch and Bitsy. 12." Repeat of 1965 but now only available in one outfit: She in full skirted cotton jumper with cotton knit short sleeved shirt and he in cotton short overall with short sleeved shirt and cap with pompom.
Janie. 12." Repeat of 1965 in A-line linen dress and long sleeved smock with leotards and boots. Carries straw bag.

Victoria. 18." Cloth body with vinyl head and limbs. Painted hair. Came in two outfits. Cotton dress edged with lace and dress and bonnet of cotton eylet trimmed with pink ribbon.

Puddin.' 21." Cloth body with vinyl head and limbs. Came in pin-checked eyelet cotton dress and nosegay printed nightie trimmed with lace.

Pussy Cat. 14," 20," 24." The 14" and 24" came in a tricot dress with lace trimming and all three sizes came in a pin-checked lace trimmed cotton dress with white collar, a pink cotton dress with front pleated panel with embroidered flowers, white collar and puffed sleeves. Also, in a pink lace edged flowr embroidered organdy dress with matching bonnet.

Sweet Tears. The 9" and 14" came with rooted or painted hair. 16." with rooted hair. All three sizes were offered in pink cotton dresses with four rows of lace edging running from shoulder to hem. Also came in christening gown. The 9" and 14" sizes came in window boxes with layette and in quilted bunting.

Baby Ellen. (Sweet Tears face). Black version. 14" size came in bunting and in same dress as Sweet Tears, cotton dress with four rows of lace.

Internationals. 8." French (790), Swedish (792), Polish (780), Spanish Boy (779), Italian (791), Dutch (791), Scottish (796), Swiss (794), Spanish Girl (795), Tyrolean Boy (799), Hungarian (797), Tyrolean Girl (798), German (763), Argentine (771), African (766), Greek (769), Mexican (776), Thailand (767), Israel (768), India (775), Irish (778), Dutch Boy (777), Peruvian Boy (770), Ecuador (787), English Guard (764), Argentine Boy (772), Bolivia (786).

Americana (Wendy face). 8." Indian Boy (720), Scarlett (725), Indian Girl (721), Hawaiian (722), Cowgirl (724), Eskimo (723), Amish Boy (726), Amish Girl (727), Priscilla (729), Miss USA (728), Bride (735), Ballerina (730).

Storyland Dolls (Wendy face). 8." Mary, Mary (751), **Red Riding Hood** (782), Hansel (753), Gretel (754), Bo Peep (783), Miss Muffet (752).

Little Women. This year 8" only. Two have changed costumes and this is first year that the boy, Laurie, is offered.

Portraits. 21." This is the only year the portraits were made using the Coco doll. Madame Doll (2060), Melanie (2050), Lissy (2051), Godey (2063), **Scarlett** (2061), and **Renoir** (2062).

20" "Coco" Plastic body and legs. Jointed waist. One piece lower torso with bent right leg. Vinyl arms and head. Rooted blonde hair and brown sleep eyes. Blue shadow and black liner. #2030-1966. Had ribbon and not tiara in hair. Marks: Alexander/1966, on head.

The real Coco was Gabrielle (Coco) Chanel, famous Paris designer of the House of Chanel on Rue Cambon since the 1920's. More than designs, she gave Europe the Coco Chanel look. Once caught in the rain, she borrowed a man's trenchcoat and women's trenchcoats were born. She walked into the Casino at Juan-les-Pins wearing pants and gave women's trousers the seal of approval. Just before an evening out, a fire singed her hair and she only had time to clip it, thus the bobbed hair look came in. She tired of people staring at her jewelry and started wearing fakes, thus costume jewelry was invented. She was the first designer to market her own perfume, Chanel #5. Coco closed up and retired just before World War II and made a comeback in 1954 at the age of 70. Perfums Chanel (1954) in exchange for her name and designs pays Coco, after taxes, 2% of global sales of Chanel #5.

Fredrick Brisson saw Coco in 1954 and said he was going to do a Broadway Musical based on her life. He talked to Alan Jay Lerner about it in 1961. (Lerner wrote the music and lyrics for the stage play) Producer Brisson began working on "Coco" in 1965. The play did not open on Broadway until 1969 and starred Katherine Hepburn as Coco Chanel. This play kept 18 dressers busy with 253 costume changes. Although a spectacular, the musical was not well received by the critics.

The Coco doll, designed by Madame Alexander, is one of her finest creations and a collector who has one in her collection is very fortunate.

17" "Leslie Bride" #1660-1966. (Polly) (Courtesy Marie Ernst)

17" "Leslie" Plastic and vinyl (Polly face). Marks: Alexander Doll Co. Inc./1965, on head. #1620-1966.

14" "Little Granny" #1431-1966. Floral print. (Mary Ann). (Courtesy Roberta Lago)

14" "Little Granny" #1431-1966. (Mary Ann) Tag: Little Granny/Madame Alexander. Also came as blonde with glasses and variation of print cotton. (Courtesy Marie Ernst)

14" "Gidgit, The American Teenager" (Mary Ann face). Plastic and vinyl with rooted black hair cut in full bangs and in twin ponytails. Blue sleep eyes. Marks: Alexander, on head. 1966. (Courtesy Jeannie Niswonger)

18" "Elise" #1750-1966. All vinyl with earrings and solitaire ring. Gown is blue. (Courtesy Sandy Rankow)

14" "Bride" Special doll made for the Marshall Field Company. 1966. (Mary Ann). (Courtesy Jeannie Niswonger)

14" "Alice In Wonderland" #1452-1966. Based on Louis G. Carroll's book "Adventures Under Ground" (Mary Ann). #1542-1966. (Courtesy Jeannie Niswonger)

8" "Cowgirl and Cowboy" Boy: 1966 to 1969.
Girl: 1966 to 1970. (Courtesy Lillianne Cook)

8" "Eskimo" 1966 to 1969. (Courtesy Connie Chase)

8" "German" Bend knees. #63-1966 to date. Some have the reverse patterns on apron/skirt. (Courtesy Marie Ernst)

8" "Thailand" Jointed knees. #67-1966. Marks: Alex., on back. Tag: Thailand/By Madame Alexander.

8" "Miss U.S.A." This is first issued one. 1966 to 1968. (Courtesy Jay Minter)

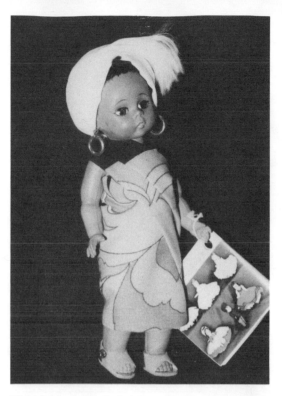

8" "Hansel and Gretel" Glued on yellowish orange wigs. Blue sleep eyes/lashes. Marks: Alex., on back. Tag: Hansel (and Gretel is same(/by Madame Alexander. #753-754-1966.

8" "African" All dark tones. Brown sleep eyes. Jointed knees. #766-1966. Came in various prints. Marks: Alex. on back. Tag: African/By Madame Alexander. (Courtesy Virginia Jones)

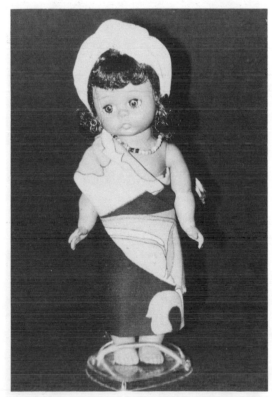

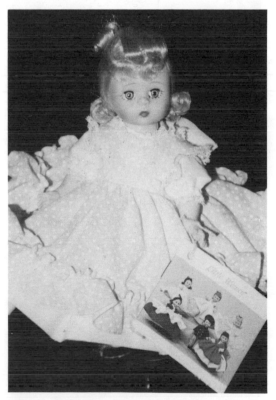

Shows variation of the print. This one from same year they were discontinued. 1971. (Courtesy Connie Chase)

8" "Amy" of Little Women. #781-1966. Jointed knees. (Courtesy Jay Minter)

8" "Scarlett" #725-1966. Green sleep eyes, brown wig and jointed knees. Marks: Alex., on back. Tag: Scarlett/By Madame Alexander.

8" "Eskimo" #23-1966 to 1969. Maggie head. (Courtesy Faye Iaquinto)

8" "Scarlett" #725-1966 to 1972. Some had a variation of the flowered print. (Courtesy Faye Iaquinto)

"Hawaiian" #722-1966. (Courtesy Joan Amundsen)

12" "Pamela" Takes wigs dressed in Polish costume made for FAO Schwarz. (Lissy). 1966. (Courtesy Jeannie Niswonger)

12" "Pamela" Takes wigs. 1966. (Lissy). Outfit is one that came in the set in trunk. (Courtesy Jeannie Niswonger)

From Marshall Field catalog of 1966. 21" "Margot" (Jacqueline) in Louis Vuitton leather-bound trunk. Sequined silk chiffon gown with velveteen wrap. Extras included mink stole and hat. This ensemble sold for $250.00 from this 1966 catalog. (Courtesy Marge Meisinger)

12" "Bitsey and Butch" #2510 and 2515-1966 with
a variation of costume that also came in various
colors. (Courtesy Betty Motsinger)

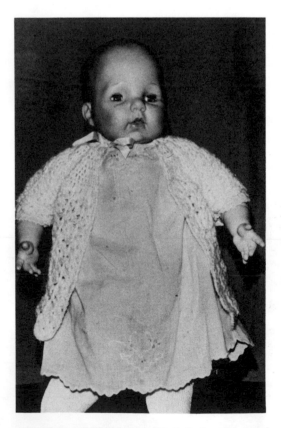

18" "Victoria" #5840-1966. Cloth body with vinyl
head and limbs. Spray painted hair, sleep eyes.
(Courtesy Marge Meisinger)

1967

Nancy Drew. 12." Plastic and vinyl. Inspired by famous little
girl series of books. Came in two outfits. 1. Linen shift under
matching coat with brass buttons. 2. Two-piece cotton
checked suit. Both wear boots, have sunglasses, camera and
pocketbook.

Poor Cinderella. 14." (Mary Ann face). Plastic vinyl. Comes
in same outfit as described for the Lissy-faced doll of 1966.

Sound of Music Dolls. Repeat from 1966.

Renoir Mother and Child. (Jacqueline and Mary Ann).

Little Women. 12." (Lisy face). Two costumes changed from
1965. First 12" boy doll, Laurie. (Lissy face).

Alice In Wonderland. 14." (Mary Ann face). Repeat from
1966.

Riley's Little Annie. 14." (Mary Ann face). Based on James
Whitcomb Riley's famous poem, "Little Orphant Annie."
Dressed in pink nosegay floral print cotton dress, pink straw
hat with flower and ribbon trim. White high button shoes
and stockings. Middle part, shoulder length blonde hair.

Muffin. 14." Cloth doll. Repeat from 1966.

Muffin. 14." Cloth doll. Repeat from 1966.

Carrot Top. 21." Trademark 269,041. All cloth with blue chenille balls for eyes, smiling mouth and carrot red yarn wig tied to sides with green ribbons. Dress of polka dot cotton.

Little Huggums. 12." Both painted and rooted hair. Repeat from 1966.

Huggums, Big. 25." Repeat from 1966.

Pumpkin. 21." Cloth with gauntlet vinyl hands. Vinyl head with large painted eyes. Wears tricot suit with attached hat. Rosebud trim. Painted hair.

Rusty. 20." Trademark 269,043. Cloth body with vinyl head and limbs. Red rooted hair and freckles. Wears jersey leotards with striped apron.

Kitten Kries. 20." Trademark 269,044. Cloth body, vinyl head and limbs. Rooted hair. Open mouth and will drink from bottle but does not wet. Place pacifier in mouth after giving her a drink of water and she cries tears. Dressed in lace trimmed pin dotted cotter dress covered with clear plastic apron which is decorated wth felt animals.

Pussy Cat. 14." 20," 24." The 14" and 20" sizes came in a tricot dress buttoned down the front with wide lace collar and all sizes came in three outfits: 1. Pin checked, lace trimmed cotton dress with white collar and tiny button trim. 2. Cotton dress with pleated front panel trimmed with flower embroidery. 3. Lace edged and flower embroidered pink organdy dress and matching bonnet.

Victoria. 20." Painted hair. Came in two outfits. White cotton dress edged with eyelet embroidery and bud trim and a pink eyelet embroidered dress with matching bonnet.

Puddin.' 21." Came in sheer batiste nightie and also in a pin checked cotton jumper effect dress with tiny white yoke, lace trimmed.

Sweet Tears. The 9" and 14" came with pillow and matching dress of pin checked cotton with three rows of lace at hem. Rooted hair. The 9" and 14" with rooted hair and the 9" and 16" with painted hair came in a pin dotted polished cotton, lace trimmed dress. The 14" size came in a christening costume. The 9" and 14" also came in a window box package with layette, and also in a travel case with layette.

Baby Ellen. 14." (Sweet Tears face). Came in two outfits this year.

Little Butch and Little Bitsy. 9." (Sweet Tears face). Open mouth/nursers and cry tears. He is in pin checked cotton short overall suit with jersey shirt and she in matching jumper dress over a jersey shirt.

Elise. 17." Came as ballerina, bride and in a formal.

Madame Doll. 14." (Mary Ann face). From Frances Cavanah's book, "The Secret of Madame Doll." Lace edged pantaloons, gown of pale pink silk brocade trimmed with pink organdy and lace ruffles. Matching organdy lace trimmed duster cap.

Leslie. 17." (Polly face). Black doll with same outfits as Elise.

That Girl — Marlo Thomas. 17." From ABC television show starring Miss Marlo Thomas. Came in two outfits: a two-tone jersey shift dress of royal blue and green with choker necklace, white lace stockings and white high heeled boots. Also in a garnet red formal that is high waisted and sleeveless. Wears three strands of crystal beads, ring and a red bow in her hair.

Renoir Girl. 14." (Mary Ann face). White organdy, lace trimmed dress with red satin ribbon at neckline and hem. Black and white high button shoes. Straw hat trimmed with lace, flowers and ribbon.

Renoir Child. 12." (Nancy Drew face). In blue cotton dress and white pinafore. Navy blue straw hat trimmed with flowers. Black and white high buttoned shoes.

Degas Girl. 14." (Mary Ann face). White eyelet embroidered two-tiered cotton dress with pink velvet sash. White organdy duster cap, lace and flower trimmed. White high buttoned shoes and long white stockings.

Internationals: English Guard (764), German (763), Argentine (771), African (766), Greek (769), Thailand (767), Israel (768), India (775), Irish (778), Dutch Boy (777), Russian (774), Brazil (773), Mexican (776), French (790), Swedish (792), Polish (780), Spanish Boy (779), Italian (793), Dutch Girl (791), Scottish (796), Swiss (794), Spanish Girl (795), Tyrolean Boy (799), Hungarian (797), Tyrolean Girl (798).

Americana. 8." Hiawatha (720), Pocahontas (721), Cow Girl (724), Scarlett (725), Hawaiian (722), Eskimo (723), Cowboy (732), Miss USA (728), Betsy Ross (731), Amish Girl (727), Amish Boy (726), Priscilla (729), Bride (735), Ballerina (730).

Storyland. 8." Mary, Mary (751), Red Riding Hood (782), Hansel (753), Bo Peep (783), Gretel (754), Miss Muffet (752).

Little Women. 8." Laurie also available. Repeat of 1966.

Portraits. 21." (Jacqueline face). Scarlett (2174), Southern Belle (2170), Melanie (2173), Renoir (2175), Godey (2172), Agatha (2171).

During 1967, the Trademark 276,076 was taken out for Rebecca but the doll was not produced until 1968.

21" "Scarlett" #2714-1967. Marks: Alexander/ 1961, on head. (Jacqueline face) Tag: Madame Alexander.

21" "Agatha" #2171-1967. Marks: Alexander/ 1961, on head. (Jacqueline face). Tag: Agatha/ Madame Alexander.

21" "Renoir Mother" A special doll for 1967 along with a Renoir child. (Jacqueline face). (Courtesy Roberta Lago)

12" "Renoir Child" #1274-1967. (Mary Ann). All good quality hard plastic except for head which is vinyl. Dress is blue and apron-pinafore is white. Hat is dark blue. (Courtesy Lucy Buffington)

17" "Elise" In Ballgown. #1755-1967. (Courtesy Jay Minter)

"Elise" #1735-1967. Ballerina. Brown pupiless eyes and dark hair. Marks: Alexander/196?— the ? could be 6, 8 or 9, yet the doll is currently available. (Courtesy Phyllis Houston)

17" "Elise Ballerina" Variation of costume style used from 1967 to 1973. Marked 1965. (Courtesy Kathryn Fain)

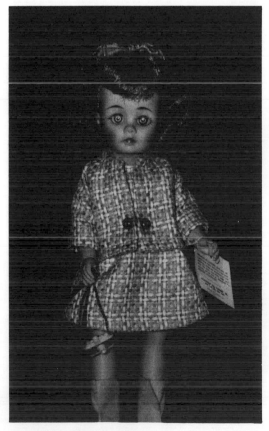

12" "Nancy Drew" #1264-1967. (Mary Ann) Original two piece suit. (Courtesy Jay Minter)

Nancy Drew in outfit #1262-1967. Linen shift dress under matching coat. (Courtesy Mandeville-Barkel Collection)

14" "Renoir Girl" #1476-1967. (Mary Ann). (Courtesy Jay Minter)

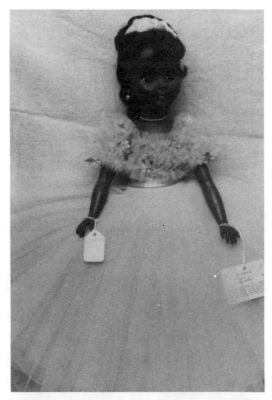

13" "Degas Portrait Child" #1475-1967. (Mary Ann face). Plastic and vinyl with blue sleep eyes/ lashes. Marks: Alexander on head. Tag: Degas Girl By/Madame Alexander. (Courtesy Kathryn Fain)

17" "Leslie" In pink formal. #1655-1967. (Polly). (Courtesy Marie Ernst)

17" "Marlo Thomas" In mod outfit. #1789-1967. (Courtesy Marge Meisinger)

17" "Marlo Thomas" From T.V. Show "That Girl" Red velvet gown #1793-1967. (Courtesy Marge Meisinger)

12" "Little Women" #1225-1967 to date. (Same dolls as the Nancy Drew) Top left to right: Marme and Meg. Lower, left to right, Amy, Laurie, Jo and Beth. These outfits to 1972. In 1972 Jo changed to dark gown and white apron and Meg went to checked gown. Alexander catalog reprint.

14" "Disney's Crest Colors Snow White" Exclusive at Disney World and Land. 1967. (Mary Ann). (Courtesy Roberta Lago)

14" "Cinderella" #1440-1967. Dressed in scullery maid outfit. (Mary Ann). Alexander catalog reprint.

14" "Riley's Little Annie" #1481-1967. (Courtesy Betty Motsinger)

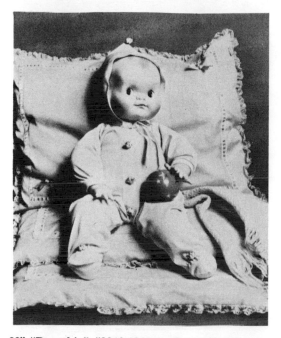

22" "Pumpkin" Cloth and vinyl. Painted hair. Painted eyes to side. Marks: Alexander on head. #8840-1967. Not original.

22" "Pumpkin" #8840-1967 to date. Cloth with gauntlet vinyl hands and vinyl head. Spray painted hair and large painted eyes to side. Alexander catalog reprint.

14" "Madame Doll" 1460-1967. Represents Civil War Era. Has secret pockets. (Mary Ann)

8" "Betsy Ross" #31-1967. (Wendy face). Jointed knees. Marks: Alex., on back. Tag: Betsy Ross/ Madame Alexander.

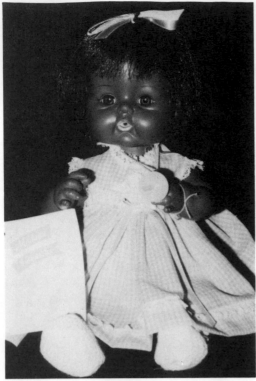

14" "Baby Ellen" #3616-1968. (Sweet Tears face). All vinyl. Open mouth/nurser. Sleep eyes and rooted hair. Marks: Alexander/1965, on head. Tag: Madame Alexander. (Courtesy Kay Shipp)

1968

Scarlett O'Hara. 14." (Mary Ann face). This year in two outfits: 1. White organdy lace trimmed gown, belted with green velvet sash. 2. Nosegay print dress with green sash. Straw hat tied with green ribbon.

Little Women. 12." Plastic and vinyl with Mary Ann faces. Laurie also available.

Cinderella. 14." (Mary Ann face). Repeat from 1967.

Alice In Wonderland. 14." (Mary Ann face). Repeat from 1967.

Madame Doll. 14." (Mary Ann face). Repeat from 1967.

McGuffey Ana. 14." (Mary Ann face). Repeat from 1967.

Milly. 17." (Polly). Offered in Marshall Field catalog.

Rebecca. 14." (Mary Ann face). Trademark 276,076, taken out during 1967. Wears a two-tiered pink and white pin dotted cotton dress with lace edging at neckline and on long sleeves. Matching pink bonnet edged with lace and flowers. Dark brown hair is braided. Carries pink parasol. High button shoes.

Sound of Music dolls. Repeat of 1967.

Victoria. 20." Came in white cotton dress edged with eyelet

and ribbon trim and also in a pink cotton dress with Irish lace trim. The lace bonnet is trimmed with rosettes on the sides.

Big Huggums. 25." Repeat from 1967.

Little Huggums. 12." Both rooted and painted hair. Repeat from 1967.

Funny. 18." Cloth doll repeat from 1967.

Muffin. 14." Cloth doll repeated from 1967.

So Big. 22." All cloth with gauntlet vinyl hands and vinyl head with painted eyes and rooted hair. Dressed in blue and white checked jumpsuit with long sleeves and white pique pinafore. Came with book, "So Big." Book illustrated by Eloise Wilkin.

Pumpkin. 22." Repeat from 1967.

Sweet Tears. 14" size came on pink and white polka dot cotton pillow with matching dress with ruffle at hem. The 14" doll also came in an organdy dress with matching bonnet. The 9," 14" and 16" sizes were released in a pin checked gingham dress and also the 9" size in this same dress came with painted hair. The 14" doll came in a christening gown and the 9" and 14" came in a window box packages with layette. The 14" was also available in travel case with layette.

Baby Ellen. 14." (Sweet Tears face). Black version available in pin checed gingham dress.

Little Butch and Little Bitsy. 9." This year both are in cotton pique.

Pussy Cat. 14," 20," 24." Available in pin checked lace trimmed gingham dress with white collar, an organdy lace edged and flower trimmed gingham dress with white collar, an organdy lace edged and flower trimmed dress and a button down the front tricot dress with a batiste eyelet ruffle trim. (This dress was on the 14" and 20" only.) All sizes came dressed in an organdy dress with pleated cotton coat and matching bonnet. Pearl buttons.

Puddin'. 21." Repeat of 1967.

Kitten. 20." Same doll as 1967 Kitten Cries. Dressed in white pique dress with matching bloomers and pink and white ruffled polka dot pinafore.

Rusty. 20." Same doll as 1967 but dressed in blue and white polished cotton polka dot dress, matching bloomers and white pique pinafore trimmed with ruffle of matching material as dress.

Elise. 17." Tulle formal, as bride and ballerina.

Leslie. 17." (Polly face). Same outfits as Elise.

Degas Girl. 14." (Mary Ann face). Repeat from 1967.

Renoir Girl. 14." (Mary Ann face). Repeat from 1967.

Renoir Child. 14." (Mary Ann face). Repeat from 1967.

Internationals. 8." German (763), Argentine (771), African (766), Greek (769), Thailand (767), Israel (768), India (775), Irish (778), Dutch Boy (777), Russian (774), Brazil (773), Mexican (776), French (790), Swedish (792), Polish (780),

Spanish Boy (779), Italian (793), Dutch Girl (791), Scottish (996), Swiss (794), Spanish Girl (795), Tyrolean Boy (799), Hungarian (797), Tyrolean Girl (798), Greece (765), Japan (770), Korea (772), Canada (760), Finland (761), Morocco (762), Rumania (786), Yugoslavia (789), Vietnam (788), Turkey (787), Norway (784), Portugal (785), English Guard (764).

Storyland. 8." Mary, Mary (751), Red Riding Hood (782), Hansel (753), Gretel (754), Bo Peep (783), Miss Muffet (752), Bride (764), and Ballerina (730).

Little Women. 8." Two costumes changed. Laurie is available.

Americana Group. 8." Hiawatha (720), Scarlett (725), Poca-

hontas (721), Hawaiian (722), Cow Girl (724), Eskimo (723), Cowboy (732), Miss USA (728), Betsy Ross (731), Amish Girl (727), Priscilla (729), Amish Boy (726).

Portraits. 21." (Jacqueline face). Lady Hamilton (2182), Melanie (2181), Queen (2185), Scarlett (2180), Gainsboro (2184), Goya (2183).

Simone. 21." (Jacqueline face). Exclusive at Marshall Field with handmade designer wardrobe including Persian lamb coat and hat. Parisian Louis Vuitton 24½" metal trunk for $325.00.

Easter Doll. 8" and 14." Special outfits (300) to West Coast.

14" "Scarlett O'Hara" Left is #1490-1968 to date. White with green sash. Right is #1495-1968 only. Nosegay print gown and natural straw hat. Alexander catalog reprint. (Both Mary Ann)

21" "Goya" #2183-1968. All in pink. (Jacqueline) Marks: Alexander / 1961. (Courtesy Phyllis Houston)

21" "Scarlett O'Hara" Green sleep eyes. Vinyl #2180-1968 Portrait. Marks: Alexander/1961. (Courtesy Sandy Rankow)

21" "Lady Hamilton" #2182-1968. (Jacqueline) Marks: Alexander/1961.

21" "Queen" #2185-1968. (Jaqueline) Marks: Alexander/1961. (Courtesy Roberta Lago)

11" "Scarlett" #1174-1968. Has white lace inside bonnet. (Cissette). (Courtesy Jay Minter)

11" "Renoir Portrette" #1175-1968. Dark blue with red hat. (Cissette). (Courtesy Jay Minter)

10" "Melinda" #1173-1968. Portrette. There were some with variations of the hat. (Cissette). Blue taffeta and white straw hat. Tag: Gold paper one over regular one: Melinda/by Madame Alexander. (Courtesy Peggy Boudreau)

11" "Agatha" #1171-1968. Portrette using the Cissette doll. (Courtesy Roberta Lago)

11" "Southern Belle" #1170-1968. (Cissette). One of the Portrette series carried for several years.

14" "McGuffey Ana" #1450-1968. (Mary Ann). (Courtesy Marie Ernst)

14" "Rebecca" #1485-1968. (Mary Ann face). Plastic and vinyl. Rooted dark brown hair in braids. Black sleep eyes/lashes. Marks: none. Tag: Rebecca/Madame Alexander. (Courtesy Phyllis Houston)

14" "Scarlett O'Hara" (Mary Ann face). #1490-1968. Plastic body and legs, vinyl head and arms. Green sleep eyes/lashes. Tag: Scarlett by/Madame Alexander, etc.

TRUNKS
FULL OF
LOVE

21" "Simone" 1968. From the Marshall Field catalog. (Jacqueline). Louis Vuitton trunk with wardrobe that included Persian Lamb coat and gold lame gouwn and cape. The ensemble cost $325.00 in 1968 catalog. (Courtesy Marge Meisinger)

14" "Portrait Children" Left: Degas Girl and right is Renoir Girl. Degas is in white with pink velvet sash. Renoir wears a pink cotton dress and white pinafore. (Both Mary Ann). Degas #1475-1967 and Renoir #1477-1968. Alexander catalog reprint.

"Jo, Little Women" 1968, 1969, 1970 and 1971. Pale blue with red polka dot pinafore. (Courtesy Mary Partridge)

8" "Yugoslavia" #789-1968 to date. (Courtesy Fay Iqauinto)

8" 'Korea" 1968 to 1970. #772. (Courtesy Connie Chase)

8" "Morocco" 1968 to 1970. #762. (Courtesy Connie Chase)

8" "Greece" #65-1968 to date. (Courtesy Jay Minter)

8" "Turkey" #787-1968. Jointed knees. 1968 to date. (Courtesy Marie Ernst)

8" "Vietnam" #788-1968. Discontinued in 1969. Jointed knees. (Courtesy Marie Ernst)

8" "Portugal" #785-1968 to date. Jointed knees. (Courtesy Marie Ernst)

8" "Canada" #760-1968 to date. Jointed knees. (Courtesy Marie Ernst)

8" "Japan" Dark tones. Jointed knees. Came with both the Maggie face and the Wendy face. #770-1968. (Courtesy Connie Chase)

8" "Finland" #761-1968. Jointed knees. Blue eyes.

8" "Rumania" #786-1968. Jointed knees. Brown eyes.

8" "Norway" #784-1968 to date. (Courtesy Faye Iaquinto)

20" "Rusty" #5261-1968 (doll dates from 1967). Freckled face, carrot red rooted hair. Cloth body with vinyl limbs and head. Sleep eyes. Alexander catalog reprint, 1968.

14" "Easter Doll" 1968. Made especially for the West Coast at the request of the Madame Alexander salesman. The dress is yellow with matching hat. Only 300 of these outfits were made. Also came in 8" size. (Courtesy Roberta Lago)

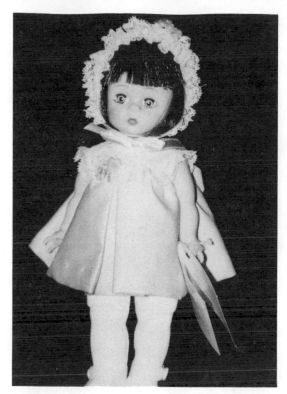

8" "Easter" 1968 only for West Coast. (Courtesy Jay Minter)

8" "Little Women and Laurie" This set of costumes are from 1968 to 1973, with change noted below. Back row, left to right: Meg, Jo, Laurie, and Marme. Front, left to right: Amy and Beth. In 1973 Marme has single row of lace on bodice and Meg has checkered gown instead of striped. Alexander catalog reprint.

"American Group" From the 1968 Alexander catalog. Top: Cowboy (732), Betsy Ross (731), Priscilla (729), Miss U.S.A. (728), Amish Girl (727), Amish Boy (726).

8" from 1968 catalog: Top: Mary, Mary (751), Hansel (753), Gretel (754). Bottom: Red Riding Hood (782), Bo Peep (783), Miss Muffet (752).

Alexander catalog of 1968 shows these: Top: French (790), Polish (780), Italian (793). Bottom: Swedish (792), Spanish Boy (779), Dutch (791).

"Americana Group" From 1968 Alexander catalog. Top: Hiawatha (720), Pocohantas (721), Cowgirl (724). Bottom: Scarlett (725), Hawaiian (722), Eskimo (723).

From the 1968 Alexander catalog. Top: India (775), Dutch Boy (777), Brazil, with hat (773). Bottom: Irish (778), Russian (774), Mexican (776).

From 1968 Alexander catalog. Top: Rumania
(786), Vietnam (788), Norway (784), Yugoslavia
(789), Turkey (787), Portugal (785).

1968 Alexander catalog. Top: Greece (765),
Korea (772), Finland (761). Bottom: Japan (770),
Canada (760), Morocco (762).

1969

Repeats from 1968. All 14." (Mary Ann face). Scarlett, Little Women (Laurie available), Cinderella, Alice In Wonderland, Madame Doll, McGuffey Ana, Rebecca.

Heidi. 14." (Mary Ann face). Print cotton dress with white bodice trimmed with ribbon and embroidery, lace edged puffed sleeves. White cotton apron. From book by Johanna Spyri. 1880.

Sound of Music Dolls. Repeat from 1968.

Victoria. 20." Repeat of two outfits of 1968, plus organdy dress with lace and feather stitching down the front.

Rozy. 12." (Janie face). Long blonde hair to below waist. Dark green leotards with shocking pink, white eyelet trimmed short shift. Straw hat with rosebud and silk band trim.

Big Huggums. 25." Repeat from 1968.

Little Huggums. 12." Repeat from 1968.

So Big. 22." Repeat from 1968.

Funny. 18." Repeat from 1968.

Muffin. 14." Repeat from 1968.

Pumpkin. 22." Repeat from 1968.

Pussy Cat. 14" and 20" sizes repeated from 1968. 14," 20" and 24" sizes have the organdy dress repeated from 1968, plus a pin checked, lace trimmed gingham dress with white yoke and a cotton dress with pink linen pleated coat with matching bonnet.

Sweet Tears. All sizes. Repeat from 1968.

Little Butch and Little Bitsy. Repeat from 1968.

Baby Ellen. Repeat from 1968.

Mary Cassatt Baby. 14" and 20" (Kitten face). From a painting by Mary Cassatt. Pink cotton, lace trimmed dress with white cotton pinafore trimmed with blue feather stitching. Blue straw hat is trimmed with flowers.

Puddin.' 21." Nosegay printed cotton jumper effect dress with tiny white yoke trimmed with buttons and lace. Also available in sheer batiste nightie with feather stitching down the front.

Portrette. 11." (Cissette face). Renoir (1175), Jenny Lind (1171), Scarlett (1174), Southern Belle (1170), Godey (1172), Melinda (1173).

Elise. 17." Tulle formal, bride and ballerina.

Leslie. 17." Same outfits as Elise.

Renoir Girl. 14." (Mary Jane face). Repeat from 1968.

Degas Girl. 14." (Mary Ann face). Repeat from 1968.

Jenny Lind and Her Listening Cat. 14." (Mary Ann face). Blue printed cotton dress with lace and velvet trim at bodice. Whie cotton eyelet apron.

Lucinda. 12." (Janie face). Blue taffeta ruffled gown. Pantaloons. Pale pink suede high buttoned shoes. Floral bud trimmed parasol. Lace edged straw hat with blue satin ribbons and pink feather.

Americana Dolls. 8." Hiawatha (720), Scarlett (725), Poca-

21" "Melanie" #2193-1969. (Jacqueline face) Marks: Alexander/1961, on head. Tag: Melanie/ Madame Alexander.

21" "Godey" #2195-1969. (Jacqueline face) Marks: Alexander/1961, on head. Tag: Godey/Madame Alexander.

hontas (721), Hawaiian (722), Cow Girl (724), Eskimo (723), Cowboy (732), Priscilla (729), Bride (735), Ballerina (730), Betsy Ross (731), Amish Boy (727), Amish Girl (726).

Storyland. 8." Mary, Mary (751), Hansel (753), Gretel (754), Bo Peep (783), Red Riding Hood (782), Miss Muffet (752).

Little Women. 8." Repeat from 1968.

Internationals. 8." African (766), Argentine (771), Thailand (767), German (763), Israel (768), India (775), Irish (778), Dutch Boy (777), Russian (774), Brazil (773), Mexican (776), Dutch (791), Swedish (792), French (790), Italian (793), Scottish (796), Swiss (794), Spanish Girl (795), Tyrolean Boy (799), Hungarian (797), Tyrolean (798), Greece (765), Korea (772), Finland (761), Japan (770), Canada (760), Morocco (762), Rumania (786), Yugoslavia (789), Vietnam (788), Norway (784), Turkey (785), Portugal (785).

Portraits. 21." (Jacqueline face) Melanie (2193), Godey (2195), Bride (2192), Jenny Lind (2191), Scarlett (2190), Renoir (2194).

Peter Pan. 14." (Mary Ann face). Dark green felt leotards with saw toothed edged light green jacket, matching felt hat, brown belt. Brown felt boots. Short red hair. From book by James M. Arrie (Ca. 1904).

Wendy. 14." (Mary Ann face). Blue taffeta gown, lace and glitter trimmed.

Michael. 11." (Janie face). Shocking pink jump suit, buttoned down the front. Holds small bear.

Tinker Bell. 11." (Cissette face). Shirred shocking pink short costume with wings. Long silk stocking and high heeled pumps with pompoms. Silver bow tying hair on top.

Tinker Bell. 8." (Wendy). Same as 11" but has white hose/slippers. Sold through stores after June and release of movie.

Jenny Lind, the Person

1970 was to be the 150th birthday of the "Swedish Nightingale," Jenny Lind's first appearance in the United States. Madame Alexander created Jenny Lind dolls in four sizes and introduced the first for Christmas, 1969. The 21" size was on display in January, 1970 at the New York's Metropolitan Opera House, where the opera Jenny starred in, Der Freischutz was revived. The 21" size was referred to as the "Prima Donna" model.

For those collectors who would like to know a little more about Jenny Lind, we have included the following. It first appeared in this author's book "Antique Collector's Dolls" Vol. II.

It was in 1850, on Sept. 1, when Jenny Lind first came to America. The "Swedish Nightingale" was famous on the Continent and England and perhaps, if it had not been for Phineas Taylor (P.T.) Barnum, she may never have reached America and the popularity she did.

Because of Barnum's great showmanship personality, the desire to see and hear Jenny Lind was more than "enthusiastic," it was wild. Over thirty thousand people lined the dock of Manhattan's Canal St. to catch a glimpse of the singer, and as the 29 year old descended the gang plank, hundreds of people were injured in the crush that resulted.

Her first American tour was a sell out and lasted through 137 cities with the first in the "Battery" area of New York at the Castle Gardens.

Johanna Maria Lind was born in Stockholm, Sweden in 1820. She was a blonde. All the china Jenny Lind dolls the author has seen have had black hair and there is a reason for

this. Jenny, herself, requested that dolls were made under P.T. Barnum's direction, to have black hair. It is a well known fact that Jenny Lind was "plain" and much ado was made about her looks because of how her looks actually transformed when she was singing and acting. Her complexion was so pale that she felt that the black hair of the china dolls would add to her attractiveness.

Once at a musical party given for the Princess of Prussia, Lady Westmorland remarked, on seeing the singer for the first time, "Why she is not only pale, thin and plain-featured, but awkward and rather nervous. Exactly like a schoolgirl! It is preposterous." When asked afterward about the performance, Lady Westmorland exclaimed, "She is simply an angel...when she began to sing her face shone like an angel. I never saw or heard anything the least like it."

It is known that Jenny Lind's interest in music was evident from the age of three. It is also a recorded fact that her parents home, when she was nine, was on a busy street leading to St. Jacobs Church and Jenny often sat at the window holding her cat and singing almost constantly. (Madame Alexander made a doll of the child called "Jenny Lind and Her Listening Cat) People moving up and down the street would stop and listen to her. One was the maid for the famous Swedish dancer, Mademoiselle Lundberg, who reported to her what she had heard. Mademoiselle Lundberg went with her maid and was amazed as she listened to the outstanding voice of the nine year old.

Mme. Lundberg visited Jenny' mother and attempted to convince her that Jenny's was a great voice that only needed training. Jenny's mother was a very bitter woman, who considered her husband a "failure," a man who moved from job to job. Therefore, she had what she considered more important things for Jenny to do...work and more work. Finally, in time, the mother was convinced that it was her "duty" to get the child training and a Master by the name of Herr Berg was hired. As the training progressed, the expense was taken over by the Swedish Government.

At age 12, Jenny's voice broke and voice exercises stopped but she did not, for she devoted herself to the study of harmony and composition. With time, of course, her voice "returned" and at age 16, Jenny had become the pupil of Swedish composer, Lindblad, who undertook to instruct her in the fullest knowledge of music known up to that time.

By 21, she had moved to Paris under the tutorage of the celebrated singer, Signor Garcia. It was from Garcia she learned the true Italian style of singing. She was recommended to the Director of the Academy of Music in Paris, after being heard by the composer Meyerbeer.

A meeting was arranged with the Director and other important, great French musicians but the Director did not appear to hear her sing. The Director, the most important man of his times in the world of music, was kept away by the very jealous lady singer of the hour, Mdlle. Rosina Stolz, and as a consequence, Jenny Lind was not offered a singing engagement in Paris. This unfair treatment so impressed Jenny Lind that she resolved never to sing in Paris and never did, although she later had many tempting offers.

Jenny Lind counted among her friends, Queen Victoria, Mendelsshon, Chopin and Hans Christian Andersen. She married her accompanist, Otto Goldschmidt in 1852 in Boston, Mass. They had three children, Walter Otton born in 1853, Jenny M.C. in 1857 and Ernst S.D. in 1861. Jenny Lind died on Nov. 2, 1887, in their home in Melvern, England, among the hills of Glouceshire, which she loved so much. She was 67 years old.

Because of P.T. Barnum's campaign for Jenny Lind, all types of items carrying the Jenny Lind name were sold. Besides dolls, these items included such things as stoves, lamps, beds, medals, buttons, clocks, trivets, sofas, caps, chairs, shawls, combs and all sorts of bric-a-brac. One such article was a tea kettle that was advertised that it "commenced to sing in a few minutes."

14" "Jenny Lind & Her Listening Cat" #1470-1969. (Mary Ann). (Courtesy Kay Shipp)

21," 14" and 11" "Jenny Lind" All in pink. (Jacqueline, Mary Ann and Cissette). 21" #2191-1969. 11" #1171-1969. (Courtesy Marie Ernst)

17" "Elise Bride" #1760-1969. (Courtesy Marie Ernst)

11" "Renoir" #1175-1969. (Cissette). Gown is pale blue. (Courtesy Doris Ermansons)

11" "Godey" #1172-1969. Jointed knees. (Cissette). One of Portrettes.

11" "Melanie" #1173-1969. (Cissette) Portrette in organdy and lace. (Courtesy Roberta Lago)

14" "Peter Pan (Mary Ann), 14" "Wendy" (Mary Ann), 11" "Michael" (Janie) and 11" "Tinker Bell" (Cissette). #1410, 1415, 1120 and 1110. All 1969. (Courtesy Roberta Lago)

Shows close up of the "Tinkerbell" (Cissette). See 8" Tinker Bell in color section.

14" "Heidi" #1490-1969. (Mary Ann), Blue eyes and blond braids.

12" "Lucinda" #1135-1969. (Janie) Marks: Alexander/1964. (Courtesy Shirley Bertrand)

12" "Laurie" (Mary Ann face) #1226-1969. Plastic body, legs and arms. Vinyl head. **Marks:** Alexander 1963, on head. Tag: A Little **Men**/ Laurie/By Madame Alexander. (Courtesy **Elizabeth** Montesano of Yesterday's Children)

12" "Rozy" #1130-1969. (Janie). (Courtesy Roberta Lago)

14" "Sweet Tears" In christening outfit. 1969 to 1975. (Courtesy Anita Pacey)

20" "Mary Cassatt Baby" #5360-1969. (Kitten). (Courtesy Roberta Lago)

8" "Ballerina" In pink and blue. #730-1969. (Courtesy Faye Iaquinto)

"Wendy" as Bride #735-1969. (Courtesy Jeannie Niswonger)

Front dress: For 14" doll. Pale blue with gold rick-rack. Tag: Cinderella/Madame Alexander. Sold in box with #140 on box, from FAO Schwarz. Back dress: Blue with rose-pink velvet ribbon. Cinderella dress for Elise (14") sold through FAO Schwarz in 1969. (Courtesy Marie Ernst)

22" "So Big" #8950 1969 to date. Painted eyes, cloth body and limbs with vinyl head and gauntlet hands. Rooted hair. (Courtesy Jeannie Niswonger)

"Victoria" With spray painted hair, #5872-1969, and is unique that she has an all cloth body and legs. (Courtesy Betty Motsinger)

Shows the Victoria doll's legs that are all cloth. (Courtesy Betty Motsinger)

1970

Repeats from 1969. All 14." (Mary Ann face). Scarlett O'Hara, Alice In Wonderland, Madame Doll, Heidi, Rebecca, Cinderella (Poor), Degas Girl, Renoir Girl, Jenny Lind and Her Listening Cat.

Little Women. 12." And Laurie. (Mary Ann faces). Repeat from 1969.

Cinderella, Rich. 14." (Mary Ann face). Ball gown of pink and silver trimmed with rosebuds. Rosebud tiara and pink ribbons in hair.

Snow White. 14." (Mary Ann face). White tulle and satin trimmed gown with silver and white full cape.

Sound of Music Dolls. Repeat of 1969.

Victoria. 20." Repeat of 1969.

Suzy. 12." (Janie face). Blue and white checked cotton dress and flowered pinafore. Straw hat and carries a basket of posies.

Big Huggums. 25." Repeat from 1969.

Little Huggums. 12." Repeat from 1969.

So Big. 22." Repeat from 1969.

Pumpkin. 22." Repeat from 1969.

Funny. 18." Repeat from 1969.

Muffin. 14." Repeat from 1969.

Sweet Tears. All are repeats from 1969.

Pussy Cat. 14," 20" and 24." Repeat of the checked gingham dress and pink organdy dress. New is silk faille trimmed coat and matching bonnet over the organdy dress.

Black Pussy Cat. Offered in the 14" and 20" sizes in checked gingham dress.

Mary Cassatt Baby. 20" and 14." (Kitten face). Repeat form 1969.

Puddin' 21." Pink and white checked, lace trimmed gingham dress with jumper effect, matching bloomers. Also in sheer batiste dress with feather stitching and lace edging.

Happy. 20." Cloth body with vinyl arms, legs and head. Open/closed smiling mouth. Dressed in short white jump suit with blue stripes and red cotton jumper dress.

Elise. 17." Formal, bride and ballerina.

Leslie. 17." Colored version (Polly face) of Elise with same outfits.

Lucinda. 12." (Janie face). Repeat from 1969.

Jenny Lind. 14." (Mary Ann face). Pink satin gown with lace

and rosebud trim. Rosebuds in hair and wears earrings.

Grandma Jane. 14." (Mary Ann face). Blue linen shift dress and matching coat. Carries beige handbag. Wears rimmed glasses.

Little Women. 8." Repeat from 1969.

Storyland. 8." Mary, Mary (751), Red Riding Hood (782), Hansel (753), Gretel (754), Bo Peep (783), Miss Muffet (752).

Americana Dolls. 8." Betsy Ross (731), Cow Girl (724), Bride (735), Scarlett (725), Ballerina (730), Pocahontas (721), Priscilla (729).

Internationals. 8." Mexican (776), Swedish (792), Irish (778), French (790), Italian (793), Argentina (771), India (775), Israeli (768), Dutch Boy (777), Brazil (773), Dutch Girl (791), African (766), German (763), Polish (780), Denmark (769), Thailand (767), Russian (774), Japanese (770), Greece (765), Korea (772), Finland (761), Morocco (762), Canada (760), Indonesia (779), Rumania (786), Portugal (785), Yugoslavia (789), Turkey (787), Norway (784), Scottish (796), Swiss (794), Spanish Girl (795), Tyrolean Boy (799), Hungarian (797), Tyrolean Girl (798).

Portraits. 21." Jenny Lind (2181), Renoir (2184), Melanie (2196), Godey (2195), Madame Pompadour (2197), Scarlett (2180).

Portrettes. 11." Renoir (1180), Melanie (1182), Scarlett (1181), Godey (1183), Jenny Lind (1184), Southern Belle (1185).

21" "Madame Pompadour" #2197-1970. (Jacqueline). Marks: Alexander/1961. (Courtesy Roberta Lago)

21" "Godey" #2195-1970. (Jacqueline). Marks: Alexander/1961. (Courtesy Roberta Lago)

21" "Renoir" #2184-1970. (Jacqueline). Marks: Alexander/1961.

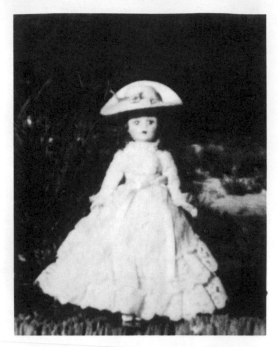

11" "Godey" #1183-1970. (Cissette). Gown and lace are pale pink. (Courtesy Doris Ermansons)

11" "Scarlett" #1181-1970. (Cissette). With black band. (Courtesy Doris Ermansons)

11" "Renoir" #1180-1970. (Cissette). Striped gown also used. (Courtesy Connie Chase)

11" "Scarlett Portrette" 1970. (Cissette). Green with light trim rather than the traditional black. This one was made same year as this trim was used on the 21" Scarlett #2180. This doll (#1180) also came with black trim.

14" "Jenny Lind" #1491-1970. Dressed in pink (Mary Ann). Blue eyes and yellow blonde hair.

14" "Cinderella Ball Gown" #1445-1970. (Mary Ann). (Courtesy Roberta Lago)

14" "Snow White" #1455-1970 to date. (Mary Ann). (Courtesy Anita Pacey)

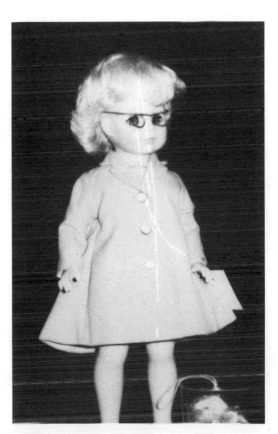

14" "Grandma Jane" #1420-1970. Plastic and vinyl with rooted grey hair, blue sleep eyes/lashes. Wire glasses. Came with hat box with hair piece and curlers. Marks: Alexander/1966, on head. Tag: Grandma Jane/Madame Alexander.

287

8" "Pocahantas and baby" #721-1970. Prior to 1970 was without the baby. Jointed knees. (Courtesy Jay Minter)

8" "Indonesia" #779-1970 to date. Bend knees. (Courtesy Marie Ernst)

8" "Red Boy" #740-1970. (Wendy face). Jointed knees. Brown sleep eyes and brown glued on wig. (Courtesy Jay Minter)

8" "Wendy Ballerina" #730 and 432-1970 to date. Prior ones have the close tucked tulle skirt. (Courtesy Mandeville-Barkel Collection)

8" "Denmarks" #769-1970 to date. Apron also came in checked pattern, sprinkled with flowers. (Courtesy Fay Iaquinto)

14" "Jenny Lind" In lavender and pink with white apron. Tag: Jenny Lind/By Madame Alexander. This is entirely different than other Jenny Linds. (Mary Ann). 1970. (Courtesy Jay Minter)

12" "Suzy" #1150-1970. (Janie). (Courtesy Roberta Lago)

20" "Negro Pussycat" #3438-1970. (Courtesy Phyllis Houston)

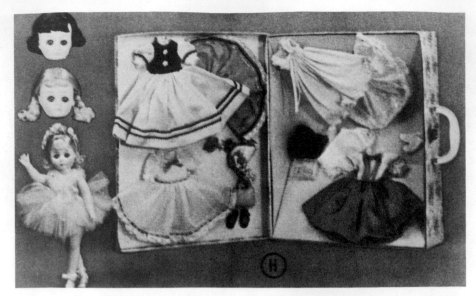

12" "Pamela" From the 1970 FAO Schwarz catalog. Called Party Kit. Doll takes wigs. (Courtesy
Marge Meisinger)

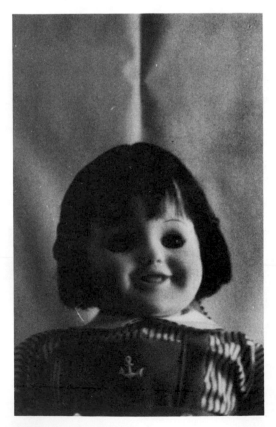

20" "Happy" #5570-1970. Cloth body with vinyl
head and limbs. Open/closed mouth with dark
brown rooted hair. (Courtesy Betty Motsinger)

1971

Repeats from 1970 are: Big Huggums, Little Huggums,
Funny, Muffin, Pumpkin, So Big, Victoria, Puddin', Sweet
Tears, Baby Ellen, Pussy Cat, Colored Pussy Cat, Elise,
Leslie, Jenny Lind and Her Listening Cat, Grandma Jane,
Degas Girl, Renoir Girl, Scarlett O'Hara, Madame Doll,
Heidi, Rebecca, 12" Little Women, Alice in Wonderland,
Cinderella (Poor) and Cinderella in Ball Gown, Snow White,
Sound of Music dolls, 8" Little Women, All 8" Storyland, all
8" Internationals except: Korea, Morocco; All Americana
except Pocahontas, Pricilla and Cow Girl.

Smiley. 20." Blonde, blue-eyed version of Happy. Pink jersey
leotards with pink pin dotted cotton dress having a round
pique collar.

Baby McGuffey. 20." (Kitten face). Pink cotton dress with
puffed sleeves and lace trim. White eyelet pinafore with
matching bonnet.

Lucinda. 14." (Mary Ann face). Same style gown, carries
parasol.

Portrettes. 11." Scarlett (1181), Southern Belle (1185).

Sleeping Beauty. 14." (Mary Ann face). Gold gown of
metallic net over gold taffeta skirt, yellow rosebuds and
bodice is trimmed with gold braid. Same braid in the tiara.

Portraits: 21." Mimi (2170), Renoir (2163), Melanie (2162),
Godey (2161).

21" "Melanie" #2162-1971. (Jacqueline). Marks: Alexander/1961, on head. (Courtesy Jay Minter)

11" "Southern Belle" #1185-1971. (Cissette). Portrette.

Shows the small set of "Sound of Music" dolls except for Maria, 12" (Mary Ann). Clockwise: 11" 'Liesl (Cissette), 8" Gretl (Wendy), 11" Brigitta (Cissette), 8" Marta (Wendy), 8" Frederick (Wendy). 1971. (Courtesy Anita Pacey)

17" "Leslie" In blue formal. #1650-1971. (Courtesy Marie Ernst)

14" "Sleeping Beauty" #1495-1971. (Mary Ann). Long curly hair. (Courtesy Jay Minter)

14" "Lucinda" #1435-1971 (Mary Ann). Marks: Alexander/1965 on head.

From the 1971 Alexander catalog. Left to right: Finland (761), Japan (770), Greece (765), Canada (760).

From the 1971 Alexander catalog. Top: Indonesia (779), Portugal (785), Turkoy (787). Bottom: Rumania (786), Yugoslavia (789), Norway (784).

The 1971 Alexander catalog shows: Top: Scottish (796), Spanish (795), Hungarian (797). Bottom: Swiss (794), Tyrolean Boy (799), Tyrolean Girl (798).

The Alexander catalog for 1971 has: Top: African (766), Polish (780), Thailand (767). Bottom: German (763), Denmark (769), Russian (774).

20" "Smiley" #5585-1971. Cloth with vinyl head and limbs. Open/closed mouth with molded tongue. Blue sleep eyes/lashes. Marks: Alexander/1970, on head.

8" "Bride" #35-1971 and 1972. (Courtesy Faye Iaquinto)

Repeats from 1971: 21" Mimi (2170), Renoir (2163), Melanie (2162), Godey (2161), So Big, Victoria, Puddin' Baby Mc-Guffey, Sweet Tears, Baby Ellen, Pussy Cat, Elise (except portrait Elise), Lucinda, Scarlett O'Hara, Grandma Jane, Degas Girl, Madame Doll, Heidi, Rebecca, Little Women (12"), Little Women (8"), Alice In Wonderland, Snow White, Sleeping Beauty, Cinderella (Poor and in Ball Gown), Sound of Music, 8" Storyland Dolls, Americana Dolls, International except added: China and Czechoslovakia.

Maggie. 17." (Elise face). Plaid skirt, short green jacket with white collar and lace edged cuffs. Straw brimmed hat with green band and bow.

Janie. 20," 14." Cloth body with vinyl head, arms and legs. Cotton dress with laced edged white organdy collar. Lace trim on dress.

Portrait Elise. 17." Full skirted nylon gown with pleated ruffled hem. Rosebud trimmed. Puffed sleeves, moire sash. Wide brimmed matching straw picture hat trimmed with lace and flowers.

Portrettes. 11." Southern Belle (1185), Scarlett (1181), Queen (1186).

Portraits. 21." Cornelia (2191), Renoir (2190), Gainsboro (2192).

21" "Gainsborough" #2192-1972. (Jacqueline). Marks: Alexander/1961. (Courtesy Marie Ernst)

21" "Cornelia" #2190-1972. (Jacqueline). Marks: Alexander/1961. (Courtesy Jay Minter)

21" "Renoir" #2190-1972. Pink with black velvet, pink sequins. (Jacqueline). Marks: Alexander/1961. (Courtesy Jay Minter)

10" "Queen" #1186-1972. (Cissette face). All hard plastic with blue sleep eyes/lashes molded. Jointed knees. Marks: Mme. Alexander, on back. Tag: Queen by/Madame Alexander.

17" "Maggie" (Elise face). Plastic and vinyl with blue sleep eyes and rooted brown hair. #1720-1972. Discontinued 1973. Marks: Alexander/1966, on head. Tag: Maggie/Madame Alexander.

14" "Renoir Portrait Child" #1477-1972. (Mary Ann). Marks: Alexander/1965, on head.

17" "Portrait Elise" #1755-1970. Pink net and lace trim. Plastic and vinyl with sleep eyes/lashes. Marks: Alexander/1966, on head. Tag: Madame Alexander, etc. Blonde hair in up-sweep.

8" "Snow White" 1972. Sold only at Disneyland-World. Dressed in what is called the Disney "Crest" colors. (Courtesy Connie Chase)

8" "Alice In Wonderland" Another exclusive with Disney Land—World. Began in 1972. (Courtesy Roberta Lago)

8" "Belgium" #762-1972. Bend knees. (Courtesy Jay Minter)

8" "China" #772-1972 to date. Bend knees issue. (Courtesy Kathryn Fain)

8" "Czechoslavakia" #764-1972. Jointed knees. (Courtesy Jay Minter)

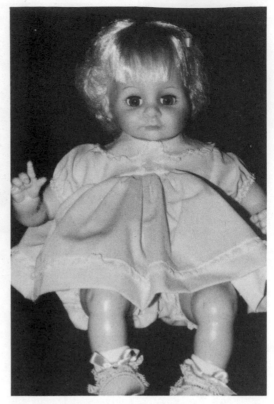

14" "Janie" Cloth and vinyl with rooted blonde hair. Blue sleep eyes. #3120-1972. Marks: Alexander/1972, on head.

1973

Repeated from 1972: Little Women (12"), Madame Doll, Heidi, Rebecca, Alice In Wonderland, Cinderella (poor and in ball gown), Sleeping Beauty, Snow White, Scarlett O'Hara, Sound of Music Dolls, Big Huggums, Little Huggums, Funny, Muffin, Pumpkin, So Big, Sweet Tears, Pussy Cat, Victoria, Janie, Baby McGuffey, Puddin', Elise (formal, bride and ballerina), Lucinda, Little Women (8"), Degas Girl, Renoir Girl, Maggie, Portrait Elise.

Blue Boy. 12." (Mary Ann face). Pale blue satin, braid trimmed suit with knee britches, ruffled lace shirt, satin beret with blue ostrich feather.

Portraits. 21." Renoir (2190), Cornelia (2191), Gainsboro (2192).

Baby Lynn. 20." Cloth body with vinyl head and limbs. Blue and white checked cotton dress with pink and white checked cotton pinafore trimmed with rick-rack. Checked poke bonnet. Also came in white organdy, and in rose and lace trimmed dress and bonnet.

Bride doll. 14." (Mary Ann face). Skirt has three wide rows of lace.

Internationals. —." Mexican (0776), Swedish (0792), Irish (0778), French (0790), Italian (0793), Argentina (0771), India (0775), Israeli (0768), Dutch Boy (0777), Brazil (0773), Dutch Girl (0791), Russian (0774), Denmark (0769), China (0772), Thailand (0767), Polish (0780), German (0763), Finland (0761), Czechoslavakia (0764), Greece (0765), Japanese (0770), Belgium (0762), Canada (0760), Indonesia (0779), Rumania (0786), Portugal (0785), Yugoslavia (0789), Turkey (0787), Norway (0784), Scottish (0796), Swiss (0794), Spanish Girl (0795), Tyrolean Boy (0799), Tyrolean Girl (0798), Hungarian (0797).

Storyland. 8." Mary, Mary (0751), Hansel (0753), Gretel (0754), Red Riding Hood (0782), Bo Peep (0783), Miss Muffet (0752).

Americana. 8." Bride (0735), Scarlett (0725), Red Boy (0740), Ballerina (0730), Betsy Ross (0731).

21" "Renoir" #2190-1973. (Jacqueline). Marks: Alexander/1961.

21" "Gainsboro" #2192-1973. (Jacqueline). Portrait.

12" "Bride" #1565-1973. (Mary Ann). (Courtesy Anita Pacey)

17" "Portrait Elise" #1780-1973. Vinyl and plastic. Marks include wrist tag: Elise. (Courtesy Jeannie Gregg)

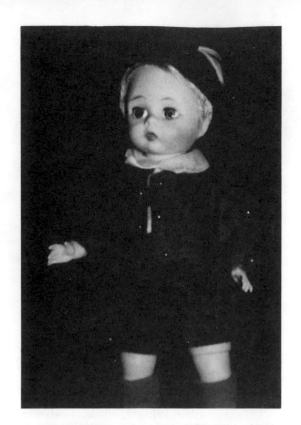

8" "Scarlett" 1973 to date. #0725. (Courtesy Connie Chase)

8" "Austria" 1973 to date. Was #399, 499 and 799 Tyrolean Boy from 1962 to 1973. (Courtesy Faye Iaquinto)

9" "Sweet Tears" All vinyl. Open mouth/nurser. Discontinued in 1973 in this size. (Courtesy Jay Minter)

20" "Baby Lynn" 1973. Cloth body with vinyl head and limbs. Rooted hair and closed mouth. (Courtesy Marge Meisinger)

20" "Baby Lynn" #7020-1973. Cloth with vinyl head and limbs. (Courtesy Betty Motsinger)

Repeats from 1973: Storybook, 8"; Americana, 8"; Little Women, 8"; Madame Doll, Heidi, Rebecca, Alice in Wonderland, Cinderella (Poor and in ball gown), Snow White, Sleeping Beauty, Lucinda, Bride Doll, Scarlett O'Hara, Big Huggums, Little Huggums, Funny, Muffin, Pumpkin, So Big, Sweet Tears, Pussy Cat, Victoria, Puddin, Baby McGuffey, Baby Lynn, Elise (in formal, as bride and ballerina), Degas Girl, Blue Boy, Renoir Girl, Little Women (12").

Portraits. 21." Cornelia (2296), Melanie (2295), Agatha (2297).

Baby Precious. 21." Pink cotton romper suit with white eyelet trimmed cotton smock. Also in pink cotton dress with wide lace panel trim. Bonnet.

Internationals. 8." Mexico (576), Italy (593), United States (559), Sweden (592), Ireland (578), France (590), Argentina (571), India (575), Israeli (568), Netherlands Boy (577), Brazil (573), Netherlands Girl (591), Russia (574), Denmark (569), China (572), Thailand (567), Poland (580), Germany (563), Czechoslavakia (564), Finland (561), Greece (565), Japan (570), Belgium (562), Canada (560), Indonesia (579), Rumania (586), Portugal (585), Yugoslavia (589), Turkey (587), Norway (584), Scotland (596), Switzerland (594), Spain (595), Austrian Boy (599), Hungary (597), Austrian Girl (598).

21" "Agatha" #2297-1974. Pink with silver sequins. (Jacqueline) Marks: Alexander/1061. (Courtesy Anita Pacey)

21" "Cornelia" #2296-1974. (Jacqueline). In blue with black trim. Marks: Alexander/1961. (Courtesy Marie Ernst)

21" "Melanie" In red and white. #2295-1974. (Jacqueline). Marks: Alexander/1961. (Courtesy Marie Ernst)

12" "Blue Boy" #1340-1974. (Mary Ann). 12" Pinkie. #1350-1975. (Mary Ann). (Courtesy Jay Minter)

17" "Elise Bride" #1670-1974 and 1975. Marks: 1965. (Courtesy Kathryn Fain)

8" "Netherlands Boy" 1974 to date. Was called Dutch #777-1964 to 1973. (Courtesy Faye Iaquinto)

8" United States. Straight legs. #559-1974. Some first issues had misspelled tags that read "Untied States." Most were re-called. Currently available. (Courtesy Jay Minter)

Shows the misspelled tag for the United States doll of 1974.

This is the 21" #9020 size Baby Precious dressed in pink. Original. 1974. (Courtesy Anita Pacey)

14" Baby Precious. Cloth with vinyl arms, legs and head. Blue sleep eyes. Pouty mouth. Original clothes. 1974. (Courtesy Anita Pacey)

Repeats from 1974: Storyland (8"); Americana (8"); Internationals (8"); Little Women (8" and 12"); Madame Doll, Heidi, Rebecca, Alice In Wonderland, Cinderella (Poor and in ball gown), Sleeping Beauty, Snow White, Lucinda, Scarlett O'Hara, Bride doll, Big and Little Huggums, Funny, Muffin, Pumpkin, So Big, Sweet Tears (all in 14" size), Pussy Cat, Victoria, Puddin, Baby McGuffey, Baby Lynn, Baby Precious, Elise (Ballerina, bride and formal), Renoir Girl, Blue Boy, Degas Girl.

Pinkie. 12." (Mary Ann face). White sheer gown, lace trimmed. Pink satin sash. Pink satin poke bonnet with long pink streamers.

Portraits. 21." Agatha (2291), Scarlett (2292), Cornelia (2290).

21" "Scarlett" (Jacqueline). Green eyes and black hair. Although marked Alexander/1961, this doll was sold in 1975 and 1976. (Courtesy Kathryn Fain)

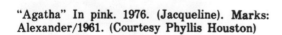

"Agatha" In pink. 1976. (Jacqueline). Marks: Alexander/1961. (Courtesy Phyllis Houston)

"Martha Washington (1789-1797)

Abigail Adams (1797-1801)

The 1976 First Ladies or Presidents' Wives will be made for a couple years with new wives added each year. They were not a Limited Edition item. Four have the Mary Ann face and two the new "Martha" face. (Photos courtesy Jane Thomas)

Martha Randolph, Daughter of Pres. Jefferson (1801-1809)

"Dolly Madison" (1809-1817)

"Elizabeth Monroe" (1817-1825)

Louisa Adams (1825-1829)

21" "Cornelia" In turquoise. 1976. (Jacqueline) Marks: Alexander/1961. (Courtesy Phyllis Houston)

8" "Betsy Ross" For 1976 with Bicentennial dress of blue stars. (Courtesy Angie Landers)

17" "Formal Elise" #1550-1975-1976. Blue with ruffle trim. Full, long bangs. (Courtesy Gloria Harris)

Available to collectors, as well as the general public, this year is the stationery notes made by the Fender Company. The boxes are exactly like the doll boxes. These first notes have color photos of the Presidents' Ladies and will be followed by other Alexander dolls.

been added to the mold. Madame Alexander assures us they did not buy this mold and we are certain the manufacturer did not add the "Alexander," so that means some place, someone is faking the Alexander name to composition dolls and evidence shows these 1946 composition dolls have been altered within the past five years. (Doll, courtesy Marge Meisinger)

18" "Personality Playmate—Sandra" All composition. Sleep eyes, dimples. This doll was originally made for Montgomery Wards. This one (see next photo) shows the "Alexander" that has

Closeup of the Alexander mold mark that has been added on the back of the Eugenia doll, Personality Playmate Sandra. (Courtesy Marge Meisinger)

Alexander Dolls available for 1977.

Portraits: Scarlett, Magnolia and Godey. (All 21")

First Ladies. Repeat of 1976.

Elise. 18" Ballerina and Bride.

Following are all the 14" dolls: McGuffey Ana (new), Lucinda, Poor Cinderella, Ball Gown Cinderlla, Alice In Wonderland, Snow White, Bride, Heidi, Rebecca, Gone With The Wind (Scarlett), Sleeping Beauty.

Blue Boy and Pinky. 12."

Little Women and Laurie. 12."

All 8" dolls with the addition of Great Britain. Dark skin dolls have a new face.
Babies: Little Huggums, painted hair and rooted hair, Big Huggums, Victoria, 14" and 20," Sweet Tears in three outfits and layette, Baby McGuffey 14," Pussy Cat, 14," 20" and 24, Black Pussy Cat, 20," Mary Mine. 14" and 20," (Baby Lynn re-named), Mommie Pet, Baby Brother (Baby Lynn re-named.)

21" Portraits of 1977. Left to right: #2298 Godey in ivory taffeta with ruby red velvet jacket. #2296 Scarlett in green taffeta and #2297 Magnolia in soft pink taffeta and lace ruffled gown with attached full length long sleeved taffeta overskirt.

1977 Alexander catalog showing new 8" "Great Britain" added this year. Top: Left to right: #590 France, #559 United States, #558 Great Britain, #76 Mexico. Bottom row: #593 Italy, #592 Sweden, #587 Ireland.

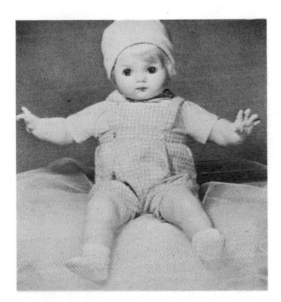

20" "Baby Brother" #6550-1977. Cloth with vinyl head, arms and legs. Alexander catalog 1977.

20" "Mommie's Pet" Cloth with vinyl head, arms and legs. The 1977 doll wears a cotton dress and pink with white pin dotted pinafore and a matching poke bonnet.

21" and 14" "Mary Mine" (Baby Lynn renamed).
#6760 and #3750-1977. Cloth with vinyl head,
arms and legs. Alexander catalog reprint.

14" "McGuffey Ana" #1525-1977. (Mary Ann).
Plaid cotton dress with white organdy pinafore
with eyelet trim. Natural straw hat trimmed
with flowers. Pigtails tied with green ribbon.

Sears, Roebuck: 1935, 36, 38, 39, 40, 42, 43, 45, 46, 47, 48, 49, 50, and 51.

Montgomery Wards: 1935, 36, 40 and 41.

John Plain: 1941, 1942, 1945.

FAO Schwarz: 1953, 56, 57, 58, 60, 61, 62, 64, 65, 66, 67, 68, 70 and 72.

Marshall Field: 1962, 66, 68, 69.

Wonderful World of Toys From Disneyland: 1960.

Screen Guild: Oct. 1939.

Town & Country: May 1964.

Toy Trader—Luella Hart: May, 55; May, June, July, Oct. 1964; Mar., May, June, July, Dec. 1965; April, June, July 1966; Jan. 1967.

Doll News (U.F.D.C.): Aug. 1970.

The Family Circle: Sept., Nov. 1942; May 1943, Feb. 1944.

Consumer Reporter: Nov. 1967.

Independent Woman: Dec. 1940.

New Yorker: Aug. 1950.

Playbill: Mar. 1953.

McCalls: Nov. 1954, June 1956, Aug. 1957.

Good Housekeeping: Nov. 1937, Dec. 1937, Nov. and Dec. 1938.

Child Life: Dec. 1938, Jan. 1939, Dec. 1940.

Plaything: Apr. 1951 to Dec. 1975.

Library Bibliography of 1957.

South Florida Today: Jan. 1976.

New York Times (Micro-film) 1935 to 1954.

New York Herald Tribune: May 26, 1963.

Palm Beach Post: Monday, Apr. 1, 1976.

Brown, Vivian. Canton Repository: Tues. March 11, 1975.

Burdick, Loraine: Celebrity Doll Journal: May, Aug. 1976; Aug. 1975; Adult Star Dolls & Toys, 1973. Child Star Dolls & Toys, 1968.

Cooper, Marlowe: Doll Home Library Series Vol. 12, 13 and 14.

Foulke, Jan: Focusing on....., Oct. 1976 Doll Reader.

Thomas, Jane Ruggles: The Most Beautiful Doll...Neyenesch Printers. 1976.

Watson, Eleanor Schwingle: Wee Friends. Midwestern Printers. 1974.

Alexander Catalog Reprints (Jane Thomas) 1942-1952 to 1975.

Bexton & Owen: Radio's Golden Age. Easton Valley Press. 1966.

Flamini, Roland: Scarlett, Rhett and a Cast of Thousands. Macmillan. 1975.

Life Goes To The Movies: Time, Inc. 1975.

Likeness, George C. The Oscar People. Wayside Press. 1965.

Scheuer, Steven H. The Movie Book. Ridge Press. 1974.

Settel & Laas. A Pictorial History of Television. Grosset and Dunlap, Inc. 1969.

Shipman, David. The Great Movie Stars. St. Martin Press. 1973.

Springer & Hamilton. They Had Faces Then. Citadel Press. 1974.

Taylor Deems. A Pictorial History of the Movies. Simon and Schuster. 1943.

Picture Index